C000301210

"Inspiring story of incredible practice that is so rich with detail. This is not just the why, but the *how*. Thoroughly recommended for anyone working with children who struggle to regulate their behaviours."

Paul Dix, *Behaviour Specialist, Educational Reformer, Author of* When the Adults Change

Relationship-based Learning

Relationship-based Learning provides a helpful range of accessible strategies, approaches, practical ideas and guidance on how to implement Behaviour for Learning for children with social, emotional and mental health issues, as well as those at risk of exclusion from school.

This essential resource explores the conceptual framework of Ellis and Tod's highly effective Behaviour for Learning conceptual framework, with each chapter featuring practical strategies and foundations that can be used at an organisational or whole-school level, as well as in the classroom. It includes tried-and-tested structures and strategies which have been proven to improve the learning and behaviour of children. The implementation of the Behaviour for Learning framework has been evidenced to have a significant impact on the quality of teaching and learning with outstanding and, in some cases, exceptional outcomes for all learners. The strategies and approaches explored in this book are relevant for teaching children in any school or alternative provision, especially those with social, emotional and mental health needs.

Relationship-based Learning is a must-read for practitioners, senior leaders, teachers and support staff, outreach services and multi-agency staff who are committed to improving outcomes for children with social, emotional and mental health needs.

Janet Packer is an experienced leader in education with a passion for children having a love for learning. Her experience, including roles as an advisor, inspector, LA manager of a Behaviour Support service and headteacher underpins her belief that all children should be provided with the best tools to enable them to thrive and be successful. It is this drive that inspired her to lead the development and implementation of Behaviour for Learning across PIDS and the Courtyard AP Academy.

Nia MacQueen is an experienced mainstream and additional learning needs teacher, headteacher and trainer who has worked effectively alongside staff in a range of settings to build capacity and improve outcomes. She also led on Behaviour for Learning and its development at the Courtyard AP Academy.

Patricia Day is an advisory teacher with extensive experience as a classroom teacher, outreach behaviour support teacher, consultant and trainer. She led on the development of assessment of Behaviour for Learning across the Primary Inclusion Development Service.

Relationship-based Learning

A Practical Guide to Transforming
Children's Behaviour

**Janet Packer, Nia MacQueen
and Patricia Day**

Routledge
Taylor & Francis Group

LONDON AND NEW YORK

Designed cover image: © Getty Images

First published 2023
by Routledge
4 Park Square, Milton Park, Abingdon, Oxon OX14 4RN

and by Routledge
605 Third Avenue, New York, NY 10158

Routledge is an imprint of the Taylor & Francis Group, an informa business

© 2023 Janet Packer, Nia MacQueen and Patricia Day

The right of Janet Packer, Nia MacQueen and Patricia Day to be identified as authors of this work has been asserted in accordance with sections 77 and 78 of the Copyright, Designs and Patents Act 1988.

All rights reserved. No part of this book may be reprinted or reproduced or utilised in any form or by any electronic, mechanical, or other means, now known or hereafter invented, including photocopying and recording, or in any information storage or retrieval system, without permission in writing from the publishers.

Trademark notice: Product or corporate names may be trademarks or registered trademarks, and are used only for identification and explanation without intent to infringe.

British Library Cataloguing-in-Publication Data
A catalogue record for this book is available from the British Library

Library of Congress Cataloging-in-Publication Data
Names: Packer, Janet, 1954– author. | MacQueen, Nia, 1985– author. | Day, Patricia, 1977– author.
Title: Relationship-based learning : a practical guide to transforming children's behaviour / Janet Packer, Nia MacQueen and Patricia Day.
Description: Abingdon, Oxon ; New York, NY : Routledge, 2023. | Includes bibliographical references and index.
Identifiers: LCCN 2022057183 (print) | LCCN 2022057184 (ebook) |
    ISBN 9780367763640 (hardback) | ISBN 9780367763671 (paperback) |
    ISBN 9781003166672 (ebook)
Subjects: LCSH: Relationship-based learning. | Children with disabilities—Education. | Behavior modification. | Teacher-student relationships. | Learning, Psychology of. | Motivation in education.
Classification: LCC LB1027.435 .P33 2023 (print) | LCC LB1027.435 (ebook) |
    DDC 371.39/3—dc23/eng/20230301
LC record available at https://lccn.loc.gov/2022057183
LC ebook record available at https://lccn.loc.gov/2022057184

ISBN: 978-0-367-76364-0 (hbk)
ISBN: 978-0-367-76367-1 (pbk)
ISBN: 978-1-003-16667-2 (ebk)

DOI: 10.4324/9781003166672

Typeset in Bembo
by Apex CoVantage, LLC

MIX
Paper | Supporting
responsible forestry
FSC
www.fsc.org
FSC® C013985

Printed in the United Kingdom
by Henry Ling Limited

Contents

Figures

Tables

Preface

Relationship-based Learning: A Practical Guide to Transforming Children's Behaviour provides strategies and approaches of how we implemented Behaviour for Learning across the Primary Inclusion Development Service (PIDS) and Courtyard AP Academy (CAPA). Our approach is based on the conceptual framework of Behaviour for Learning developed by Simon Ellis and Janet Tod.

The Behaviour for Learning framework has been fundamental to promoting learning and improving behaviour in our school, The Courtyard AP Academy (CAPA). The framework also influenced the way in which the Primary Inclusion Development Service worked in partnership in schools to improve behaviour. We offer practical ideas and guidance on how to implement Behaviour for Learning for learners with social, emotional and mental health (SEMH) issues, as well as those at risk of exclusion from school. Each chapter includes practical strategies and frameworks that can be used at an organisational or whole school level, as well as in the classroom. It includes structures and strategies which we believe will improve the learning and behaviour of children.

We believe that the strategies and approaches we have used continue to be relevant for teaching children in any school or alternative provision, especially those targeted at children with SEMH needs.

Please note that all the children's names have been altered to protect confidentiality. Names of parents, carers, professionals and schools have been anonymised.

Acknowledgements

We thank all the staff who joined us on our journey implementing Behaviour for Learning through our interventions in the Primary Inclusion Development Service and the Courtyard AP Academy.

We say thank you to all headteachers across Hammersmith and Fulham primary schools who worked in partnership with us and helped us to develop and refine our approach to Behaviour for Learning in the Primary Inclusion Development Service.

To the colleagues who helped us from the local authority, Education Psychology service, Tri-Borough Alternative Provision (TBAP) thank you for your advice, suggestions and encouragement. Our knowledge and understanding of early years increased as a result of the support we received from the early years adviser. It was brilliant having an educational psychologist attached to our team and working closely with a senior educational psychologist, we gained a deeper understanding of children with SEMH and received training and support which strengthened the team.

Thank you, Fiona, for suggesting that we focus on learning to improve the behaviour of children and for all your support when PIDS started.

A special thank you to Seamus Oates for giving us the opportunity to develop Behaviour for Learning at the Courtyard AP Academy and share our approach across TBAP.

It was a privilege to work with staff who were committed to improving outcomes for children and supporting them to develop a love for learning. We thank all the staff who worked at the Courtyard AP academy who created an ethos and culture where Behaviour for Learning permeated the whole school and had a significant impact on children's lives. We thank you for being willing to try out new ideas and the contributions that you made.

Of course we thank the children with whom we worked. They are not mentioned by name but we learnt so much from them and they are the inspiration for this book.

Thank you to Paul Dix for reading our manuscript and for your constructive and encouraging feedback. It was particularly valuable, as you had followed our journey throughout.

Thank you Simon Ellis and Janet Tod for suggesting that we write a book to capture the work that we were doing. Your book *Behaviour for Learning* provided us with the unique conceptual framework that underpinned our work.

A special thank you to Simon for reading our manuscript and the detailed advice that you gave which has helped us to keep focused on the purpose of our book, to share the strategies and approaches that were significant throughout our work in implementing Behaviour for Learning.

Thank you to our families.

For Gary, Lizzie and Rory for their patience, love and support.

Thank you to Archie, Bonnie and Valentine for your love and support.

Thank you Alaina for reading the manuscripts and for your ongoing love, support, suggestions and editing. Thank you Steve for your ongoing support.

I would like to thank the editors at Routledge. Thank you Alison for giving us the opportunity to write this book and for your encouragement and advice. Thank you Rhea for your support and advice.

Relationship-based learning

Introduction

Relationships are a crucial factor in promoting a positive learning environment for everyone in the school community including children, staff and parents. The importance of positive relationships is widely recognised as the most vital tool to support learners (DFEE and McBer, 2000; Hattie, 2009; Roffey, 2011). The impact of these relationships cannot be underestimated and begin with the professional responsibility of the adult to create opportunities where relationships can thrive (Pianta and Walsh, 1996; Hornby and Atkinson, 2003; Jennings and Greenberg, 2009; DFE, 2011).

Positive relationships help to build children's self-esteem, foster their mental health and enhance their learning. They also have an influence on well-being, motivation and the performance of both students and teachers (Desforge and Abouchaar, 2003; Martin and Dowson, 2009; Roffey, 2011). One of the key themes identified by the Education Endowment Foundation (EEF) in their report on improving behaviour in schools (EEF, 2019) was the importance of relationships in promoting positive behaviours, focusing on building good relationships so that children feel valued and supported.

Teachers must make a conscious effort to support the personal and cultural identities of the children in their classes. To ensure this happens, they are required to reflect on their practice and to gain insight into any cultural misunderstandings or bias that they may hold about different cultural groups which may affect their perception and expectations of children's learning and behaviour. As adults we must be able to understand ourselves as cultural beings, 'practitioners must enter their classrooms with a sound grasp of how their own socialization, experiences, values and perceptions shape who they are as professionals' (Monroe, 2006, p. 4).

Relationships between peers are also fundamental as children can contribute positively to the social and emotional development of others, including skills such as empathy, cooperation and problem solving.

Positive interactions between parents and teachers are essential to ensuring a child's success long term (Olender et al., 2010; Roffey, 2004). This positive support enables them to support and encourage their child at home and can also increase parental confidence in their role (Hampden-Thompson and Galindo, 2017).

Working in partnership with external agencies can be complex and challenging. For this reason, productive relationships are of particular importance here (Cheminais, 2009). Where professionals come together to share knowledge and expertise to support and meet the needs of children and their families, collaboration is required in order to secure and improve positive outcomes for children.

DOI: 10.4324/9781003166672-1

Within this book, we recognise the importance of developing positive relationships in schools and focus on the relationships for learning based on the Behaviour for Learning conceptual framework. We explore the ways in which this can be influenced by adults and describe how working within the framework can offer a dynamic approach to improving learning, teaching and behaviour.

Our inspiration for writing this book is our passion and belief in the implementation of the Behaviour for Learning framework and its impact on outcomes for children, on the quality of teaching and learning and on the academic achievement and progress of individuals. In addition to this its contribution to improved well-being and behaviour was clear at our school – The Courtyard Alternative Provision Academy, formerly the Primary Pupil Referral Unit and specialist provision for children with Social Emotional and Behavioural Difficulties (SEBD).

> The culture of the school is one of success through learning. All members of the school community, pupils, parents, carers and staff buy into the culture.
>
> OFSTED report, 2015

It is evident that the implementation of this approach had a phenomenal impact on the ethos and culture of our school. This extended beyond the children and staff to parents, carers, services and partner agencies that were involved with supporting our families.

The Behaviour for Learning approach also influenced the way in which the Primary Inclusion Development Service (PIDS) worked in partnership with schools to improve behaviour. The focus on the identified learning behaviours in the PIDS process helped to reframe behaviour management and encouraged staff to develop strategies that would support individuals and groups to increase their positive learning behaviours. As a result, during our time as a local authority service, we began to see a reduction in exclusions.

The Behaviour for Learning approach places significant emphasis on the three relationships – the child's relationship with self, others and the curriculum. Its implementation supported us to explore ways in which to improve and sustain positive behaviour. It also allowed us to develop ways to implement a personalised curriculum, firmly based within an equalities framework, supporting all children, especially those with social, emotional and mental health (SEMH) needs.

We cannot discuss the success of the implementation of the Behaviour for Learning approach without first acknowledging the professional learning environment created, where staff became committed, developing a deep-seated belief in the approach and a strong desire to ensure the best outcomes for all children.

Our journey with the Behaviour for Learning (BFL) approach began in the context of the Primary Inclusion Development Service in 2009. We had a unique opportunity to start from the beginning and to develop a new strategy to improve behaviour across a range of mainstream schools and in the Primary Pupil Referral Unit. The knowledge and experience gained throughout the journey was instrumental in identifying the structures, strategies and approaches that improved outcomes for children, especially those who attended the Courtyard AP Academy. There were a number of key lessons that we learnt, and we believe practitioners can learn from them also. Some of these include:

- How we adopted a shared understanding of BFL
- How BFL was incorporated into the interventions that we used in schools
- How the staff learning programme empowered staff to use the BFL framework
- How the assessment process enabled staff, parents and children to track the progress of the learning behaviour relationships
- How BFL permeated all aspects of the Courtyard AP Academy and transformed the culture and ethos
- The most effective strategies that helped to build capacity
- How we developed strong links with parents so that they were actively involved and participated fully in the processes to support their child's learning behaviours

Our work as classroom practitioners, with schools and across the local authorities, focused on improving behaviour. We reflected on our practice and looked at models that linked learning and behaviour. At the time there was only one approach that really stood out for us – an approach that was well established and had a clear focus on learning. This was the Behaviour for Learning conceptual framework developed by Ellis and Tod (2009). We decided to develop and implement Behaviour for Learning within the context of the work that we were undertaking across mainstream schools and in the Primary Pupil Referral Unit (PPRU).

A key feature of our book is that we aim to demonstrate how moving away from a focus on improving behaviour and behaviour management, to one where learning and behaviour are linked can transform children's learning.

There are many books that address different aspects of improving behaviour in schools, two of which focus in particular on Behaviour for Learning: *Behaviour for Learning: Proactive Approaches to Behaviour Management* by Simon Ellis and Janet Tod (2009) and *Promoting Behaviour for Learning in the Classroom: Effective Strategies, Personal Style and Professionalism* by Simon Ellis and Janet Tod (2015). These particular books written by Ellis and Tod were instrumental in helping us to develop and implement the Behaviour for Learning framework at the Primary Inclusion Development Service and the Courtyard AP Academy.

In writing this book, we hope not only to provide an additional perspective on promoting children's positive behaviour but also to share practical suggestions and a range of strategies that transform the behaviour of learners in both a specialist provision for children with SEMH needs and for all children in the classroom.

This is a book aimed at educational practitioners including senior leaders, teachers, support staff, Special Educational Needs Coordinators (SENCOs), pastoral support teams, outreach services and multi-agency staff who are committed to improving outcomes for children with SEMH needs. It is based on the Behaviour for Learning conceptual framework by Ellis and Tod (2015, 2018), which we adopted, adapted and implemented for the children in our provision and our outreach work in mainstream schools. Each chapter includes a variety of practical strategies and frameworks that can be employed at an organisational or whole school level, as well as more specifically in the classroom. It also includes structures and suggestions that we believe will improve the learning and behaviour of children.

The key message that we wish to convey is that the implementation of the Behaviour for Learning framework can have a significant impact on the quality of provision including teaching and learning resulting in outstanding, and in some cases, exceptional outcomes for learners with SEMH needs. From our experience, it is a tool that can make a difference for all children as well as address the inequalities that may exist within the classroom.

We believe that the systems and structures we put in place to implement Behaviour for Learning was highly effective and continues to be relevant and adaptable to supporting children in any school or alternative provision, especially those targeted at improving the quality of learning for children with SEMH needs.

Chapters

Chapter 1 'The best thing about our school is learning!'

We start this chapter with a child talking about their experience at the Courtyard AP Academy. We identified Behaviour for Learning as an area of excellent practice which was consistently endorsed by reviewers of our provision. This chapter focuses on the excellent practice, the impact of Behaviour for Learning at the Courtyard AP Academy where Behaviour for Learning permeated all aspects of our school. We include the BFL model that our approach was based on and the learning behaviours that we used based on the three relationships – relationship with self, relationship with others and relationship with the curriculum. We include children's reflections on their learning and how parents were actively engaged. We see how children's learning experiences were transformed, the educational gap was closed and they all made progress.

Chapter 2 Vision to action

This chapter focuses on the journey that we took starting from the development of the Primary Inclusion Development Service (PIDS). We developed and implemented Behaviour for Learning in PIDS and show how we incorporated the framework into the structures and processes that we developed. We include the national context, the nature and concerns about behaviour in schools and share our response. We discuss the ways that we worked in partnership in schools to build capacity and empower staff. The final section of this chapter is about transition. We were involved in transition from the Courtyard AP Academy to mainstream school, Key Stage 2 to 3 and Year 6 to 7. These were very important stages for children and their parents/carers. Transition was usually a challenge, trying to reintegrate children who had had a history of exclusions or had been permanently excluded from school back into mainstream. We show how the Behaviour for Learning approach supported the reintegration process, often leading to a successful transition of children back into a mainstream school.

Chapter 3 Professional learning

Professional development is critical when new concepts and approaches are being introduced, adopted and implemented. This chapter focuses on the professional learning programme where we capitalised on a national programme that all staff took part in. We highlight how the programmes, key strategies and actions influenced and empowered staff on the team. We include the role of peer supervision and solution-focused approaches. We describe the learning that we were engaged in that transformed the ethos and culture of our service. There is a specific reference to strengthening families and communities, the parenting programme that we did with parents/carers.

Chapter 4 Developing our assessment tool

This chapter focuses on the assessment tools that we implemented based on the three relationships: 'relationship with self,' 'relationship with others' and 'relationship with the curriculum' of the Behaviour for Learning framework. We explain the assessment procedure that we used, the graphical analysis and how we interpreted them to track the progress of the learning behaviours for each child. We worked in partnership with schools and parents to review the assessments and identify next steps. Readers will be interested to see how the analysis of the assessments can be used effectively to track a child's learning behaviours and see the relationships between them.

Chapter 5 The golden thread

This chapter explores how we implemented Behaviour for Learning at the Courtyard AP Academy and reflects on both the successes and challenges. It includes the development of additional strategies that we used to support the model. The implementation of Behaviour for Learning influenced our approaches to learning which helped to improve outcomes for children. It includes specific strategies that were used to promote positive learning behaviours. We include the personalised curriculum, our approach to Behaviour for Learning, the social, emotional aspects of learning (SEAL) programme.

Chapter 6 Changemakers

This chapter outlines the development of additional strategies that we used to support the Behaviour for Learning model. Within this chapter, you will see how the implementation of Behaviour for Learning can influence approaches to learning that support improved outcomes for children. It includes specific strategies and practical ways to promote positive relationships and learning behaviours that contributed to an engaging curriculum.

Chapter 7 Promoting Behaviour for Learning across schools

In this chapter we ask the question: Was the focus on Behaviour for Learning making a difference across schools? We look at the tools that we used to monitor and evaluate the outreach service and the robust systems that we put in place to review the impact of Behaviour for Learning on the interventions. We share our review process where the contribution of parents/carers and the child was valued and provided a way where all those involved worked together collaboratively. We include case studies to show the impact of Behaviour for Learning and the role of the staff involved.

Chapter 8 Transforming learning

In Chapter 1 we shared the impact of the implementation of Behaviour for Learning on the children who attended the Courtyard AP Academy. In this chapter we look at the evidence that we used to assess the impact, that is how we monitored and evaluated the implementation of Behaviour for Learning. We describe how our approach created a positive learning environment for the whole school community. We highlight a tapestry of strategies that positively impacted children's progress, learning and behaviour.

We started with a child talking about their experience in Chapter 1 and we end with children sharing their experience at the Courtyard AP Academy.

References

Cheminais, R. (2009). *Effective Multi Agency Partnerships: Putting Every Child Matters into Practice.* London: SAGE.

Department for Education (DFE). (2011). *Review of Best Practice in Parental Engagement.* London: DFE.

Department for Education and Employment (DFEE) and McBer, H. (2000). *Research into Teacher Effectiveness: A Model of Teacher Effectiveness.* London: DfEE.

Desforge, C. and Abouchaar, A. (2003). *The Impact of Parental Involvement, Parental Support and Family Education on Pupil Achievement and Adjustment: A Literature Review.* DES Research Report for Education and Skills.

EEF. (2019). *Improving Behaviour in Schools: Guidance Report.* https://d2tic4wvo1iusb.cloudfront.net/eef-guidance-reports/behaviour/EEF_Improving_behaviour_in_schools_Report.pdf?v=1635355216 (accessed 29/07/22).

Ellis, S. and Tod, J. (2009). *Behaviour for Learning: Promoting Positive Relationships in the Classroom.* Abingdon, UK: Routledge.

Ellis, S. and Tod, J. (2015). *Promoting Behaviour for Learning in the Classroom: Effective Strategies, Personal Style and Professionalism.* Abingdon, UK: Routledge.

Ellis, S. and Tod, J. (2018). *Behaviour for Learning: Promoting Positive Relationships in the Classroom* (2nd ed.). Abingdon, UK: Routledge.

Hampden-Thompson, G. and Galindo, C. (2017). School-family relationships, school satisfaction and the academic achievement of young people. *Educational Review,* 69(2), 248–265. Sussex.

Hattie, J.C. (2009). *Visible Learning: A Synthesis of over 800 Meta-analyses Relating to Achievement.* London and New York: Routledge.

Hornby, G. and Atkinson, M. (2003). A framework for promoting mental health in school. *Pastoral Care in Education,* 21(2), 3–9.

Jennings, P.A. and Greenberg, M.T. (2009). The prosocial classroom: Teacher, social and emotional competence in relation to student and classroom outcomes. *Review of Educational Research,* 79, 491–525.

Martin, A. and Dowson, M. (2009). Interpersonal relationships, motivation, engagement, and achievement: Yields for theory, current issues and educational Practice. *Review of Educational Research,* 79(1), 327–365.

Monroe, C.R. (2006). Misbehaviour or misinterpretation? Closing the discipline gap through cultural synchronization. *KAPPA Delta Pi Record,* 161–165.

OFSTED. (2015). *Courtyard Alternative Provision Academy: Inspection Report.* London: OFSTED.

Olender, R.A., Elias, J., and Mastroleo, R.D. (2010). *The School-Home Connection Forging Positive Relationships with Parents.* Thousand Oaks, CA: Corwin Press.

Pianta, R.C. and Walsh, D.C. (1996). *High Risk Children in Schools Constructing Sustaining Relationships.* New York: Routledge.

Roffey, S. (2004). The home – school interface for behaviour. A conceptual framework for co-constructing reality. *Education and Child Psychology,* 21(4), 95–107.

Roffey, S. (2011). *Changing Behaviour in Schools. Promoting Positive Relationships and Wellbeing.* London: Sage Publications.

1 'The best thing about our school is learning!'

The impact of Behaviour for Learning at the Courtyard AP Academy

Introduction

This chapter starts with a quote from the children who attended the Courtyard AP academy. Their response about learning was often a positive one and was reflected in the feedback they gave in writing and verbally. The vision at the Primary Pupil Referral Unit which then became reorganised as the Courtyard AP Academy did not change – it was that children would have a love for learning. This was based on a quote by John Holt:

> Since we cannot know what knowledge will be needed in the future, it is senseless to try to teach it in advance. Instead our job must be to turn out young people who love learning so much, and who learn so well, that they will be able to learn whatever needs to be learnt.
>
> (Holt, 1964, p. 173)

One of the main impacts of implementing Behaviour for Learning was that the children developed a love for learning and staff developed ways of motivating and inspiring children to learn.

In this chapter we share the impact that Behaviour for Learning had on the school community, children, parents/carers and staff. We include the learning behaviours that we developed in the Primary Inclusion Development Service (PIDS) to use across schools and the Courtyard AP Academy. We listen to what the children had to say and use good news stories about children to share the outcomes.

'My Behaviour for Learning is amazing'

Learners were given a great opportunity when invited to speak at the 'Alternative Provision; Pupil Referral Unit Network' conference at City Hall London. Luke was the youngest participant and had been at The Courtyard AP Academy (CAPA) for 18 months. The way in which he spoke, with such confidence and conviction, was a strong reflection of the progress that he had made when just a year earlier, he had been struggling to engage with any form of learning and was experiencing great difficulty engaging at school. To hear him speak about his journey (see Figure 1.1) with such clarity and pride was testament to the growth and development that he had experienced whilst being supported within an environment dedicated to using a Behaviour for Learning approach.

DOI: 10.4324/9781003166672-2

> Hello everyone, my name is Luke, and I am 7 years old. I am in Year 3, the Raspberry class, the Courtyard AP Academy.
>
> When I was at my mainstream I wasn't focused that much on my learning and got into trouble for not doing learning. Sometimes, I felt annoyed and upset when this happened at school and sometimes I was unsafe.
>
> Then I started at the Courtyard and I made a lot of progress and a lot of friends. My behaviour for learning is amazing because I always show self-control and independently make choices. Also I have self-belief and I believe I can be successful in all my learning.
>
> With my learning I am very good at Maths because my progress is great and now I can work by myself and use the grid method. I have also got 1124 coins on study ladder because I've been excellent at finishing the tasks in Maths and English.
>
> The things that help me at school are the teachers because they are amazing and help me all the time if I need it. Next when I get stickers and tokens I feel motivated. If I work well the teachers tell me I'm an impeccable and outstanding learner. This is what I get tokens for. Now I always listen, and I am a role model to others. I always try my best in learning, and I am proud of myself and my work.

Figure 1.1 Luke, a learner from the Courtyard AP Academy talking about his experience

Luke's speech (Figure 1.1) inspired many people at the conference, and he received a variety of positive feedback as a result. What followed was a wide interest from other professionals in how Behaviour for Learning underpinned our practice at the Courtyard AP Academy. It was refreshing and unusual to the audience that Luke did not talk about 'good' or 'bad' behaviour, but instead he spoke confidently about the progress he had made with his learning. It was clear that he had a sound knowledge and understanding of his learning behaviours and this was reflected in his speech.

Luke's experience was not unusual for a child who attended our school; the key messages from his talk about learning and Behaviour for Learning could be echoed by all the children who attended The Courtyard AP Academy. Figure 1.2 show some examples of children talking about their learning.

The feedback from children consistently showed that they had a good understanding of their own learning behaviours and the progress they had made and continued to make. These were children who had histories of poor behaviour, SEBD and fixed term exclusions. They were categorised as 'disadvantaged' and having a disability or special educational need, usually with a background of social, emotional and mental health needs. Children often entered the Courtyard AP Academy with standards much lower than typically expected for their ages and despite these factors, were able to make excellent progress academically, socially and emotionally.

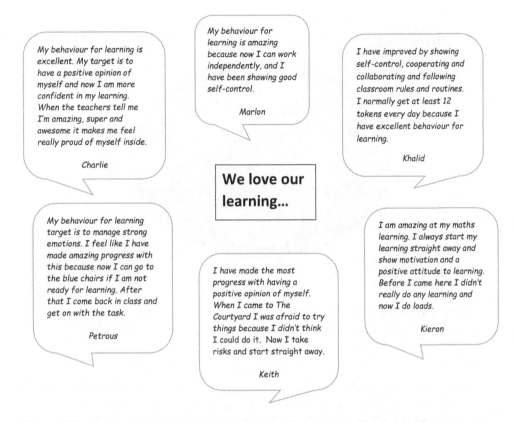

My behaviour for learning is excellent. My target is to have a positive opinion of myself and now I am more confident in my learning. When the teachers tell me I'm amazing, super and awesome it makes me feel really proud of myself inside.

Charlie

My behaviour for learning is amazing because now I can work independently, and I have been showing good self-control.

Marlon

I have improved by showing self-control, cooperating and collaborating and following classroom rules and routines. I normally get at least 12 tokens every day because I have excellent behaviour for learning.

Khalid

We love our learning...

My behaviour for learning target is to manage strong emotions. I feel like I have made amazing progress with this because now I can go to the blue chairs if I am not ready for learning. After that I come back in class and get on with the task.

Petrous

I have made the most progress with having a positive opinion of myself. When I came to The Courtyard I was afraid to try things because I didn't think I could do it. Now I take risks and start straight away.

Keith

I am amazing at my maths learning. I always start my learning straight away and show motivation and a positive attitude to learning. Before I came here I didn't really do any learning and now I do loads.

Kieron

Figure 1.2 Examples of children sharing about their love for learning at The Courtyard

So, what was our approach to Behaviour for Learning based on?

The approach to Behaviour for Learning that we adopted was based on the conceptual framework by Ellis and Tod (2009) (Figure 1.3).

The Ellis and Tod model is adapted from a previous framework from Powell and Tod in 2004 and is shown in Figure 1.3.

In this model, the term 'learning behaviour' is placed at the centre of the triangle indicating that the promotion of learning behaviour provides a shared aim for teachers and others who have responsibility for providing appropriate learning experiences for children and young people. The identified learning behaviour provides the focus for assessment, intervention and positive change.

The triangle surrounding the term 'learning behaviour' is used to indicate that the development of learning behaviour is influenced by social, emotional and cognitive factors. This triangle is sometimes referred to as the triangle of influence. Explicitly recognising the influence of social, emotional and cognitive factors allows the learning behaviour to be explored and addressed through the three relationships (with self, others and the curriculum) experienced by the individual within the classroom. The arrows that surround the triangle represent the dynamic nature of learning and reflect the reciprocal influence that these social, emotional and cognitive factors have on the development

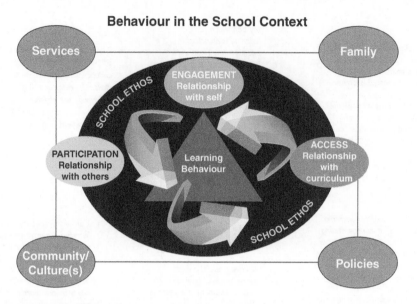

Figure 1.3 The Behaviour for Learning conceptual framework
Source: adapted from Powell and Tod, 2004

of learning behaviour. The terms access, engagement and participation in the diagram are an indication of effective inclusion in groups settings. The learner is not viewed as a passive recipient but placed at the heart of effective practice. The circle surrounding the triangle of influence named school ethos and the terms that lie outside the circle, services, parents/carers, community and policies acknowledge that that the development of learning behaviour takes place in a wider context. The overall purpose of the framework is that it encourages staff teachers to look at what learning behaviour they need to develop in order to reduce the problematic behaviour that is being shown by the child (Ellis and Tod, 2018, pp. 37–38).

What is a learning behaviour?

A learning behaviour can be described as a behaviour that a child is required to possess in order to learn effectively in the group setting of the classroom. It should not be assumed that a child already possesses the ability to effectively carry out this positive behaviour; therefore it is the role of the adult to recognise this and to identify the necessary areas for development so that a child might be successful throughout their schooling. The Behaviour for Learning framework is based on the premise that there are particular behaviours necessary for learning and it is therefore important for teachers to think consciously about how they create opportunities for children to develop the learning behaviours (Ellis and Tod, 2015, pp. 37–38).

In their work, Ellis and Tod (2009, 2015, 2018) make the point that there is not a finite, definitive list of learning behaviours and encourage practitioners to focus on the individual child to determine what learning behaviours they have currently mastered, what that reveals about each of the three relationships and the necessary learning behaviours that are

Table 1.1 The learning behaviours developed and used within each of the relationships

Learning Behaviours

Relationship with self	Relationship with the curriculum	Relationship with others
RS1. Is interested in learning	RC1. Is willing to engage with the curriculum	RO1. Is willing to work independently as appropriate
RS2. Has a positive opinion of self	RC2. Can take responsibility for own learning	RO2. Socially aware of what is going on around him/her
RS3. Can manage strong emotions such as anger and/ or sadness	RC3. Is able to access the curriculum	RO3. Is willing and able to empathise with others
RS4. Has a belief that he/she is capable of being successful	RC4. Is willing to try new things and 'take risks'	RO4. Is willing to ask for help
RS5. Can independently make choices	RC5. Can make mistakes and 'move on'	RO5. Is willing to behave respectfully towards adults in school
RS6. Can take responsibility for own behaviour	RC6. Is self-aware, knows how and when to get help	RO6. Is willing to behave towards peers
RS7. Shows good self-control	RC7. Motivated to complete tasks	RO7. Is able to listen to others and be attentive
	RC8. Able to work unaided	RO8. Can cooperate and collaborate when working and playing in a group
	RC9. Follows classroom rules and routines	

a priority to develop. As a local authority, we took the decision to change the diagnostic assessment that had been previously used by staff as it was not rooted in Behaviour for Learning and in particular, the three relationships (with self, others and the curriculum). A decision was taken to develop specific sets of behaviours associated with each of the three relationships in order to support not only staff assessments of learner progress but also children's self-assessments. These can be seen in Table 1.1.

During their time at The Courtyard AP Academy, children became very self-reflective about their relationships with self, others and the curriculum. As well as knowing and understanding these behaviours, it was important that every member of the staff also had a shared understanding of Behaviour for Learning and how it was being implemented in The Courtyard AP Academy. As a result of a rigorous staff training programme and a strong staff commitment, Behaviour for Learning permeated the entire culture, ethos and curriculum. It was evident in daily practice and was a language that the entire school community spoke. Staff promoted the learning behaviours at every opportunity available to them, for example, during breakfast time, in and out of the classroom, on school trips and during assemblies. Figure 1.4 provides examples of the way in which staff incorporated the language into feedback. The children were clear about the learning behaviours, and this was achieved in a variety of ways which will be discussed in the coming chapters such as discreet Behaviour for Learning lessons as well as being modelled consistently in staff practice.

Children made significant progress at the Courtyard AP Academy – in fact they made outstanding progress academically, behaviourally, socially and emotionally. They also developed a strong love for learning and had ample experiences of being successful.

The shift from a focus solely on behaviour and behaviour management to one which linked learning with behaviour, transformed our approach to behaviour, teaching and learning. The Behaviour for Learning framework, including the three relationships, led

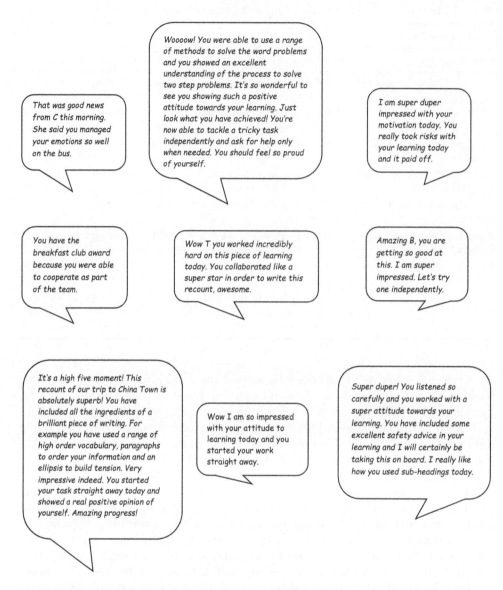

Figure 1.4 Examples of feedback that staff gave to the children at the Courtyard AP Academy

the initiatives and developments that took place throughout the Courtyard AP Academy and in our partnerships with parents/carers, schools and other agencies.

Within a short space of time, usually 8 weeks of a child attending the Courtyard AP Academy, children's learning and behaviour could be seen to be changing, and we were able to see a measurable change in children's attitude to learning and their relationship with the curriculum. The personalised curriculum which was carefully planned taking account of the child's detailed assessment of their previous learning and Behaviour for Learning assessments was fundamental to their success. Children made rapid progress especially within reading, literacy, and numeracy skills. We could confidently say that given children's low starting points when they came to The Courtyard AP Academy, that outcomes were consistently judged by us and validated externally as being outstanding (OFSTED, 2015, 2018) and that the achievement gap was closing quickly. Pupil's Attitudes to Self and School (PASS) data revealed that children saw themselves as capable to meet the curriculum demands and had very positive views of themselves as learners.

The feedback children received from staff (see Figure 1.5) had a significant impact on their relationship with themselves, their emotional well-being and the progress they were making. They thrived on the high-quality and purposeful feedback they received which was consistent and provided throughout the day. Such feedback included comments about the children's self-esteem and self-efficacy which led to them feeling more positive about themselves, growing in self-confidence and becoming more resilient.

The quality of work in children's books was a testament to their love for learning. They took great care in their presentation and work. They enjoyed reading the feedback and as time went on, they would respond with their own comments. The children's work and the classroom environment were evidence of the progress they had made, especially in their relationship with self and relationship with the curriculum. It did not matter where children started academically, they made rapid progress and showed great improvements over time.

As the children became more motivated and successful, they took risks and tried new things more frequently. There was no longer a barrier when presented with a task which may have appeared to be a challenge. Children felt safe and secure in class, and this was reflected in their engagement and positive attitudes to learning. They were immensely proud of their work, and they would sit with pride as they showed their books to their parents/carers at child-led progress meetings. They talked about the work they were most proud of, their targets and what they needed to improve. Children sharing work was also a highlight for visitors, especially when it was a member of staff from their mainstream school. For some children, there was a startling difference between the achievements that they were making at The Courtyard AP Academy and the work they had done in their previous school. For the children it was such an achievement to be able to demonstrate

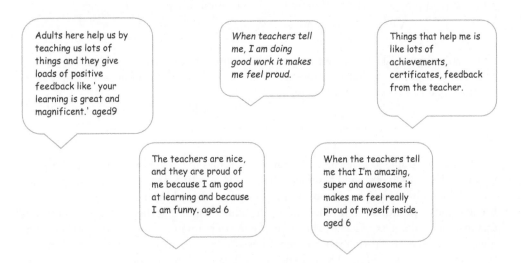

Figure 1.5 Children from the Courtyard AP Academy talking about staff feedback

what they could do, how much they had achieved and talk about their progress. This created a shared sense of pride.

As children made progress in their relationship with the curriculum, they made strong progress in the social and emotional aspects of their learning too. We could see how the cognitive, emotional and social aspects of the children's learning were interdependent.

Children's attendance also improved over time which we believe is related to the fact that they enjoyed coming to school as it was such a positive experience for them. For some children their attendance was very impressive, for some it improved rapidly within a short space of time and for others it was 100%. Learners loved coming to school. Figure 1.6 shows one child's feedback.

> My attendance at school this term is 95%. I feel really proud of this because last year it was much lower. Now I am at school more. I participate in more learning, actually all my learning. That means that when I do assessments, I feel confident.   - Khalid

Figure 1.6 Khalid from the Courtyard AP Academy talking about his attendance

Positive relationships amongst peers and between children and adults developed as their relationships with the curriculum strengthened. Within the school day, there was an abundance of communication and the dialogue was ongoing. Children were also provided with many opportunities to learn how to relate to each other in positive ways.

> Relationships at all levels are exemplary. The obvious mutual trust that exists between adults and pupils is rarely demonstrated so overtly. A typical pupil comment was 'I feel like I'm part of a family here.'
>
> Challenge Partners March 2015

Children were able to maintain and repair relationships in a restorative way. They learnt to get on well with each other and developed this in a range of situations such as in the classroom, at breakfast club, in the playground, during games lessons and in music lessons. They were friendly and respectful to each other and to the adults supporting them. This did not mean that that they did not experience conflict but the use of restorative conversations, and children giving compliments and feedback to each other as part of their daily reflection time meant that conflict was resolved quickly and effectively. The development of strong and respectful relationships resulted in the environment at the Courtyard AP Academy being calm, peaceful and purposeful. Daily routines were well established, and children knew what to expect.

Impact of Behaviour for Learning on parental engagement

'They've given me my son back.'

This was the response from a parent when asked to give feedback about his experience of The Courtyard AP Academy and his son's progress. The reason for this response is illustrated in the case study in Table 1.2.

Table 1.2 Case study of child who attended the Courtyard AP Academy

Case Study

Bradley was permanently excluded from his primary school for a serious violent incident. He physically assaulted his headteacher. It was stated that he was unable to manage his strong emotions and found it difficult to be safe within the mainstream setting. He was below the expected level for his age academically. Following his permanent exclusion and concerns at home he was put in foster care. Bradley settled well with his carers.

Feedback from Carer:

He is a very happy little boy who enjoys coming to school. He is helpful at home and always follows instructions. His behaviour has improved significantly since attending the PPRU and they would like to thank the staff at the PPRU for this.

Over a period of time, he went back to live with his parents and settled well back into his home environment. He made progress academically and in his Behaviour for Learning.

During his time at The Courtyard, he was able to manage his emotions such as anger and sadness. He could access his learning mostly independently but required ongoing praise and sometimes required additional support at the start of the lesson so that he was clear about the task. He always engaged with the curriculum and had a positive attitude to learning. His relationships improved and he always behaved respectfully towards adults and his peers.

This is his feedback from his review before starting mainstream school on a part time basis initially.

Feedback from Bradley:

I'm so reliable, my name from Miss N is Mr Reliable.

I am better at writing especially using WOW words like amazing, wonderful and fabulous.

I'm nervous about my mainstream but I think I'm ready.

After 2 years he was successfully reintegrated into Year 6 of a mainstream primary school. His parents were incredibly pleased. Bradley was a different boy. Bradley was now ready to go to secondary school and with support in place, he made a successful transition. His dad was so overwhelmed by the changes that had taken place with his son both academically, socially and emotionally while he was at the Courtyard that when asked to give feedback about the Courtyard AP Academy as part of the review process, he said,

'They have given me my son back.'

We regularly received encouraging feedback from parents and carers once their child had settled at the Courtyard AP Academy; however, initial communications were not as consistently positive and could vary to a great degree; some negative, some suspicious. It is important to remember the history of race equality and parental experiences (Demie and McLean, 2017). There were parents who had themselves had a negative experience of school and as a result were cautious and not keen on sending their child to a Primary Pupil Referral Unit (PPRU). However, perceptions often shifted quickly during their first visit to the Courtyard AP Academy as the environment was calm and the quality of children's work both in their books and on display changed their attitudes for the better. There was almost an element of surprise at the standard of work that the children were doing. The displays in and out of the classroom were impressive, especially the artwork. Parents/carers were introduced to Behaviour for Learning by the children as they visited the school and the three relationships were on display in every classroom.

Our parents/carers valued the way they were treated and appreciated how we cared for their children. They knew that we wanted the best for them and this was reflected in both the formal and informal feedback that we received from them. We had high expectations for every child and that was evident throughout the school. The focus on learning and the positive feedback about school from the children and staff daily meant that we were able to engage parents/carers very quickly in a positive way. We personalised our support for parents/carers and created an ethos of mutual trust and support. We broke the negative cycle that had existed and worked effectively in partnerships, problem solving and sharing ways to promote learning and improve Behaviour for Learning. Incidents still occurred; however, daily feedback to parents/carers was always balanced. An incident did not dominate the whole conversation but was included as part of the journey of the day. some examples of feedback (see Figure 1.7) we received from parents/carers.

Figure 1.7 Parents' and Carers' feedback

Staff and parents/carers worked collaboratively to problem solve any issues that arose. They were also assisted in accessing additional support for their children, for example, with the process of seeking an Education Health Care Plan (EHCP) or access to Child and Adolescent Mental Health Services (CAMHS).

We also had fun experiences with families and engaged them in ways that meant they felt part of the school community. Parents/carers enjoyed attending the tea parties organised by their children and this became a family event also attended by grandparents and younger siblings. Families sat together while the children served them afternoon tea – this was an event not to be missed.

Home life improved for most children, partly as a result of improved feedback from school phone calls and conversations were no longer dominated by talk of 'bad behaviour' or 'being disruptive.' Parent/carers regularly talked about how their children's behaviour had been transformed by the work of the school.

> Parents spoke passionately about how staff had listened to and nurtured their child so that they were now more confident and engaged in learning.
>
> Chalenge Partners review 2017

It is the responsibility of the leadership to ensure that all aspects of work in schools are underpinned by equal opportunities and inclusion (DCSF, 2008). Rigorous policies and procedures that promote equal opportunities and inclusion are key components in supporting the development of the three relationships, and must be made explicit to the whole school community and external partners they work with.

Children's ethnic, cultural and personal identities are an integral part of a child's relationship with self, others and the curriculum. At the Courtyard AP Academy, ensuring ethnic and cultural diversity was promoted throughout our school was one of our strengths. As well as incorporating the spiritual, moral, social and cutural values into our curriculum, we included ideas from the cultural, spiritual and historical rites of passage (Steele and Marigna, 1994) which was one way we could ensure that ethnic, cultural, family and spiritual roots were explicit across the curriculum. It is not enough just to assume that there will be a multi-ethnic, multi-cultural approach to a curriculum. If children are going to develop their learning behaviours, then it is important to look at ways in which the curriculum has a multi-ethnic and multi-cultural dimension that helps support and affirm the development of children's cultural and personal identities.

Every child or young person needs to develop a sense of identity:

- Confident, strong and self-affirming, as distinct from uncertain, ashamed or insecure;
- Open to change, choice and development, as distinct from unreflective, doctrinaire and rigid;
- Receptive and generous towards other identities, and prepared to learn from them, as distinct from wishing to exclude or to be separate. (Runnymede Trust, 1993)

As well as responding to children's diverse learning needs, we had a responsibility to develop the personal and cultural identity of each child who attended the Courtyard AP Academy. It was important that children were learning from a diverse range of cultural experiences and perspectives and had a positive view of themselves and their heritage. Children took part in a rich cultural calendar and were proud to share and talk about their own faith and beliefs. This helped the children to build good relationships with each other. There were many opportunities provided throughout the curriculum for children to explore, celebrate and gain a deeper understanding of different cultures. The staff, parents and visitors played an important role in this. Children enjoyed learning about each other's heritage as well as taking part in specific activities such as djembe drumming, taiko drumming as part of the Japanese day and doing Kente designs.

A member of staff shared her feedback after working on black role models and historical figures and as part of a final piece of work where children had to choose an inspirational person to research and explain why they were role models.

> Learners were able to identify with them culturally and were inspired by their success. They felt ambitious and positive about their futures especially the children who wanted a career in the field of their role models.
>
> Middle leader feedback

'It is important that children see themselves as integral parts of the rich diverse mosaic of traditions, faiths and ethnicities which make up the UK today' (DFE, 2022). We have a responsibility to make that a reality for all children.

Reintegration: back to mainstream

We became very successful at reintegrating children back into a mainstream setting, especially when we were able to offer part time placements.

The Behaviour for Learning framework played a major role in the children's ability to access mainstream education and was instrumental in helping us to prepare them for reintegration either back to their primary mainstream school, secondary school or to a specialist provision more suited to the child's individual needs. We were dedicated to providing the children with mainstream experience where possible and we were very grateful to the headteachers who worked in partnership with us and enabled this to happen. We built up a trust with headteachers who understood how we worked and knew that the reintegration process was supported by the regular review process that we used. Table 1.3 shows the feedback that was taken from the class teacher, deputy headteacher and learner as part of the review process. Sometimes it was not the right time for the child to return to mainstream, but that was built into the reintegration process, and this removed any sense of failure.

Table 1.3 Feedback from a class teacher, deputy headteacher and learner who attended the Courtyard AP Academy part time.

Mainstream feedback from class teacher and deputy headteacher	Feedback from Oliver during follow up visit
• Good attitude towards the curriculum • Daily reflections help with decision making • Circle time for whole class re: transition has supported him • Accepting praise more which is a huge positive • More able to make mistakes and move on • Looking forward to break times more – broader circle of friends • Making good progress in learning	• I'm feeling confident about my SATs • I've been finding mainstream really good • I'm getting better at English because I've developed an imagination from all the books that I've been reading • I'm much better at division • I've been showing more self-control and more interest in my learning • On a scale of 0–10 I was on a 2 when I first started CAPA but now I am a 9 with my Behaviour for Learning • I am looking forward to secondary school • I feel great because I have been working hard and doing better

The use of coaching strategies, joint observations and feedback based on Behaviour for Learning supported the reintegration process for children, parents/carers and staff.

Good News

Table 1.4 shows a range of 'good news stories' of children who given their starting points made excellent progress, improved their learning behaviours and a number of them were successfully reintegrated into a mainstream school.

Table 1.4 'Good news' stories of children who attended the Courtyard AP Academy, background information and the progress that each child made

Name	Background	Outcome
Asiff	• Permanent exclusion from mainstream school (Year 5) • Significant SEMH difficulties • Self-harm • Significant communication and processing difficulties • Difficulties maintaining peer relationships	– Accelerated progress – Achieved over and above expected at the end of KS2 – Re-integrated into mainstream school full time – Transitioned successfully into mainstream secondary school – Currently making good progress in Year 8 and is working at national expectations
Petrous	• 2 x permanent exclusions from mainstream schools (Year 5) • Significant SEMH difficulties • School refuser • Persistent disruption including aggressive and violent behaviour and significant damage to property	– Reintegrated into a local mainstream school full time – Transitioned successfully into mainstream secondary school – Continues to make significant progress (currently Year 9) – Mother reports improved relationship between the two and a more 'settled' home life as a result where the family are now 'happy and we have a new life' – Improvement in attendance from 57% to 96%
Matthew	• Permanent exclusion from mainstream school (Year 2) • School refuser • Physically and verbally abusive to staff and learners • Poor relationships with peers and often involved in conflict • Inability to manage strong emotions • Working significantly below national expectations	– Accelerated progress – Reintegrated into mainstream primary school full time where he continues to do well in Year 3 – Feedback from Matthew – 'I feel great because I have been working hard and doing better!' – Feedback from external agencies is that Matthew is a 'different character' – Improvement in attendance from 19% to 98%
Benjamin	• EHCP – SEMH difficulties • Attended 3 mainstream schools • Verbally and physically aggressive to adults and peers • Inability to manage strong emotions • 6 x fixed term exclusions	– Exceeded expectations in reading, writing and SPAG at the end of KS2. – Continues to make good progress academically and socially and emotionally. – Transitioned into mainstream secondary school (Currently Year 7) – Has developed positive relationships with peers and adults. – Reports that he is enjoying his new school and feels confident that he will do well.
Shiroh	• Permanent exclusion from mainstream school (Year 6) • Significant SEMH difficulties • Difficulties relating to forming and maintaining relationships with others, both learners and adults • Required significant support in order to manage strong emotions	– Achieved level 5s at the end of KS2 – Transitioned successfully into mainstream secondary school (currently Year 8) – Feedback from secondary school is that he shows a consistently positive attitude to his learning and is accessing the curriculum well. – He is currently exceeding national expectations

(Continued)

Table 1.4 (Continued)

Name	Background	Outcome
Clive	• 7 x fixed term exclusions for physical assaults (Year 6) • Managed move from one mainstream to another • Permanent exclusion from mainstream school • Twice weekly support from CAHMS due to ongoing mental health difficulties • Significant difficulties when relating to others	– Achieved 1x level 5 and 2x level 4 at the end of KS2 – Transitioned successfully into mainstream secondary school (currently Year 8) – No serious incidents since attending secondary school – Has been able to form a friendship group and maintain this – Feedback from mainstream is that Clive follows classroom rules and routines
Donald	• Permanently excluded from mainstream primary school • Difficulties relating to personal space • Poor relationships with others • Tendency to steal objects from others and school • Often involved in physical altercations	– Exceeded expectations in reading, writing and SPAG and met his maths expectation. – Transitioned into a mainstream secondary school (currently Year 7) – Feedback from link worker and mainstream is that Donald is learning positively in all lessons and has a number of achievement points – Mum reports that Donald is happy and achieving well
Hussein	• 11x fixed term exclusions from mainstream school (Year 6) • Part time placement at CAPA • Significant SEMH difficulties • Difficulties relating to forming and maintaining relationships with others, both learners and adults	- Achieved level 4s at the end of KS2 – Reintegrated into mainstream primary school full time – Feedback from the mainstream school was that Hussein was more respectful towards adults, was happier to be at school and developed more positive relationships with adults. – Transitioned successfully into mainstream secondary school (currently Year 8)
Henry	• 6 x fixed term exclusions for mainstream school (Year 6) • Part time placement at CAPA • Significant SEMH difficulties • Ongoing refusal to engage with the curriculum • Inability to form and maintain friendships • Difficulties when managing strong emotions	– Achieved level 4s at the end of KS2 – Reintegrated into mainstream primary school full time – Feedback from the mainstream school was that Henry was engaging well with the curriculum, accepting more praise and was more able to make mistakes and move on – Transitioned successfully into mainstream secondary school (currently Year 8) – Parent's reported that they are 'thrilled' with the progress made and thank TBAP for the support provided.
David	• 7 x fixed term exclusions from mainstream school (Year 3) • Part time placement at CAPA • Inability to manage strong emotions • Physically aggressive towards others • Disengaged from the curriculum • Speech and language difficulties	– Reintegrated into mainstream primary school full time – Continues to be successful at mainstream in Year 6 – Feedback from the mainstream school was that David became a lot more interested in learning and developed a more positive opinion of himself. – Carer reported that the relationship between them had improved and that David was now able to follow instructions and listen more often.

Elliot	
• 3 x fixed term exclusions (Year 2)	– Accelerated progress (1c to 2a in 18 weeks in numeracy)
• Physical and verbal aggression	– Reintegrated into mainstream primary school full time
• Very low self-esteem affecting his ability to engage with the curriculum	– Continues to be successful at mainstream in Year 5
• Lack of social boundaries	– Feedback from mainstream was that Elliott 'Shows a strong interest in learning and is more able to work in a group. He is proud of his learning and is getting better at managing his emotions.' He is able to ask for help when needed and has got lots of friends.'
• Inability to maintain relationships with peers and adults	
• Rejection of support provided	
Jermaine	
• Permanently excluded for the use of dangerous weapons (Year 6)	– Reintegrated into a new mainstream primary school full time
• Difficulties when managing strong emotions	– 100% attendance
• Physically aggressive towards others	– Transitioned successfully into mainstream secondary school (currently Year 9)
• Poor attendance	
Marco	
• 4 x fixed term exclusion from mainstream school (Year 5)	– Reintegrated into mainstream primary school full time
• Part time placement at CAPA	– Mother reported a transformation in their relationship
• Ongoing emotional outbursts	– Transitioned successfully into mainstream secondary school (currently Year 9)
• Significant SEMH difficulties	– Continues to make good progress at mainstream school – science teacher & head of year reports that he has a positive attitude towards his learning.
• Ongoing refusal to enter the classroom	
Simone	
• 3 x fixed term exclusion from mainstream school (Year 4)	– Reintegrated into mainstream primary school full time
• Part time placement at CAPA	– Feedback from Simone, 'I am so confident now. I always work on my own, it's much better and I am proud.'
• Significant SEMH difficulties	– Feedback from the mainstream school 'Simone is more engaged in her work and the intervention has had a big impact. She is more able to work in a group and is sharing her work with others which she enjoys.'
• Very low self-esteem affecting her ability to access the curriculum	
• Inability to operate within the systems and boundaries of a mainstream school	
Hakim	
• Permanent exclusion from mainstream school (Year 5)	– Reintegrated into a new mainstream primary school full time
• Difficulties with interacting appropriately with others	– Father reported, 'He has changed since coming to his new school and is now more motivated to attend school. He is delighted to be going to a mainstream school.'
• Significant social and emotional difficulties	– Transitioned successfully into mainstream secondary school (currently Year 9)
• Inability to manage strong emotions	
• Regular physical and emotional outbursts	
Kieron	
• 7 x fixed term exclusion from mainstream school (Year 2)	– Reintegrated into mainstream primary school full time
• Part time placement at CAPA	– Accelerated progress (1c to 1a in 14 weeks in reading)
• Unable to be included safely at mainstream school	– Continues to be successful at mainstream in Year 6
• Significant lack of social awareness	– Staff at the mainstream school reported a considerable improvement in Kieron's attitude to learning
• Violent outbursts	

(Continued)

Table 1.4 (Continued)

Name	Background	Outcome
Maria	• Significant difficulties when interacting with others including violent tendencies. • Verbal and physical abuse towards staff and other learners. • Unable to operate within the boundaries of a mainstream school. • Difficulties accepting responsibility for own choices and move on after mistakes. • Significantly below age-related expectations.	– Significant progress in relationship with self, others and curriculum. – Strong progress across the curriculum. – Successfully reintegrated into mainstream for a session each week. – Positive mainstream feedback. – Improved sense of self – PASS data is extremely positive.
Jordan	• At risk of permanent exclusion from mainstream school (Year 2) • 9 x fixed term exclusions • Violence towards adults and peers • Inability to remain in class • Verbal abuse towards peers and adults • Ongoing damage to property	– Strong progress in relation to his ability to remain in class – reduction in ready for learning exits. – Significant reduction in serious incidents – Improved relationships with adults and peers – Successfully reintegrated into mainstream school following a 20 week placement
Leandros	• At risk of permanent exclusion (Year 2) • Significant SEMH difficulties • Difficulties when managing strong emotions • Almost daily violent outbursts • Inability to self-regulate • Unable to be included safely at mainstream school	– Mother reports she is pleased with his progress and ability to manage his emotions at school – No serious incidents since attending CAPA – Improvement in B4L data – Increased ability to work independently – Currently being reintegrated into local mainstream school
Jerome	• Had been moved between 3 schools by the age of 7 • 6 x fixed term exclusions • Was permanently excluded from mainstream school • Violent outbursts and an inability to be included safely at school • Difficulties with interacting appropriately with others	– Improvement in attendance from 58% to 76% and rising – Good progress across the curriculum – A significant improvement in self-control and ability to remain in class – Reintegration into the primary school on a Thursday afternoon – Progress with B4L progress

Excellent practice at the Courtyard AP Academy

As part of the Challenge Partners review process in September 2014, we identified Behaviour for Learning as an area of excellent practice. This was confirmed by the review team of three senior practitioners.

'The consistently outstanding Behaviour for Learning is a testament to leaders' tenacity and determination to follow through with what they believe to best for pupils at CAPA. The positive impact of the strategy is clearly evident in so many ways, including pupils' outcomes, attitudes to learning, high self-esteem, high attendance, good self-control and understanding of what successful learning looks and feels like.'

Feedback from Challenge partners review 2014

Our Behaviour for Learning approach was recognised and endorsed by a range of practitioners, teachers, support staff, headteachers, local authority inspectors and OFSTED as excellent practice which we shared with schools and local authorities.

Summary

In this chapter we have shared the children's experience of The Courtyard AP Academy and how the implementation of Behaviour for Learning impacted their lives and experiences at school. The impact was evident in many ways such as pupil outcomes, attitudes to learning, high self-esteem, high attendance, good self-control, improved relationships and an understanding of what successful learning looks like.

We shared the learning behaviours that we used across schools and in the Courtyard AP Academy.

We looked at the role that staff had to play and how they reinforced the learning behaviours for each child.

We shared parents' experience and feedback.

Finally, we have shared the good news stories of some of the children, giving background information about each child and highlighting the impact on their academic achievement, personal development and Behaviour for Learning.

Takeaways

- Leaders, be passionate and determined about the vision you have for your school/provision and the strategies that are going to make a difference.
- A focus on learning can effectively transform children's behaviour as well as make a significant difference to their learning and learning experiences.
- Children's feedback gives insight into the ethos of the school and the specific factors which impact on their learning.

Reflective questions

- In what ways is your vision for children's Behaviour for Learning evident throughout your school?
- What do the children in your school/provision have to say about the impact of improving Behaviour for Learning on their lives and experiences?

'When I started at The Courtyard I did not have a positive opinion of myself, I was a 2, now I am an 8 and feel much more positive about my learning.'

'When I started at The Courtyard I found it hard to manage my strong emotions I was a 1 and now I am now an 8, I feel much happier.'

- Here are two children talking. How involved are the children in your school/provision in assessing their Behaviour for Learning? Do they understand what it looks like when it is good, and do they know what happened for it to improve?
- How do you use solution-focused approaches to support a child to improve their learning and behaviour?
- Do all staff know what to do to improve a child's specific learning behaviour identified as a cause for concern?

References

Demie, F. and McLean, C. (2017). *Black Caribbean Underachievement in Schools in England.* Published by Schools Research and Statistics Unit Lambeth Education and Learning.

Department for Children, Schools and Families (DCSF). (2008). *The National Strategies Primary. Excellence and Enjoyment: Learning and Teaching for Black Children in the Primary Years.* London: DCSF.

Department for Education (DfE). (2022). *Inclusive Britiain: Government Response to the Comission on Race and Ethnic Disparities.* London: HMSO.

Ellis, S. and Tod, J. (2009). *Behaviour for Learning: Proactive Approaches to Behaviour Management.* Abingdon: Routledge.

Ellis, S. and Tod, J. (2015). *Promoting Behaviour for Learning in the Classroom: Effective Strategies, Personal Style and Professionalism.* Abingdon: Routledge.

Ellis, S. and Tod, J. (2018). *Behaviour for Learning: Proactive Approaches to Behaviour Management* (2nd ed.). Abingdon: Routledge.

Ellis, S. and Tod, J. (2022). Behaviour for Learning. In H. Cooper and S. Elton-Chalcraft (eds.), *Professional Studies in Primary Education* (4th ed.). London: SAGE.

Holt, J. (1964). *How Children Fail.* London: Penguin.

OFSTED. (2015). *Courtyard Alternative Provision Academy: Inspection Report.* London: OFSTED.

OFSTED. (2018). *Courtyard Alternative Provision Academy: Inspection Report.* London: OFSTED.

Powell, S. and Tod, J. (2004). *A Systematic Review of How Theories Explain Learning Behaviour in School Contexts.* London: EPPI-Centre, Social Science Research Unit, Institute of Education, University of London.

Steele, M. and Marigna, M. (1994). *Strengthening Families, Strengthening Communities: An Inclusive Parent Programme.* London: Race Equality Foundation.

The Runnymede Trust. (1993). *Equality Assurance in Schools: Quality, Identity, Society, a Handbook for Action Planning and School, Effectiveness.* London: Trentham Books for the Runnymede Trust.

2 Vision to action

Introduction

In the introduction we shared that the implementation of Behaviour for Learning started in the Primary Inclusion Development Service (PIDS). In this chapter we provide more detail about PIDS, the setting up of the service designed to meet the needs of children with social, emotional and behavioural difficulties (SEBD) across schools. We describe the structure of the service, the roles and responsibilities of the staff team in the Primary Inclusion Development Service (PIDS) and the processes that we put in place.

We share how we reframed our approach to improving behaviour by being intentional about incorporating Behaviour for Learning into our structures, systems and processes. The reader will be able to identify how the Behaviour for Learning framework, including the three relationships, became an integral part of our work. A fundamental part of the team's role was to build capacity and empower staff so that they became even more effective at improving the behaviour of children in their schools.

Transition is an important process in any school and specialist provision. We developed approaches for reintegration back into mainstream school and from key stage 2 to 3 and refer to the five bridges of transition (Galton et al., 1999) and how we incorporated it into our process.

Social, emotional and mental health

In 2015 the Special Needs and Disability code of practice (DFE, 2015) replaced social, emotional and behavioural difficulties (SEBD) with social, emotional and mental health difficulties (SEMH). The rationale for the change being that SEBD put a lot of emphasis on the presenting behaviours which were not ameliorated by the behaviour management strategies in the school. We found that children with SEMH difficulties presented challenges to schools even when schools had consistent approaches to managing behaviour and the teacher was experienced. We had requests for interventions from a range of schools and from staff with varying levels of experience.

There is often a tension or dilemma for teachers who are anxious about supporting children with SEMH, whilst needing to meet the needs of the rest of the class at the same time given the negative effect of the behaviour of those with SEMH (Cooper, 2008). We found that all teachers wanted to be inclusive in their practice and wanted to look at ways to effectively meet the needs of children with SEMH.

For the remainder of this book, we will use the terms SEMH and SEBD interchangeably.

DOI: 10.4324/9781003166672-3

The journey begins

The priority for the local authority was to develop a service which focused on learning and not just on improving behaviour. The service was targeted at supporting primary schools to enhance their own capacity to respond even more effectively to the needs of primary school-aged children with SEBD and to secure each child's entitlement to learning within their own mainstream school. This was a challenge as the experience and expertise of the team largely focused on behaviour as a separate entity to learning. We used the Behaviour for Learning framework by Ellis and Tod (2009) to develop the approach that we would use across schools.

Where did we start?

Covey (1989) identified 'Begin with the end in mind' as one of the seven habits of highly effective people. It was important that as we were embarking on a new project that if we did not have a clear vision it could result in confusion and a lack of clarity of what we were trying to achieve. Beginning with the end in mind was a positive place to start and provided a focus of what we wanted to achieve as a team. The priority was certainly to improve children's outcomes, to reduce exclusions and to empower staff so that they were developing the skills, knowledge and understanding of children with SEBD. The support to be provided by PIDS was for children who were identified by the school as having SEBD. This was a crucial provision, as it meant that children without a statement could access high-quality interventions. There was already a specialist full time provision for children with a statement for SEBD. The Primary Inclusion Development Service widened the scope of children who would be supported across the borough.

Our vision is to provide a high-quality service which is personalised and achievement driven to ensure pupils with SEBD are supported to achieve high outcomes and reach their full potential.

The key words that encapsulate our vision are:

- Learning
- Empower
- Partnership

To achieve this we will:

Promote and provide a professional, dedicated and specialist support service which works closely with teams services.

Work in partnership using solution focused approaches so that schools develop their own capacity to respond even more effectively to the needs of primary aged children with SEBD.

Lead on the development of processes and practices that are specifically targeted at reducing exclusions.

Work in effective partnerships to secure each child's entitlement to learning within their mainstream school.

Review and evaluate the purpose and practice of the service to ensure that it meets current expectations with enough flexibility to meet future challenges.

Figure 2.1 The vision and aims of the Primary Inclusion Development Service

It was an opportunity to look at how staff could work in a way where they were empowering others and share their knowledge and skills. We defined our vision and then looked at ways to make it a reality.

We focused on the vision and looked for different ways in which we could incorporate the Behaviour for Learning framework in PIDS and across schools.

Background to the Primary Inclusion Development Service

The Primary Inclusion Development Service was set up following the reorganisation of the Primary Behaviour Support Team (PBST), Behaviour Education Support Team (BEST) and the Primary Pupil Referral Unit (PPRU). The school specialist provision for children who had a statement for SEBD was redesignated to a primary school. In the Primary Inclusion Development Service (PIDS), there was a move away from a 'traditional approach' to outreach to try and establish a more developmental model with schools; one where staff would be developing and coordinating work across schools and different services to secure better outcomes for children. The title of 'inclusion development team' more closely described its function in developing and coordinating work across professional and agency boundaries to secure better outcomes for children.

Within the PIDS, the focus was going to be on learning, and we started by exploring the following question:

'Is it possible to transform a child's behaviour by focusing on learning?'

This was a particularly interesting question for us to explore with specific regard to children who were perceived by schools as the 'most challenging' in relation to their behaviour and at risk of fixed term and permanent exclusion. Few would disagree that learning and behaviour are inextricably linked; our challenge was to research and find a model that would enable us to implement our vision whilst maintaining a focus on learning.

The staff in the PIDS team needed to develop an understanding of how learning could be a central focus to improving behaviour. The training and literature that had influenced our practice had focused on behaviour and behaviour management including a range of strategies that could be used to improve behaviour in class and throughout the school (DCSF, 2009; DFE, 2012 a,b, 2014, 2015; DFES 2001, 2003b, 2003c, 2004; OFSTED, 2014, 2006). The book *Behaviour for Learning* (Ellis and Tod, 2009) was a turning point in our journey. It was exactly what we were looking for; an approach that was not only explicit in the way behaviour and learning were linked, but also one that maintained a focus on learning as a key approach to transforming children's behaviour. Following a discussion with the leadership team, we implemented the Behaviour for Learning conceptual framework based on the model by Ellis and Tod (2009). It was a framework that we could use to develop our service and became the foundation for our practice.

Behaviour: Is it improving?

The concerns about poor behaviour in schools has been on the agenda in education for decades. Our development of the Behaviour for Learning approach within the Primary Inclusion Development Service took place in the wider national policy context of pupil behaviour as an ongoing concern for policy makers and schools. At the start of the service, the Steer report (DFES, 2005a, 2009) which had been commissioned by the government, reported that the standards of behaviour were good or outstanding in the vast majority of schools (DFE, 2012a). Ofsted had also painted the picture that behaviour was improving (Ofsted 2005). However, by 2017, Tom Bennet concluded 'there is sufficient evidence to suggest that there is enough of a problem nationally with behaviour for it to be a matter of concern' (Bennet, 2017, p. 21).

The Elton report (DFES, 1989) was a key document widely recognised as being critical in establishing the importance of whole school behaviour (e.g., Hallam and Rogers, 2008; DFES, 2005a, 2006, 2009; Chambers and Olsson Rost, 2020) The Elton report was commissioned as a result of public and parliamentary concern about indiscipline and bullying in schools.

Successive governments have also produced numerous guidance documents (DFES, 2003c; DCSF, 2008a, 2009; DFE, 2010, 2014, 2016) on school discipline and pupil behaviour. Even though the purpose of the plethora of reports and guidance documents produced over the three decades since the Elton Report (DFES, 1989) has been to address concerns over the standards of behaviour in schools, a key question is whether the problem of misbehaviour has changed for better or worse or not changed at all (Davey, 2016).

There is a strong focus on delivering high standards of behaviour in the Government white paper, 'Strong schools with great teachers for your child' (DFE, 2022). The paper stresses the importance of developing strong cultures that reduce poor behaviour. The view is stated that no matter how brilliant a school's curriculum, children will not achieve their potential if there are poor standards of behaviour (DFE, 2022, p. 25). Even though few would argue with this statement, the section on better behaviour and attendance does not give sufficient attention to the role of curriculum and pedagogy in influencing standards of behaviour and attendance. To some extent it reinforces the idea viewed by Ellis and Tod (2009, 2015, 2018, 2022) as problematic, that 'promoting learning' and 'managing behaviour' are separate issues for schools. The EEF (2019) report recommends teaching learning behaviours alongside managing behaviour in the 'Improving Behaviour in schools guidance.'

Throughout our work across schools, we found that promoting high standards of behaviour was essential. Schools were keen to uphold and promote an inclusive environment where children and staff felt supported to improve the behaviour and meet the needs of children with SEBD. There is always the tension of promoting high-quality teaching and learning while supporting and meeting the needs of children who are perceived as having a 'negative' impact on the learning experiences of other children in the class.

Changing the focus

The team all had experience of working to improve behaviour across schools in the local authority. They were very experienced and skilled, having been trained in a whole range of strategies and approaches to improve behaviour in schools. They were involved in developing behaviour policies and supporting schools to follow the government guidelines. That had been their job. The focus of their support had been mainly about 'getting children to behave' so that teachers could teach. There was a common view held by some staff and members of the team that you had to get the behaviour right before you could teach. Our experience in schools and in the PPRU/Courtyard AP Academy showed us that this was not the case. We were encouraged and influenced by the emphasis that Alan Steer puts in the report of the practitioners' group that 'the quality of teaching and learning and behaviour are inseparable' Steer report (DFES, 2005a), OFSTED (2005) also reports that an appropriate curriculum and effective teaching can enhance and encourage good behaviour.

Our next step was to train staff in the Behaviour for Learning framework, to move away from focusing on the behaviours that were becoming a barrier to learning to those learning behaviours which would promote positive behaviour. The learning behaviours were those behaviours which the children had to develop to be able to engage fully and learn effectively.

Of course, there was anxiety and uncertainty amongst the staff. Behaviour for Learning and the important link between behaviour and learning was a new concept and approach. There were also new roles and responsibilities. The requests from schools changed and the way we were going to respond was going to focus on capacity building, that is, empowering staff in schools. Everyone was expected to work in a new and different way. There were several tensions which arose as we embarked on a different approach to promoting positive behaviour and as we started to explore the following questions:

- How would staff in schools respond to a focus on Behaviour for Learning?
- Would we be able to work across professional boundaries, for example, a development worker modelling strategies for a class teacher?

Implementing Behaviour for Learning

We were convinced from the outset that implementing the Behaviour for Learning framework across the PIDS would have a positive impact not only on children's behaviour but also on their learning. There were two priorities; first to look at how we could fulfil the vision and aims of the service, and second to look at ways in which we could strengthen the links between teaching, learning and behaviour using the Behaviour for Learning framework.

Our rationale for developing and implementing Behaviour for Learning was:

- It promoted the development of positive learning behaviours.
- It provided opportunities to use specific positive praise and reinforcement.
- It enabled us to identify the learning behaviours for each child and implement strategies to develop the learners and staff.
- It promoted and enhanced relationships with self, others and the curriculum, that is, the social, emotional and cognitive aspects of learning.
- It provided the opportunity to focus on the personal and cultural identities of children.
- It provided a way to break down 'good behaviour' into small manageable steps.
- It provided a specific focus for interventions.
- It developed a language of learning.
- It provided a way that we could measure the impact of the strategies that we were using.
- It promoted accountability and independence for staff and learners.

Following extensive training for staff on how to implement Behaviour for Learning, it was clear early on that the framework was having a positive impact on the children's three relationships: 'relationship with self,' 'relationship with others' and 'relationship with the curriculum.' For those individual children from mainstream schools involved in a PIDS intervention and children who attended the PPRU we were witnessing changes in children's learning behaviours.

A new service

To fully understand how we were able to transform our way of working and implement Behaviour for Learning it will help to understand the Primary Inclusion Development Service (PIDS), the staffing structure and the processes that we implemented.

It was important to involve staff in the vision and to begin to create a culture where staff could be open. The academic term before PIDS started provided a good opportunity to visit all the primary schools and meet with headteachers to identify the schools' needs and discuss the service. Meetings were also held with the PIDS staff team to find out more about their roles and responsibilities.

Quality standards

The process and development of PIDS was based on a review of the processes implemented by the Behaviour Education Support team using the first 6 of the quality standards related to improving the outcomes for children (Figure 2.2).

The standards were drawn up by the South East Regional partnership in association with the South West Regional partnership (DCSF, 2008c) and were designed to support improved outcomes for children and young people with special education needs (SEN). To improve the quality of outcomes for children supported by the service, we focused on section one: outcomes, standards 1–6 (see Figure 2.2).

The quality standards helped us to identify the strengths of the previous service and the areas for development. Having the opportunity to reflect back on positive aspects of the team's work and look ahead was an excellent place to start. The next stage was to draw up the targets and action plans with success criteria to ensure that all the areas that we had identified would include Behaviour for Learning.

These were the key questions that we used to help us reflect on our progress in meeting the quality standards:

Where are we now? How do we know?
Where do we want to be? 1 year? 5 years?
How are we going to get to where we want to be? What actions do we need to take?
How will we know that we have been successful?

Standard 1: Progress towards outcomes is systematically recorded and monitored.

Standard 2: The Service promotes the use of interventions based upon up to date specialist knowledge and expertise of suitably qualified professional staff.

Standard 3: Parents should always be consulted and where appropriate, involved in supporting the learning and development of their child as part of any intervention.

Standard 4: Clear outcomes are agreed on by the service and user, and steps are taken to avoid the development of a culture of dependency.

Standard 5: Services have a clear purpose which takes into account local authority policies, the Children and Young People's plan, the needs of particular schools, early years settings and other provision in the area and the range of CYP needs.

Standard 6: The service regularly collects feedback about its interventions and uses it to improve the quality of service.

DCSF, 2008c

Figure 2.2 Section one of the quality standards: Outcomes, standards 1–6 identified in the quality standards for special education needs (SEN) support and outreach services

Table 2.1 Areas that PIDS identified for development

Areas identified for development following the review based on the quality standards 1–6

1. Data from the school is collected systematically, recorded and analysed
2. The outcomes for the interventions are agreed on with the school staff, includes the headteacher, class teacher, parents and in most cases the child
3. The progress the children make is monitored during the intervention and after it is finished. The progress of groups and classes is also tracked.
4. Interventions are based on Behaviour for Learning and promote the development of learning behaviours. There are systems and structures in place to monitor the impact of the interventions
5. Parents are involved in all stages of the intervention process
6. All the information and process is accessible to parents/carers
7. The process of PIDS is designed to increase the capacity of schools
8. Training is provided to ensure that staff can fulfil their roles
9. The service works with the local authority, the primary strategy team to identify schools so that support can be prioritised according to the needs of schools
10. The service works collaboratively with other services to improve outcomes for children
11. All INSET completed by PIDS in schools or across the LA is collated, evaluated and analysed by PIDS
12. Evaluation of the service is used to improve the quality of the service

---

Table 2.2 A section taken from the PIDS service plan, the priority and targets for the academic year 2009–2010

PRIORITY: To establish a Primary Inclusion Development Service which is focused on achieving high outcomes for pupils with BESD

TARGETS

1. To develop an effective strategy to meet the vision and aims of the service
2. To ensure that there are clear direction and priorities identified for the service
3. To implement effective management systems
4. To ensure that interventions are bespoke, that is, programmes and support are tailored to meet the needs of the school within its context
5. To ensure that staff have the experience, knowledge competencies and skills to work in partnership with schools and other services/agencies
6. To ensure that there is partnership working with other services

---

We were aiming to be an outstanding service where outstanding was defined as 'can consistently demonstrate high rates of progress in the majority of Children and Young People and provide evidence of continuous improvement in service management and delivery in most areas over a three year period' (DCSF, 2008c, p. 6).

Table 2.1 shows the areas that we identified as needing to be developed in the Primary Inclusion Development Service (PIDS) following the review using the quality standards.

The areas needing development across the service were incorporated into the PIDS service improvement plan (Table 2.2).

Each of the targets included actions, success criteria, monitoring and evaluation with names of staff allocated to each target and action.

As well as drawing up a service improvement plan for PIDS, we also produced an improvement plan for the PPRU because it was seen as a discrete unit.

Table 2.3 An extract from the Quality Improvement Plan 2011–2012

Target	Success Criteria	Evidence	Strategies/Action What has to be done	Who	By whom? Timescale	Resources
To ensure that assessment supports the development of high-quality learning and impacts on pupil progress	Rigorous and accurate assessment supports the implementation of high-quality teaching and learning AFL and APP enables pupils to play a significant part in making improvements in their work Analysis of Behaviour for Learning Assessment supports the pupils' personal development and well-being A rigorous and robust system is in place to track progress across the curriculum	• Joint implementation tool • APP/AFL assessment • Pupil Books • Work Scrutiny • Behaviour for Learning assessment • Lesson Observation • PPRU panel update	Share assessment data with mainstream school Continue to implement APP Behaviour for Learning assessment implemented. Use at start of placement and half termly to track progress of pupils' personal development and well-being Analyse and evaluate Behaviour for Learning assessment with key staff (Mainstream school); identify key focus areas with pupil			

Light grey: Information deleted

Key

A key was used to indicate the progress made in each of the targets of the action plan. The target is shaded dark grey in the table above to indicate that progress towards the target is good or better in all areas.

An extract from the PPRU quality improvement plan

Incorporating Behaviour for Learning throughout the service improvement plan and the PPRU improvement plan was a way of ensuring that it was evident throughout the work of the teams. This was more effective than just having one target which said, 'implement Behaviour for Learning.' It helped us to include Behaviour for Learning into more targets, actions and success criteria and involve more staff. In this way the team were putting the actions in place, and we were monitoring the success criteria and providing evidence showing the impact. The evaluation of the service improvement plan, the school self-evaluation form (SEF) and reports both internal and external, gave us feedback about Behaviour for Learning.

The structure of the Primary Inclusion Development Service (PIDS)

Teams, roles and responsibilities

There were two teams in PIDS, the extended PPRU provision and inclusion development team, (see Figure 2.3). Although the PPRU had a distinct identity, it remained an integral part of the Extended PPRU provision team. There were different roles and responsibilities in the teams. The role of 'Teacher Consultant' was introduced to demonstrate that there was an enhanced expectation about the level of expertise that would be required from the teacher, as well as the additional responsibility of building capacity in schools. The redesignation of learning mentors and teaching assistants to 'development workers' was twofold. It clearly indicated their role in developing provision across the schools and separated the role from that which was currently in schools and any preconceived views of what their roles would be in practice. Each member of staff had an area of work that they had oversight of with responsibility for the development and dissemination of this area, with or on behalf of their colleagues.

Even though Figure 2.3 shows the staffing structure for PIDS, it was never fully implemented because of staffing and budget constraints. The head of service took on responsibility for the extended PPRU team and inclusion development team and the structure changed to include a business support officer.

The staff were divided into teams which was based on their roles and responsibilities, the extended primary pupil referral team and the inclusion team. The staffing in the PPRU did not change.

1. The extended PPRU team focused on:

    *   Leading and raising achievement of pupils with SEBD
    *   Supporting the development of interventions and strategies for schools causing concern
    *   Providing leadership and leading on developing processes and practices targeted at reducing exclusions

2. The inclusion development team focused on:

    *   Schools becoming even better at managing pupils with SEBD
    *   Developing the continuing professional development strategy designed to increase capacity
    *   Using specific areas of responsibility for building capacity in schools

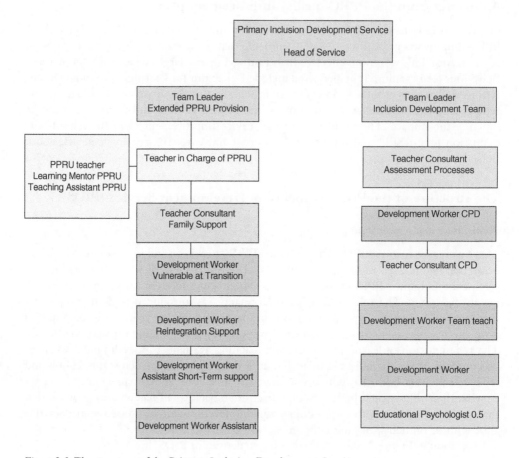

Figure 2.3 The structure of the Primary Inclusion Development Service

The rationale for having an extended PPRU team was to support the reintegration and/ or transition of children back into their mainstream primary school or secondary school if they were in Year 6. Alongside the PPRU placement there would be support for families, hence the role of a member of staff with additional responsibility for working with families, primarily parents/carers.

The staff in this team would be able to enhance and further individualise the provision for pupils in the PPRU or work in schools to further enhance the provision for pupils who are at risk of being permanently excluded. Although staff had specific responsibilities within their roles, in practice staff worked across a range of interventions according to their strengths, experience and development needs. For example, some staff wanted to gain experience of working with families and therefore worked alongside the teacher consultant with responsibility for families.

Building capacity

Throughout the vision and the role of the Primary Inclusion Development Service (PIDS) there is a reference to 'enhancing the capacity of schools' and the role of the inclusion team being responsible for 'building capacity.'

The role of the team was to engage school staff, individually and collectively in learning how to become even better at meeting the needs of children with SEBD. Stoll (2009) describes building capacity as 'the power to engage and sustain learning of people at all levels in the educational system for the collective purpose of enhancing student learning' Stoll (2009).

Capacity building was complex. The team had to work in such a way that staff in schools would learn and acquire the knowledge and skills to deal with the challenging behaviours they were facing. This was not just about working with the class teacher or teaching assistant but looking at ways in which we could personalise staff support and involve the whole school community, to ensure that any strategies implemented would be embedded and sustainable.

Capacity building brought a different approach to the way that the PIDS team was going to work. Whilst there was uncertainty about a new approach to supporting schools, they received it in a very positive way as they focused on improving outcomes for children and empowering staff in schools. They would have the opportunity to work in such a way that staff across the whole school would be learning strategies to positively impact children's behaviour, and thus reduce the number of exclusions.

To build capacity it was important to involve everyone in the vision that we had and what we were trying to do. Learning together helped as everyone was new to this approach – there were no experts. A culture of trust and professional respect had to be developed with staff who were willing to share and take risks. It was important that teachers were as equally valued as development workers.

Staff needed opportunities to see Behaviour for Learning in action and try things out with feedback. Collaboration among staff was important to work together, share and learn. In Chapter 3 we look at how this was achieved.

Working as a team

When the service started, staff were allocated to interventions in pairs according to experience and expertise. This was a deliberate strategy to provide opportunities for staff to learn together and from each other. The PIDS process (see Figure 2.4) was carried out in teams for a term so that staff gained an understanding of the expectations and requirements of each stage A to E. Senior leaders of PIDS led the interventions and focused on Behaviour for Learning throughout the process.

The PIDS process in practice

Working in an outreach capacity, it was important to recognise the unique ethos of each individual school and ensure that the key principles of the three Behaviour for Learning relationships could be embedded with respect to that. A personalised approach was used. Moving from a *referral* form to a joint intervention tool which was the *request for*

The Primary Inclusion Development Service: the process

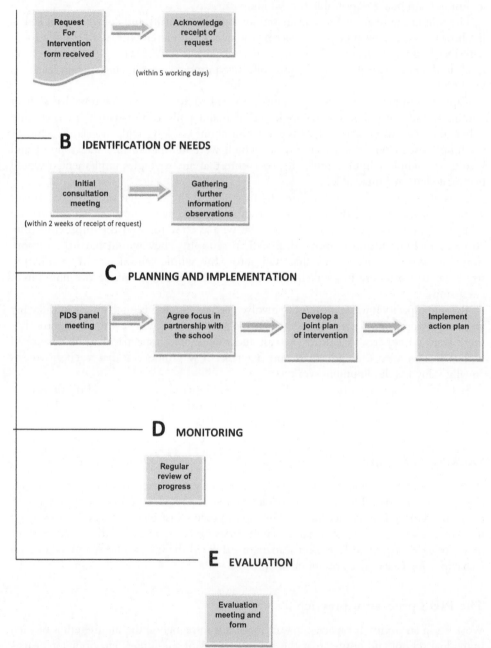

Figure 2.4 The PIDS process for interventions

intervention form was intentional in terms of partnership working, as interventions took on a joint approach, members of the team collaborating with school staff. To enable effective capacity building we were drawing on the existing knowledge and skills within the schools. We needed to play a role of facilitating this through coaching, modelling and training.

The process that was used for PIDS incorporated the Behaviour for Learning framework and included solution-focused approaches. We were intentional about incorporating Behaviour for Learning into the structures and processes that we had developed in PIDS. As we go through the process we show how we shifted the focus to Behaviour for Learning and the three relationships of the learning behaviours.

Request for Intervention

The joint intervention tool (Appendix 3) was the initial form that was sent to schools. It was usually completed by a member of staff, then signed by the headteacher and had to be signed by the parent/carer showing that they agreed for the intervention to go ahead.

The reasons for the request for the intervention for children varied but tended to be more general. Figure 2.5 gives some examples.

Table 2.4 shows specific examples of requests received for two children completed by teachers in different schools.

The inclusion of the assessment form which was part of the intervention tool helped to change the focus of the interventions. All staff completed a Behaviour for Learning assessment for a child and identified the pupil's strengths and areas of concern. This meant that the focus was now Behaviour for Learning and promoting positive learning behaviours.

– Physically aggressive: kicking, biting, hitting, punching other children, hitting staff
– Verbally abusive: unkind language, swearing, use of racist language, frequently shouting
– Persistently angry outbursts, damaging furniture, trashing displays, tearing own work, running out of class, tantrums
– Unable to control emotions

Figure 2.5 Some of the common reasons given on the requests for intervention received from schools across the local authority

Table 2.4 Examples of two reasons for requests completed by two different schools

Reason for request for intervention from school	
Child X Stuart	*Child Z Genevieve*
Aggressive towards other children, fighting	Refuses to complete work she does not want to do
Verbally abusive, swearing and refusing to follow requests	Abusive to staff especially if they persist and make a reasonable request
Underachieving, little work completed in class	Abusive to some of the other children in the class
Becomes angry and frustrated in lessons	Poor relationship with peers
Unwilling to accept support	Has had a fixed term exclusion
Unpredictable/threatening behaviour	Refuses to accept support offered in the classroom
Refusing to follow adults' instructions	Refuses to remove outdoor clothing
Fixed term exclusions from school	Happy to draw pictures but reluctant to write
	Very poor attendance

The assessment was accessible to all staff and parents found it helpful, the language of the learning behaviours was clear, precise and more meaningful.

Tables 2.5, 2.6 and 2.7 give examples of Behaviour for Learning assessments received for children completed by class teachers as part of the request for intervention.

The inclusion of the Behaviour for Learning assessment completed by staff became the focus for the intervention and was different from the initial requests. The assessments of Genevieve, Tobi and Stuart centre around the shared Behaviour for Learning framework and the identification of learning behaviours. Staff identified a lot of concerns for some

Table 2.5 BFL strengths and areas of concern identified by the class teacher for Genevieve

List the pupil's strengths from the assessment

Relationship with self (RS)	Relationship with others (RO)	Relationship with curriculum (RC)
RS1. Is interested in learning		

List of concerns from the assessment

Relationship with Self (RS)	Relationship with others (RO)	Relationship with Curriculum (RC)
RS2. Has a positive opinion of him/herself	RO1. Is willing to work independently as appropriate	RC1–RC9
RS3. Can manage strong emotions such as anger and/or sadness	RO2. socially aware of what is going on around him/her	RC2. Can take responsibility for own learning
RS4. Has a belief that he/she is capable of being successful	RO3. Is willing and able to empathise with others	RC3. Is able to access the curriculum
RS5. Can independently make choices and try to solve problems	RO4. Is willing to ask for help	RC4. Is willing to try new things and 'take risks'
RS6. Can accept responsibility for own behaviour	RO5. Is willing to behave respectfully towards adults in school	RC5. Can make mistakes and 'move on'
RS7. Shows good self-control	RO6. Is willing to behave respectfully towards peers	RC6. Is self-aware, knows how and when to get help
	RO7. Is able to listen to others and be attentive	RC7. Motivated to complete tasks
	RO8. Can cooperate and collaborate when working and playing in a group	RC8. Able to work unaided
		RC9. Follows classroom rules and routines

Table 2.6 BFL strengths and areas of concern identified by the class teacher for Tobi

List the pupil's strengths from the assessment

Relationship with self (RS)	Relationship with others (RO)	Relationship with curriculum (RC)
RS1. Is interested in learning	RO4. Is willing to ask for help	RC4. Is willing to try new things and take risks

List areas of concerns from the assessment

Relationship with self (RS)	Relationship with others (RO)	Relationship with Curriculum (RC)
RS2. Can manage strong emotions such as anger and/or sadness	RO5. Is willing to behave respectfully towards adults in school	RC8. Is able to work unaided

Table 2.7 BFL strengths and areas of concern identified by the class teacher for Stuart

List the pupil's strengths from the assessment

Relationship with Self (RS	Relationship with Others (RO)	Relationship with Curriculum (RC)
RS1. Is interested in learning RS2. Has a positive opinion of him/herself	RO4. Is willing to ask for help RO5. Is willing to behave respectfully towards adults in school RO6. Is willing to behave respectfully towards peers RO7. Is able to listen to others and be attentive	RC1. Is willing to engage with the curriculum RC9. Follows classroom rules and routines

List areas of concern from the assessment

Relationship with Self (RS)	Relationship with Others (RO)	Relationship with Curriculum (RC)
RS3. Can manage strong emotions such as anger and/or sadness RS4. Has a belief that he/she is capable of being successful RS5. Can independently make choices and try to solve problems RS6. Can accept responsibility for own behaviour RS7. Shows good self-control	RO1. Is willing to work independently as appropriate RO2. Socially aware of what is going on around him/her RO3. Is willing and able to empathise with others RO8. Can cooperate and collaborate when working and playing in a group	RC2. Can take responsibility for own learning RC3. Is able to access the curriculum RC4. Is willing to try new things and take risks RC5. Can make mistakes and move on RC6. Is self-aware, knows how and when to get help RC7. Motivated to complete tasks RC8. Able to work unaided

children, for example in Figure 2.7. School staff would then prioritise 1 or 2 following an observation.

The shift from general reasons for a request shifted to learning behaviours which was evident on all requests for interventions that we received.

Gathering information

As well as gathering information from the request for intervention form we carried our classroom observations using the Behaviour for Learning framework, that is the learning behaviours that we had identified as the focus. The purpose was to get any additional information that would help to identify the focus for the intervention. This turned out to be a particularly important part of the process. Observations were carried out in pairs focusing on the learning behaviours of the child and on the strategies used by adults in the classroom which were having a positive effect on the child's relationship with self, others and the curriculum. One member of the PIDS team focused on the child and another member of the team focused on the class. This was insightful as we were able to share our perspective of the child's learning behaviours and feedback with the teacher on the strategies that were being used in the classroom which were promoting positive learning behaviours and those that needed to be developed. The discussion with the class teacher was a good opportunity to reframe behaviour management and focus on the learning behaviours that were going to be prioritised. This approach was also a way of helping teachers and the support staff to focus on what was going well, the approaches and strategies that were having an impact on the child's learning behaviour.

Staff also brought their own cultural knowledge and expertise, and this was evident sometimes in the observation or meeting to discuss the initial request. For example, there were sometimes children who were described as having an attitude problem and or being feisty; this was not necessarily evident to some of the observers, but it provided a good opportunity to share teachers' perceptions of the different cultural groups in the classroom.

Planning and implementation

The meeting and discussions with school staff and the parent(s) provided a good opportunity to share the information that had been collated and identify the next steps. It was now at the stage where the staff from the school, parent/carer and PIDS would create a joint action plan, detailing what they were going to do after they had agreed on the focus of the intervention.

The joint action plan (Appendix 4) was based on the information gathered from the request for intervention form which included the BFL assessment and classroom observation. Figure 2.6 shows the questions that were discussed.

What are the anticipated outcomes of the intervention?
What changes will you be looking for?
What are your expectations of the Primary Inclusion Development Service?
Specific actions, Personnel, Timescale, Training, Development, and other resources
How will you know that the actions are having an impact?

Figure 2.6 The questions on the joint action plan

A solution-focused approach was incorporated into the action plans by referring to 'anticipated outcomes' and the 'changes you will be looking for' meant that there was an expectation that there would be differences in the child's learning behaviours. Once the action plan was completed a programme of intervention was put in place which would include a regular visit to the school at least one session a week, a session being half a day initially.

The staff leading the intervention in the school kept a regular record of support which was based on the joint intervention and the support provided. The record of support was a record of the actions that had taken place and follow up for the following week. This was shared and discussed with the class teacher and provided an opportunity on a regular basis to discuss any concerns, progress and next steps. The PIDS team used a range of strategies to support school staff, which included observing teacher behaviours and classroom structures that were promoting learning behaviours, modelling strategies and coaching staff. Using a solution-focused approach empowered school staff to reflect on existing good practice.

Even though there were learning behaviours across the three relationships that were causing concern, schools tended to identify relationship with the curriculum as a focus at the start of the intervention. A considerable number of the action plans focused on the relationship with the curriculum, especially, is willing to engage with the curriculum 'is able to access the curriculum.' The focus on the curriculum had an impact on children's relations with self and others highlighting the interdependence of the three relationships.

Monitoring

Every 6–8 weeks there was a review of the intervention. This was an important stage in the process, tracking progress and measuring the impact of the intervention. This process took the form of a meeting and was attended by the staff, parent, head of service, head of school and the intervention lead from PIDS. The 6–8-week review included the format shown in Table 2.8.

The review process was an effective way of keeping track of whether the strategies being implemented were having an impact on improving the Behaviour for Learning of a child. It was usually after 8 weeks, the child's Behaviour for Learning assessment would be completed by the same teacher who did the initial assessment, and it would then be analysed. If the child had completed an assessment at the start of the intervention then they would also complete one. The analysis would be a clear indication of whether the child had made progress in any of the targeted learning behaviours. In Chapter 4 we show the analyses of the initial assessment and those taken as part of the review process. The assessment was very clear to the parents/carers and to the child. The staff would reflect

Table 2.8　6–8-week review format

Work completed	Progress against outcomes
School/Service/Agency Hours	Targets/Success criteria
Specify actions that have taken place – see action plan	What progress has the pupil made following analysis of the BfL assessment by the school and school staff
	What academic progress has the pupil made? Level of attainment
	Has attendance/punctuality improved?
	What is the pupil's view
	What is the parent's view?

Barriers	Next Steps and timescales
Is there anything getting in the way of action work identified on the action plan?	Specific actions with times
	What is the focus going to be following the analysis of the assessment?
	Will it change or stay the same?

on the analysis and decide whether to continue with the strategies or make changes. On some occasions the review was evidence of the strategy not being effective and the strategy would have to be changed. The teacher consultant would support the class teacher to implement the strategies and for some interventions the development worker would work with the pupil and Learning Support Assistant in class to enable the child to improve in the areas identified on the assessment. The role of the development worker would also include sharing, modelling and coaching strategies. As described in an evaluation from one school SENCO wrote about the team, we were 'walking the walk and not just talking the talk.'

The partnership between the PIDS team and teacher was helping to build capacity. The intervention usually continued until the classroom teacher believed that the child had made sufficient progress and the teacher no longer required the intervention.

If the data analysed and evaluated showed that the intervention was having a limited impact on promoting the learning behaviour of a child, as part of the review process, we would discuss whether a placement at the PPRU would enable the pupil to make progress with the development of their learning behaviours. This approach was an effective strategy and one we adopted.

The evaluation

Figure 2.7 includes the questions asked as part of the evaluation process at the end of the intervention.

What have been the outcomes of the intervention?
How has the input from the Primary Inclusion Development Service contributed to this?
Strategies/Systems/Actions that have made an impact
Sustainable next steps
Agreed date of follow up meeting

Figure 2.7 Evaluation questions

It was critical that the actions in place to improve the learning behaviours of the child were sustainable. The follow up meeting provided the opportunity to reflect on the progress the child was making in relation to their learning behaviours.

Schools that requested interventions

The PIDS service was available to all schools across the borough. The service was used by a wide range of schools from those outstanding to those requiring improvement. Requests for intervention included teachers who were very experienced to those who were newly qualified teachers (NQTs). There was often training and support needed for teachers new to the profession. There were a range of different reasons for requesting an intervention but what was common was that there was a child for whom the strategies being used by the school were not having the desired impact. Staff had tried a range of strategies and approaches and they needed support as they had exhausted the strategies that they had tried or used.

All of the headteachers in the borough, and over time, neighbouring boroughs were aware of the service, the vision and aims and the way that we were working. It was important to develop an effective partnership with headteachers in schools.

Behaviour for Learning provided a fresh approach, looking at how we could improve behaviour with a focus on capacity building. The involvement of a headteacher in the development of PIDS and a headteacher representative as part of the PPRU, Courtyard AP Academy management committee was valuable input. The head of service was a member of the headteachers forum and there were many opportunities to share and get feedback about the service, structure and processes as well as Behaviour for Learning that we had adopted.

Within the first year the PIDS received 53 requests for intervention. The requests were from 22 different schools across the local authority with two schools making five or more requests. The majority of the requests were for individual children, the majority boys and the others for either classes, teachers or whole school. In our first academic year 2009/2010 the requests across year groups were reasonably even. All the requests were for children in Years 1–6.

Table 2.9 and Figure 2.8 show the PIDS requests from September 2000–2013, the majority being for individual children.

Table 2.9 Types of requests received from September 2009 to June 2010

PIDS Request by Type September 2009 through June 2010	
Type	*Number of Interventions*
Individual	42
Group/class	6
Teacher	3
Whole School	2
	53

Interventions

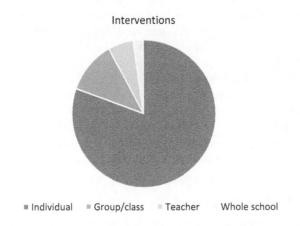

■ Individual   ■ Group/class   ■ Teacher   Whole school

Figure 2.8 Pie chart showing the requests for intervention from September 2009 to July 2010

The children we received requests for were all identified as children having SEBD but how that was defined varied from school to school, and from teacher to teacher; there was not a clear definition. What was clear, however, was that these children needed support to improve their behaviour and a significant number were at risk of being excluded from school.

The severity of the incidences varied from school to school. All the children on the requests were described as having SEBD. We were aware that some of the behaviours children exhibited did not necessarily come under SEBD; however, we still responded to all requests from schools.

Even though there was no clear definition from the schools, every request for a child had a completed Behaviour for Learning assessment which was the focus for the intervention for all staff involved in the school.

Parental involvement

Parents played an important part in the intervention process. They had to agree to the intervention before it went ahead. Some parents were ambivalent about the involvement of the team and did not always understand the reason for the request or the team's involvement. There were some black parents who were very concerned about any involvement with external agencies and concerned about their child being labelled. Nationally a disproportionate number of black children were being excluded; this was a familiar trend (Gilborn, 1995; DCSF, 2008a; DFE, 2019, 2012a; DFES, 2005a, 2009). An intervention was not seen initially as positive by these parents; however, spending time going through the process, the role of PIDS and the focus on Behaviour for Learning helped us to work in partnership, improve learning behaviours and reduce exclusions. What was clear from all parents was that they did not want their child excluded and were willing to receive support. It was very important here to ensure that all parents were always consulted and where appropriate, involved in supporting the learning and development of their child as part of the intervention. Positive communication with parents is important and adopting a personlaised approach so that they are fully engaged (Campbell, 2011). A meeting was always held with parents once they had signed the request for intervention to discuss the request and listen to their views. The Behaviour for Learning assessment helped parents gain a broader understanding of the needs of their child's learning behaviours in terms of the three relationships. These were very accessible to parents and more meaningful than being told, for example, 'your child is disruptive!' The focus on learning behaviours was more positive. The regular reviews kept parents in touch with the progress their child was making and also meant if there were concerns or strategies not working or any issues at home, these too could be raised. The focus was always moving to the next steps on the assessment and agreement from everyone involved what the next steps would be. This process was extremely positive, as rather than focusing on the things going wrong, the focus was on what was going well and what to do next. Even though progress seemed small to start with, the parents contributed and participated fully in the process.

Organisational changes

In 2010 the PPRU moved to a purpose-built premises on the site of a local primary school. The PPRU was renamed the Courtyard AP Academy in 2013 and amalgamated with the provision for children with SEBD. PIDS and the Courtyard became part of the Tri-Borough Alternative Provision (TBAP). The Courtyard AP Academy was the first primary provision within the trust and PIDS became part of Commissioning and School Support services (CSS) which had a broader remit providing support for challenging learners within their existing schools. The staffing structure of PIDS changed, the teacher consultants continued in their role and joined with a primary team from a neighbouring borough, providing a range of interventions for primary schools. There was a significant change in the role and responsibilities of development workers in the PIDS, all support staff across the organisation TBAP, were renamed Learning Support Professionals and there was no longer an extended PPRU team. The staff continued to provide school-based interventions in primary schools.

The Courtyard AP Academy

The Courtyard AP Academy had places for 16 children, those with statements, permanently excluded and those at risk of permanent exclusion. The number of children attending the Courtyard AP Academy varied throughout the year, and sometimes, due to demand, the numbers of children exceeded the 16 spaces. For example, in 2015 in its inspection there were 20 pupils ranging from Year 1 to Year 6, 15 pupils attending full time and 5 part time. Most of the pupils attending were described as disadvantaged and were eligible for additional funding from pupil premium. Pupils came from a variety of ethnic heritages, the largest group at the time of the inspection in 2015 were from White British backgrounds.

Part time placements at the PPRU and the Courtyard AP Academy

The relationship built with parents as part of the PIDS process supported the transition of children who attended the Courtyard AP Academy for a fixed time. The regular review process meant that parents/carers had a good understanding of the progress their child was making.

We had a good record for reintegrating children back into their school, especially when they attended the Courtyard AP Academy part time. The visit to the PPRU removed the myths and fears that some parents had, one of the key ones being that only 'badly behaved' children attended and little learning took place. This perception was often changed in one visit and certainly after their child attended for a period of time. The attitudes of parents changed and they developed a positive outlook as their child made progress in their learning behaviours. Parents had a much more positive perspective of school and what their child could achieve. Part time places was a positive incentive for parents, especially those who had concerns of their children being labelled or underachieving. In fact, children returned to school in line with their expected age academically. Personalisation of the curriculum in a small setting provided the opportunity to close the academic gap.

Transition

Returning to mainstream school – reintegration

Transition can be a worrying and anxious time for children and their parents/carers. It is important that they are carefully planned and take into account the needs of children so that the process is successful (Galton et al., 1999; Ellis and Tod, 2018; DFE, 2015). Transition to a mainstream school provided us with many challenges, especially when the child had been permanently excluded. We often approached headteachers with a specific package that we put in place which involved support from a member of the PIDS team for a regular time each week. We were highly effective at preparing children who attended the PPRU part time to return to their mainstream primary school. The success was due to the process that we used. The member of staff with responsibility for reintegration attended the PPRU on a regular basis and observed the structures in place and strategies that were being used to promote positive learning behaviours of the child. They would also spend time providing in class support for the child, gaining confidence in the strategies that were being used and building relationships. Throughout this process there was ongoing feedback to the member of the PIDS team from the PPRU class teacher. The child's progress in their Behaviour for Learning assessment would be the indicator for when he/she was ready to be reintegrated and they would then be supported back into school. The development worker with responsibility for reintegration was able to model the strategies for the class teacher and teaching assistant. The children attending the PPRU part time had made such progress in their Behaviour for Learning on a part-time basis that they were able to make the adjustments with support so that they could attend school full time.

The reintegration process was a good model of how an outreach service could work in partnership with a PPRU to support reintegration into a mainstream school.

The reintegration of children who had been permanently excluded and were ready to return to a mainstream school was always more challenging. The process that took time was finding a school willing to take a child who had been permanently excluded; however, we did find schools who were willing to accept children with support provided by the team. The role of the development work and approach was the same as for children who had attended the PPRU part time. In this case the reintegration process often took longer.

Transition from key stage 2 to key stage 3

Transition for children from the Courtyard AP Academy to secondary school was more of a challenge, especially if they did not have mainstream school experience. It was always

---

1. **Administrative or bureaucratic bridge** – sharing information about pupils, good working relationships between primary and secondary schools, feedback to primary schools of Year 7 progress. This also includes sharing information between mainstream and specialist provision and alternative provision.
2. **Social and personal bridge** – induction days, open evenings, visits to special schools, alternative provisions for example PPRUs, pupil peer mentoring, pupil and parents' guides, parents have opportunities to meet key staff to discuss the process and arrangements to support the child, especially vulnerable learners.
3. **Curriculum bridge** – effective use of pupil data, work samples shared, cross-phase projects, exchange of curriculum maps, joint planning.
4. **Pedagogical bridge** – shared understanding of effective teaching and learning, observations of teaching and learning, team teaching, teacher exchanges between primary and secondary schools, also special schools and alternative provision.
5. **Management of learning bridge** – pupils are active participants in transition and their own learning, pupil portfolios, passports, transition plan.

Figure 2.9 Five bridges of transition

a priority where possible to arrange mainstream experience for children in Year 6 which might be part time or a reintegration to a full-time place. Parents often wanted their child to go to a mainstream school and there was a reluctance from some secondary schools to accept a child who had attended an alternative provision. A member of staff in the team had responsibility for supporting the transition process of children from the Courtyard AP Academy to secondary school. She developed the transition programme and met with children weekly to support and prepare them for the move that they would be making to secondary school. We used the 5 learning bridges of transition (Galton et al., 1999; DFES, 2005b) to inform what we needed to have in place for children moving from key stage 2 to 3. This can be seen in Figure 2.9.

The transition process, Figure 2.10 for children with SEMH was drawn up following a review of what was in place and what we needed to do to support the children and their families (DFES 2001; DFE 2015).

TRANSITION PROCESS FOR VULNERABLE PUPILS IN YEAR 6 WITH SEBD

1. IDENTIFICATION OF SEBD PUPILS FOR TRANSITION

- ✓ Pupils identified by SNAPT, PPRU, schools
- ✓ Information stored on database
- ✓ PIDS panel meeting

2. IDENTIFICATION OF NEEDS OF INDIVIDUAL PUPILS

- ✓ Initial meeting with key school staff
- ✓ Gathering further information
- ✓ Identify SEBD needs, triggers, strategies, parent and pupil views

3. PLANNING AND IMPLEMENTATION

- ✓ Amend transition plan with the school
- ✓ Implement transition plan from January to December

4. REVIEW

- ✓ Weekly review of the transition intervention

5. EVALUATION

- ✓ Evaluation meeting in July with primary school and in December with the secondary school

6. FOLLOW UP

- ✓ Observations, meetings to review progress of pupil. Approx 1 term later

---

Figure 2.10 Transition process for children with SEBD

The transition plans and process were adopted by the Special Needs Assessment Panel of the local authority. The key features of the transition plan can be seen in Figure 2.11.

- General information about the pupil
- Interests of the pupil
- Child's perspective, self-assessment
- Behaviour for Learning assessment of vulnerability at transition
- Triggers that might lead to poor behaviour
- Strategies that had been successful in promoting positive behaviour and learning
- Observations by the development worker so that they had an understanding of the strategies that were used by the teaching assistant who worked very effectively with the pupil
- 1:1 session with the pupil to discuss transition and any areas they were concerned about
- An observation by the Head of school and teacher in charge of the PPRU so that we could identify the teaching and learning strategies that were used by the class teacher to support learning and progress.
- Visits to a secondary school
- Meeting with key staff from the primary school and secondary school
- Meeting with the parent

Figure 2.11 The features of the transition plan

Transition plan

The transition plan would always start with what we were trying to achieve for the child – the outcomes.

Table 2.10 is an example of the agreed outcomes of a Year 6 child's transition plan discussed with the Mainstream school SENCO, head of the PPRU, parent and child.

Table 2.10 The agreed outcomes identified on the transition plan for a Year 6 child

What are we trying to achieve?
Outcomes

XV has a team of adults in secondary school who know and understand his needs and the strategies to manage his Behaviour for Learning, so that he can make progress.

All staff in the secondary school, especially those who teach him, implement the strategies, structures and approaches that will enable XV to learn effectively.

XV makes friends and has a 'buddy' who supports and looks out for him.

XV has identified adults who he can go to when there is an incident or crisis.

XV continues to make the progress he has made from primary school in terms of his learning and behaviour.

Information for the plan was collected from the primary school staff, that is the Year 6 class teacher and SENCO, other staff supporting the child, the child, the parents and staff from the PPRU/Courtyard AP Academy. Data collected included Teacher's assessment of pupil attainment, attendance, special education needs and an updated Behaviour for Learning assessment. The Behaviour for Learning assessment was also used to identify the areas where the child was vulnerable at transition so that strategies could be in place to support the process. Children from the PPRU/Courtyard AP Academy went to different provisions from Year 6, mainstream secondary schools, special schools and the secondary PPRU. Some of these schools were out of borough so the plan that we implemented had to be relevant to different settings and providers. If the child had been at the Courtyard AP Academy or was supported through an intervention, then the child would have a good understanding of their learning behaviours. In addition to this, staff would have information about the approaches and strategies that promoted the positive learning behaviours of the child.

The learning support professional for transition played a key role in supporting Year 6 children from the Courtyard AP Academy into mainstream secondary school. As well as providing resources and teaching children so that they were prepared to move to secondary school, staff gained a good understanding of the strategies that promoted their learning behaviours. If needed they would go into the Year 7 class providing support discretely.

The Behaviour for Learning assessment provided a positive way to identify a child's vulnerability and what support one could put in place. The areas which were mainly a concern for these children was knowing that there was someone they could go to if they were unsure or needed help. Secondly that they were going to be able to do the work, that is, access the curriculum.

In a secondary school the Behaviour for Learning assessments were able to be used as a tool to look at the progress of the child in different subjects as these sometimes differed. We found that the kind of discussion that they were able to have was very valuable. Staff would share their perspective and identify strategies that were working and having a positive impact in different subjects.

We identified areas of effective practice and areas for further development so that we had an effective transition process for children going to secondary schools. As a result of this we were asked by the Special Needs Assessment panel for the local authority to produce transition plans for children with SEMH difficulties who might be vulnerable at transition.

The impact of the transition plan was:

1. The child had a key involvement in the transition planning process and had a good knowledge and understanding of their learning behaviours and the progress they had made which they could share and talk about. They were able to discuss their academic and attendance and what support they believed they needed to be successful.
2. The development worker had a good understanding of the strengths and the areas for development of the child's learning behaviours. They also knew the strategies that had effectively been used to promote the learning behaviours.
3. Secondary school staff gained a good understanding of the needs of the child and the Behaviour for Learning assessment, the progress and strategies that promoted positive behaviour following their meeting with the Development worker for transition.
4. A senior member of staff from the secondary school visiting the provision to gain insight into the child's learning experience; for example, a visit by the headteacher of a provision for children with ASD and a SENCO from a mainstream secondary school supported the transition process so that it was successful.
5. The member of staff with responsibility for transition supported children during induction days if they requested it.

6. Strategies that were effective in supporting the learning of children were shared and provided for staff, transition mentors and learning mentors.
7. Additional adult support was provided by the Development worker for the child in the classroom (for the class), teachers and support staff during the autumn term to support the implementation of the transition plan.
8. Feedback was provided to the SENCO on the child's progress, especially on the areas that had been identified on the transition plan.
9. There was always an opportunity for the child to reflect on their learning behaviours and the outcomes of the transition plan.

Partnerships

It was our intention to develop strong working relationships with a wide range of services in order to achieve good outcomes for children and young people. The 'Every Child Matters' agenda, (DFES, 2003a) strengthened the requirement for agencies to work together to improve outcomes for Children and Young people (Cheminais, 2009). It was the role of the team to support schools in working to achieve the five Every Child Matters outcomes, identified as Being healthy, Staying safe, Enjoying and Achieving, Making a positive contribution and Achieving economic well-being within the context of the interventions that were going to take place in schools.

PIDS worked in very effective partnerships across the local authority which enabled the team to enhance their practice in the classroom, that is teaching and learning, and helped us to be more effective in meeting the needs of children with SEBD.

Effective partnerships were made with the following agencies: Education psychologist, social work teams, Child and Adolescent mental health services (CAMHS), speech and language team, looked After team, Education welfare team, Special education needs, Exclusion team, primary improvement and inclusion team. Not only did working in partnership improve outcomes for the children we worked with, but the team benefited as they gained a greater understanding of the needs of the children, further developed skills and strategies to support and empower staff in schools and in the Courtyard AP Academy. The Behaviour for Learning framework was used as a basis for all written reports requested such as Education health care plans (EHCP), Child Protection meetings, CAMHS, transition plans and other agencies that required a report for a child who attended the Courtyard AP Academy.

Every Child Matters

Every Child Matters (ECM) was launched in 2002 partly in response to the failure of Schools in England to prevent the abuse and death of Victoria Climbe, the 8-year-old child who died in 2000. The intentions of ECM were to improve children's care, protect children and maximize their potential. The five outcomes identified were being healthy, staying safe, enjoying and achieving, making a positive contribution and economic well-being. Two of the key strategies from the white paper Every Child Matters, 2003, were to develop a common assessment framework and the introduction of a lead professional. The aim was to have more integrated services and sharing between professionals. This involved all organisations who provided services to children, teaming up, working collaboratively and sharing information to protect children from harm.

Some teachers felt the move went too far as they would often be the lead professionals with responsibility for looking after all aspects of children's lives.

In 2010 with the Coalition government there was a shift from well-being to achievement and Every Child matters was renamed as Helping Children to Achieve More.

As a team with responsibility for a significant number of vulnerable children it was an advantage to work with other agencies and to have a coordinated approach to support them. For example, working with social services helped us to understand why a child may be struggling with his learning behaviours associated with relationship with self.

We worked in very effective partnerships across the local authority which enabled the team to enhance their practice in the classroom, that is, teaching and learning, and helped us to be more effective in meeting the needs of children with SEMH.

Education psychology team

Working in partnership with the Education Psychologist was one of the most valuable and significant partnerships that we had. As well as having an Education psychologist in the Primary Inclusion Development Service we worked with different members of the local authority team. In addition to training the team in Peer Supervision they were involved in joint observations with members of the team focusing on the three Relationships in the Behaviour for Learning framework. We did some joint interventions and work with parents. Training on meeting the needs of children with social, emotional and behavioural issues strengthened the work of the team; for example, we gained a good understanding of attachment theory and how it impacted the children we were working with. This meant that when there were gaps identified in relation to how the team worked or in their understanding of the needs of the children they provided training for the team. A good example of this is the training that we received on Blanks questioning by the Education Psychologist who had carried out some observations. As a result of the training staff became more effective at developing children's language and their use of questioning. Blank's level of questioning was developed by Blank, Rose and Berlin in 1978 (Blank et al., 1978). The framework, which is based around four different levels of questions, helps to develop children's language, vocabulary and comprehension skills. There are four levels of questioning which start from simple, concrete questions to more difficult, abstract questions. We had opportunities to reflect on the language that we were using to ensure that our questions were at the right level, simplifying and restructuring them so that the child/children understood.

CAMHS (Child Adolescent Mental Health Services)

We developed a good relationship with staff from the child and adolescent mental health service who provided specialist support for the team, especially for those children receiving support from the team. We developed a good relationship with the primary mental health worker who supported our provision. In this way we gained further support in meeting the mental and emotional needs of the children at the PPRU and Courtyard AP Academy. It was important for all staff to be involved in supporting the children's relationship with self.

Social work teams

The team had a greater understanding of the concerns around families and needs of the children, which enabled us to respond more quickly as well as to understand the response and behaviours of the child. We were also able to gain a holistic picture of the child within the context of their family. The relationships, especially relationship with self and relationship with others, also gave a different language to use when we liaised with social workers and their families which helped to provide a focus for intervention.

School improvement and standards team

The role of the school improvement and standards team was to support the improvement of standards across schools ensuring every child had a chance to reach their potential. The Head of the PIDS met with staff from this team which helped us to get an oversight of the needs of the schools and those that would benefit from support. This included schools where behaviour was a concern across the school. It was an opportunity to share Behaviour for Learning, how we were using the framework to implement interventions and support schools. There was also an opportunity to give and receive feedback on the success of interventions in schools.

Tri-Borough Alternative Provision (TBAP)

The Courtyard AP Academy was one of five schools and the only primary school in the trust in 2013. As TBAP expanded there was an increase in primary provisions.

The Courtyard AP Academy benefited from being part of an academy trust for alternative provision. The systems and structures adopted by the trust, Bluewave swift, enabled us to effectively gather data on pupil achievement and to use the information to secure high-quality teaching. As a result, the achievement of learners was outstanding. We had increased access to a range of specialist resources to support the curriculum; for example, the primary school curriculum was enriched by having a weekly timetabled session with an art specialist from the secondary provision. All children were taught Spanish as part of their weekly timetable.

The children needed support to remove barriers that were negatively impacting their emotional and mental health. Inhouse therapeutic support provided by TBAP increased support for children on a regular basis.

Children experienced a wider range of extra-curricular activities, for example, circus skills, theatre visits and residential experiences.

As an alternative provision it is important for all staff to have an understanding of the needs of children with SEMH difficulties and how to promote children's mental health and well-being. The continuing professional development (CPD) pathways introduced by TBAP enabled staff to continue to develop their knowledge and understanding, especially staff who were new to the provision. Staff chose pathways according to their personal development needs; for example, there were courses on attachment theory and anger management. There was also a pathway about Behaviour for Learning led by the primary leadership team at the Courtyard AP academy. This was attended by primary school staff and secondary school staff.

Partnerships with headteachers

We developed effective partnerships with headteachers across the local authority from a wide range of schools. The feedback from the annual report helped to develop our practice and identify areas for improvement and further development, for example, 'better ways of contacting in crisis points for advice (which is so useful) but sometimes not available.'

We had a headteacher who was involved in the development of the Primary Inclusion Development Service. She was a member of the management committee, and her involvement was valuable to the development of PIDS and the Courtyard AP Academy. With regular feedback and evaluation not only on the structure and implementation of our processes, she was instrumental in supporting us to modify and further develop our practice.

Table 2.12 shows the partnership agreement that was drawn up between the Courtyard AP Academy and primary schools, which was used effectively to ensure that there was progression and continuity for each child who attended on a part-time basis.

Courtyard partnership agreement

Table 2.11 Courtyard partnership agreement

School:	Year group:
Learner:	Date of Entry:

The Courtyard will:

- Provide skilled staff who can provide alternative short-term education provision.
- Promote a positive learning experience through a balanced and personalised curriculum and supportive and caring staff.
- Provide a safe learning environment where the learner can explore their difficulties and learn from experience.
- Work collaboratively with schools in developing their capacity to be the most effective they can be in responding to learners with SEMH difficulties.
- Communicate regularly with mainstream staff to review progress and the impact of the strategies implemented.
- Train mainstream staff to ensure a consistent approach if necessary.
- Lead a review of the learner's progress and readiness for reintegration following a six week placement.

The Mainstream School will:

- Complete the referral form and provide the CAPA with any relevant information, including the completion of a Behaviour for Learning questionnaire, SATS or teaching assessment results which may be useful to the CAPA staff.
- Provide CAPA with appropriate learning and curriculum information for the learner to maintain continuity in learning on a weekly basis.

- Provide opportunities for the class teacher and any other key adults to visit CAPA during the placement.
- Make any reasonable adjustments necessary, including those under the Disability Discrimination Act 2005, for the pupil to be able to succeed in the mainstream environment.
- Attend review meetings.
- Participate fully in the learner's reintegration to mainstream school.
- Work in partnership with the staff in the CAPA.

HOS Mainstream: HOS CAPA:
Class Teacher: Class Teacher:

Summary

We have shared our journey as a Primary Inclusion Development Service. We discussed how we reframed behaviour management and implemented an approach to improving behaviour based on Behaviour for Learning.

We stressed the importance of involving parents in the process.

We discussed the structure and process of PIDS showing how we incorporated Behaviour for Learning into specific areas of the intervention so that it was an integral part of our work.

We described the transition process and key steps to support an effective transition or reintegration back into school.

Developing partnerships with other professionals and agencies to learn and share practice has an important part to play in improving outcomes for children. The partnerships also developed the skills of staff. It is important to effectively target the support required to meet the needs of children.

Takeaways

- Incorporating Behaviour for Learning so that it was an integral part of the structures and processes that we used provided an effective strategy to involve all staff in a different approach to improve behaviour.
- It is crucial to involve parents/carers at every stage so that you work in partnership to improve the learning behaviours of children.
- All schools/provisions need to be explicit about how equal opportunities and diversity are addressed, monitored and evaluated.
- A transition plan based on the five bridges and the Behaviour for Learning framework will support children with SEMH to move from key stage 2 to key stage 3.

Reflective questions

- How can staff be provided with more opportunities to work in partnership with external agencies so that they develop more skills and knowledge to meet the needs of children with SEMH?
- Learning and behaviour are inextricably linked. How do you use your knowledge and understanding of quality teaching and learning to improve behaviour?
- Are there any other ways that the transition process in your school needs to be adapted to meets the needs of all children?
- Do you have any concerns about the behaviour of a child in your class? Have a look at the learning behaviours and identify the strengths. What would your concerns be?
- Which learning behaviours are you promoting in your class? Which strategies are most effective?

References

Bennet, T. (2017). *Creating a Culture: How School Leaders Can Optimise Behaviour: Independent Review of Behaviour in Schools.* London, UK: DfE.

Blank, M., Rose, S.A., and Berlin, L.J. (1978). *The Language of Learning: The Preschool Years.* New York: Grune and Stratton.

Campbell, C. (2011). *How to Involve Hard-to-Reach Parents: Encouraging Meaningful Parental Involvement with Schools.* Nottingham: NCSL.

Chambers, C. and Olsson Rost, A. (2020). The history of behaviour management: Key theories and current context. In E. Overland, J. Barber and M. Sackville-Ford (eds.), *Behaviour Management: An Essential Guide for Student and Newly Qualified Teachers.* Abingdon: Routledge.

Cheminais, R. (2009). *Effective Multi-Agency Partnerships: Putting Every Child Matters into Practice.* London: Sage.

Cooper, P.N. (2008). Nurturing attachment to School: contemporary perspectives on social, emotional, behavioural difficulties. *Pastoral Care in Education,* 26(1).

Covey, S.R. (1989). *The 7 Habits of Highly Effective People: Powerful Lessons in Personal Change.* New York, NY: Simon and Schuster.

Davey, A. (2016). Behaviour in schools – is it bad as they say – or is it worse. In A.O.' Grady and V.E. Cottle (eds.), *Exploring Education at Postgraduate Level: Policy, Theory and Practice.* London: Routledge.

DCSF (2007) The National Programme for Specialist Leaders of Behaviour and Attendance ; Inducting new staff in behaviour and attendance. Nottingham: DCSF available for download from http://www.teachernet.gov.uk/npslba

DCSF(2007) The National Programme for Specialist leaders of Behaviour and Attendance. The role of senior leadership in behaviour and attendance. Nottingham: DCSF
available for download as above

Department for Children, Schools and Families (DCSF). (2008a). *Excellence and Enjoyment: Learning and Teaching for Black Children in the Primary Years.* Nottingham: DCSF.

Department for Children, Schools and Families (DCSF). (2008b). *Improving Behaviour and Attendance: Guidance on Exclusion from Schools and Pupil Referral Units.* Nottingham: DCSF.

Department for Children, Schools and Families (DCSF). (2008c). *Quality Standards for Special Educational Needs (SEN) Support and Outreach Services.* https://dera.ioe.ac.uk/8552/1/00582-2008DOM-EN.pdf (accessed 29/07/22).

Department for Children, Schools and Families (DCSF). (2009). *School Discipline and Pupil Behaviour Policies – Guidance for Schools.* Nottingham: DCSF.

Department for Education (DFE). (2010). *The Importance of Teaching. The Schools White Paper.* Nottingham: DFE.

Department for Education (DFE). (2012a). *Pupil Behaviour in Schools in England.* London: DFE.

Department for Education (DFE). (2012b). *Behaviour and Discipline in Schools; A Guide for Headteachers and School Staff.* London: HMSO.

Department for Education (DFE). (2014). *Behaviour and Discipline in Schools. Advice for Headteachers and School Staff.* London: DFE.

Department for Education (DFE). (2015). *Special Needs and Disability Code of Practice; 0–25 Years.* London: DFE.

Department for Education (DFE). (2016). *Behaviour and Discipline in Schools. Advice for Headteachers and School Staff.* London: DFE.

Department for Education (DFE). (2019). *Timpson Review of School Exclusion.* London: DFE.

Department for Education (DFE). (2022). *Opportunity for All: Strong Schools with Great Teachers for Your Child.* England: DFE.

Department for Education and Science (DFES). (1989). *Discipline in Schools (The Elton Report).* London: HMSO.

Department for Education and Science (DFES). (2001). *Special Education Needs Code of Practice.* London: DFES.

Department for Education and Science (DFES). (2003a). *Every Child Matters.* Nottingham: DFES.

Department for Education and Science (DFES). (2003b). *Excellence and Enjoyment: A Strategy for Primary Schools.* London: HMSO.

Department for Education and Science (DFES). (2003c). *Improving Behaviour and Attendance: Guidance on Exclusion from Schools and Pupil Referral Units.* London: DFES.

Department for Education and Science (DFES). (2004). *Primary National Strategy: Behaviour and Attendance Materials.* Nottingham: DFES.

Department for Education and Science (DFES). (2005a). *Learning Behaviour: The Report of the Practitioners on School Behaviour and Discipline (The Steer Report).* London: HMSO.

Department for Education and Science (DFES). (2005b). *The London Challenge KS2 – Key 3 Transition Project.* Mouchel Parkman. Nottingham: DFES.

Department for Education and Science (DFES). (2006). *Learning Behaviour: The Report of the Practitioners Group on School Behaviour and Discipline.* London: DFES.

Department for Education and Science (DFES). (2009). *Learning Behaviour: Lessons Learned (The Steer Report).* Nottingham: HMSO.

Education Endowment Foundation (EEF). (2019). *Improving Behaviour in Schools.* https://d2tic4wvo1iusb.cloudfront.net/eef-guidance-reports/behaviour/EEF_Improving_behaviour_in_schools_Report.pdf?v=1635355216 (accessed 29/07/22).

Ellis, S. and Tod, J. (2009). *Behaviour for Learning: Proactive Approaches to Behaviour Management.* Abingdon: Routledge.

Ellis, S. and Tod, J. (2015). *Promoting Behaviour for Learning in the Classroom: Effective Strategies, Personal Style and Professionalism.* Abingdon: Routledge.

Ellis, S. and Tod, J. (2018). *Behaviour for Learning: Proactive Approaches to Behaviour Management* (2nd ed.). Abingdon: Routledge.

Ellis, S. and Tod, J. (2022). Behaviour for Learning. In H. Cooper and S. Elton-Chalcraft (eds.), *Professional Studies in Primary Education* (4th ed.). London: SAGE.

Galton, M., Gray, J., and Ruddock, S. (1999). *The Impact of School Transitions and Transfers on Pupil Progress and Attainment.* Homerton College, Cambridge Research Report No. 131.

Gilborn, D. (1995). *Racism and Antiracism in Real Schools: Theory, Policy, Practice.* Buckingham: Open University Press.

https://d2tic4wvo1iusb.cloudfront.net/eef-guidance-reports/behaviour/EEF_Improving_behaviour_in_schools_Report.pdf?v=1635355216

https://dera.ioe.ac.uk/8685/1/010862a7282189a539b5765bf5280fa6.pdf Inducting new staff in behaviour and attendance

https://dera.ioe.ac.uk/8687/1/5614a0a07b35847e5384f0f591ef0e26.pdf Specialist leaders in behaviour and attendance role of senior leaders

OFSTED. (2005). *Managing Challenging Behaviour*. London: Ofsted.

OFSTED. (2006). *Improving Behaviour*. London: Ofsted.

OFSTED. (2010). *The National Strategies: A Review of Impact*.

OFSTED. (2014). *Below the Radar: Low Level Disruption in the Country's Classroom*. London: HMSO.

Quality Standards. https://dera.ioe.ac.uk/8552/1/00582-2008DOM-EN.pdf. Sent from My iPad.

Stoll, L. (2009). Capacity building for school improvement or creating capacity for learning: A changing landscape. *Journal of Educational Change,* 10(2), 115–127, May. University of London, Institute of Education.

3   Professional learning

Introduction

In this chapter we share the learning programme that enabled us to empower staff so that they were prepared to fulfil their leadership roles and lead interventions in schools. We identify specific programmes which were fundamental to everyone's knowledge and understanding of leadership as well as the skills that they would need to work in a more developmental way. Understanding and experiencing the five-stage learning model (Joyce and Showers, 1980) supported staff with any training that they would lead in schools.

A model of learning competencies and the situational leadership model (Blanchard et al., 1985) provided an understanding of the needs of the team and how to respond and support the development of staff individually and as a whole service.

We spend time talking about the use of peer supervision which provided a climate where staff openly shared and were supported by each other. We adopted solution-focused approaches throughout our journey, when we were drawing up our vision as a service in the Primary Inclusion Development Service (PIDS) process, and we used it with staff and children in schools, the Primary Pupil Referral Unit (PPRU) and Courtyard AP Academy.

We end the chapter by talking about how we used restorative approaches to develop work in schools and support children in the PPRU/Courtyard AP Academy to resolve conflict and develop their relationships with each other. Peer supervision was key to developing a climate where staff developed trust and learned from each other.

Our professional development learning programme was based on the following target which was crucial to improving outcomes for children in our Primary Inclusion Development Service/Primary Pupil Referral Unit improvement plan.

Target: To ensure that staff have the knowledge, competencies and skills to work in partnership with schools and other services/agencies.

If we were going to build capacity in schools and the PPRU based on the Behaviour for Learning framework, the team would have to have a shared knowledge and understanding of Behaviour for Learning; this was a priority. As a leadership team, we had all been involved in leading continual professional development and had led in-service training for schools. We wanted to broaden our perception of 'training' and so we decided to focus on professional learning.

Professional learning can be described as:

> An ongoing process encompassing all formal and informal learning experiences that enables all staff in schools individually and with others to think about what they are doing, enhance their knowledge and skills and improve ways of working so that pupils'

DOI: 10.4324/9781003166672-4

learning and well-being are enhanced as a result – creating opportunities for adult learning, ultimately for the purpose of enhancing the quality of education in the classroom.

Bubb and Earley, 2007, p. 4

We fully embraced this definition and what followed was the development and implementation of an intense learning programme. The five-stage learning model (Joyce and Showers, 1980) was instrumental in supporting the training programme for the team so that we could implement the target. To build capacity across schools and the PPRU all staff would need to be competent to support and work collaboratively with staff in schools.

The five-stage learning model (Joyce and Showers, 1980) included the following stages:

1. Acquisition of knowledge; at this stage the theory is presented, and the new skill described.
2. The second stage is where good practice is modelled. Behaviour for learning was demonstrated and modelled so that it could be seen and be evident to staff.
3. At the third stage there is application. Applying to practice. Staff are learning the skills required and have the opportunity to get involved and try out the new skills.
4. In the fourth stage there is feedback and reflection. This is an important stage as it is in the feedback that learning is taking place. The feedback is structured and focused on the skill that is being developed and the person learning the skill has opportunities to reflect.
5. The fifth stage is referred to as embedding the experience and includes coaching from a member of staff who has a good knowledge and understanding of the skills and approach being implemented. This is where staff put what they had learned into practice.

Effective training strategies provided opportunities for a member of staff to know and understand the theory of Behaviour for Learning; it enabled them to see it in practice – demonstrated in the classroom with small groups and then practice using coaching and feedback to support the learning that was taking place. Our professional learning programme for the team included a range of activities:

• Lectures
• Discussions
• Focused observations – small groups and whole classes
• Structured feedback
• Self-assessment
• The use of videos for observations
• Staff sharing their own knowledge and expertise
• Reflective and problem-solving activities
• Modelling and coaching
• Structured feedback
• Use of case studies
• Peer supervision
• Solution-focused approaches

It was important that all staff were involved, we did not draw a distinction between teachers and development workers – they were all valued equally. Staff also led sessions which were based on their experience and expertise. If we were going to implement Behaviour for Learning then *all* staff would have to be involved; this was important and was reflected in the feedback by a member of the team in the Courtyard AP Academy.

'Teachers really value my input. I feel totally empowered. The head of school and the lead teacher run training between them, such as the successful leverage learning, ensuring that no one missed out' (learning support professional).

Throughout our programme we developed a staff learning culture where there was openness and trust. All staff were willing to share, be vulnerable, make mistakes, receive feedback and learn from each other. We were all starting from the same place.

What did we include in our staff professional learning programme?

Our staff professional learning programme had two dimensions. Firstly to know and understand Behaviour for Learning and how to implement the framework. Secondly to develop the leadership roles of the team and further develop their skills knowledge and understanding to enable them to work confidently in partnership with schools.

We carried out our own training weekly and used the reflective tasks suggested throughout the book on Behaviour for Learning by Ellis and Tod (2009). The tasks were instrumental in challenging our personal views and perspectives about behaviour management, as well as the approaches that were used across schools where the focus had been solely on behaviour. There was an opportunity for the team to develop a shared understanding of Behaviour for Learning and to look at ways that we could implement the Behaviour for Learning conceptual framework. Following the identification of the learning behaviours (see Table 1.1, Chapter 1, p. 11) that we had adopted, we spent time identifying and focusing on the strategies and approaches that were promoting the learning behaviours.

The National Programme for Specialist Leaders of Behaviour and Attendance (NPSLBA)

All staff in the team took part in the National Programme for Specialist Leaders in Behaviour and Attendance (NPSLBA) (DCSF, 2007a; DFES, 2004). The course was intended for all those who wanted to develop their knowledge, understanding and skills in behaviour and attendance to improve outcomes for children and young people. The NPSLBA was fully incorporated into the National Strategies' behaviour and attendance and SEAL programme in May 2007 and came to an end in 2011. The National Strategies supported the national outcomes for children in Every Child Matters (ECM) and is described as representing one of the 'most ambitious change management programmes in education' (DFE, 2011). The resources were high-quality training materials which were accessible to a wide range of professionals.

This programme played a very important part in the team's development of their leadership skills and their knowledge and understanding of teaching, learning and behaviour.

The advantages of using the NSPLBA were:

1. It was accessible to everyone in the team.
2. It was based on an effective learning model and included activities that all staff could engage in.
3. The study topics focused on the work situation, giving participants the opportunity to look at how the learning could be applied in their own work situation.
4. It was a personalised course with opportunities for each member of staff to work collaboratively and learn from each other in the team.

5. The focus on leadership provided everyone with the opportunity to develop their leadership skills, knowledge and understanding.
6. There were 28 study topics related to behaviour and attendance and so a wide range to choose from.
7. The study days were an opportunity for the staff to explore different leadership styles and develop an understanding of leadership theory and some of the key theories of leadership practice.
8. There were opportunities to be reflective which was one of the key features of the programme.

In what ways did the NSPLBA support the development of the team?

The implementation of the 'Five Stages of learning' model, (Joyce and Showers, 1980) supported the learning of the team and provided the team with further insight into how adults learned, which was then used to support our team and schools.

It was important for each member of the team to see themselves as leaders. The programme enabled the team to become more equipped in their leadership roles and to gain an understanding of how to become emotionally intelligent.

We were engaged in a programme that was informing the work that we were engaged in. The Study topics chosen were bespoke to our team and covered the areas identified by individuals and the team. The study topics that we covered can be seen in Table 3.1. Each member of the team had the opportunity to work collaboratively and lead sessions on the programme. Everyone further developed their knowledge and gained a deeper understanding of the social and emotional needs of children with SEBD and a wider range of strategies that could be used.

Table 3.1 NPSLBA Programme for the Primary Inclusion Development Service

NPSLBA		
Group	Date	Title
Study Day 1	22.02.10	Study day 1
Cluster 1	17.03.10	1a) Creating an ethos for Social Inclusion
Cluster 2	30.03.10	8c/6b) Working with Parents & Carers in settings that include children with SEBD
Study day 2	19.04.10	Study day 2
Cluster 3	30.06.10	3b) Applying Learning theories to Behaviour and Poor Attendance
Cluster 4	14.07.10	7c) Reducing the risk of violence
Cluster 5	29.09.10	3a) Underlying causes of Challenging behaviour and Poor Attendance
Cluster 6	13.10.10	4g) Using counselling Skills with Staff, Children and Young people, Parents and Carers
Study day 3	1.11.10	Study day 3
Cluster 7	24.11.10	Reflective log
Cluster 8	8.12.10	8a) Establishing Peer Support systems for staff that include children with SEBD
Cluster 9	26.01.11	Reflective log
Cluster 10	2.02.11	Children, Young People and the Law
Cluster 11	16.02.11	Reflective log
NPSLBA	04.03.11	Evidence files
NPSLBA	07.03.11	Moderation

Emotionally intelligent leader?

The leadership aspects of this course are important for anyone who has a leadership role. The literature on Emotional Intelligence certainly indicates that self-awareness, self-management, empathy and relationship management impacts and influences the school culture, climate and ethos.

Goleman's leadership styles and being emotionally intelligent were included in the training. The focus was what it meant to be an emotionally intelligent leader.

Emotional Intelligence is referred to as 'the capacity for recognising our own feelings and those of others, for motivating ourselves, and for managing emotions well in ourselves and in our relationships' (Goleman, 1998, p. 317). It is important to prepare leaders with the emotional skills and behavioural leadership competencies of Emotional Intelligence so that they positively impact all aspects of the school climate (Goleman et al., 2002; Gomez-Leal et al., 2021; Bullock, 2009; Gray, 2009). These are important skills for any leader but essential when going into schools with different contexts and needs of staff. Throughout the programme and work-based activities there was an opportunity to reflect on one's development as a leader.

The learning model stressed the importance of providing structured learning experiences and the opportunities for anyone learning a new skill to have opportunities to practice and get feedback. We looked at ways of providing more structured learning experiences into our training with opportunities for feedback.

We completed the Course in March 2011. It was a formal process for the team. Our workplace testimonies included the following:

- A description of how the participant had developed as a leader by taking part in the NPSLBA.
- The evidence to show that the participants' leadership skills had been developed.
- Whether the NPSLBA had enhanced the participants' opportunities for career progression.

Being a reflective practitioner was important and crucial. The opportunity to reflect on experiences and learning was incorporated into each module. The reflective log was a critical part of the process in the NPSLBA course, all participants having the opportunity to link the theory they had acquired to their practice. This provided everyone with the chance to reflect on their leadership role, skills and understanding in learning behaviour and attendance. We looked at the impact of our work on our leadership role and of course on the children and people we were working with. As part of this process, it was critical to ensure that the actions or activities that were implemented were embedded and sustainable. The following two questions were particularly important in enabling staff to reflect on roles, responsibilities and the impact that they were having across provisions.

- What impact has the work had on my workplace, children and young people and colleagues?
- What actions need to take place to ensure change is embedded?

The National strategies NPSLBA participant pack 2009

It was important for the team to take hold of the fact that they were having an impact in the schools they supported and could be specific about the actions that they had taken. Headteachers and staff provided feedback on the work as well as the witness statement provided by the line manager. We wanted to know that staff had been empowered and that the approaches implemented based on Behaviour for Learning would be embedded and sustainable.

The reflective logs from each member of staff who had taken part in the course included work that they had taken part in, where they had had a significant role or responsibility for leading an intervention. The evidence collected included weekly records of support, half termly reviews, feedback from staff and headteachers, records of in-service training and evaluation by staff, parental feedback and feedback from children. Evidence was also included where staff worked with other agencies, for example, the primary strategy team, localities, the looked after team, local authority teams who analysed exclusion data and attendance data and school OFSTED (2009) inspection reports. Even though we had been working for the Primary Inclusion Development Service for a short space of time there was ample evidence to show the impact that the service was having on children, parents, staff and schools.

These are examples of activies undertaken by staff from our cluster:

Activity undertaken: Developing a transition programme for pupils with BESD
Activity undertaken: Inducting a member of staff in the Primary Inclusion Development Service
Activity undertaken: Using observations to review behaviour in a school
Activity undertaken: Working with parents and carers in settings that include children with BESD

Moderation and a workplace testimony statement by the line manager validated the work and evidence that had taken place. Figure 3.1 is an example of information taken from a section of a witness statement which follows the key leadership activities which had taken place throughout the year.

Workplace testimony

A brief description of how the participant has developed as a leader by participating in NPSLBA, making reference, where possible, to the impact on the workplace and/or pupils
  Specific areas of skills identified in the member of staff's job.
  As a result of the above there is:

- An increased focus on quality first teaching and Behaviour for Learning, rather than on the individual.
- A reduced number of exclusions at primary school and in Year 7.
- Positive feedback from headteachers on the work of the team involvement of PIDS staff is having.
- A body of evidence from schools showing that the involvement of PIDS staff is having an impact on pupils, behaviour and learning.

What evidence have you seen that the participant's leadership skills have been developed or enhanced by the NPSLBA?

- Line management and performance management meetings.
- Participation in Inclusion meetings.
- Feedback from headteachers.
- PPRU Management committee.
- SIP report.

(Witness statement written by line manager LA officer)

Figure 3.1 An example of information from a witness statement written for a member of staff

Developing as a Behaviour for Learning practitioner?

We gained a good understanding of Behaviour for Learning from focusing on working through the text and reflective exercises (Ellis and Tod, 2009). We now had to focus on structured experiences, coaching and feedback so that staff were able to work with staff in schools on identifying behaviours that promoted the learning behaviours of children.

Learning through experiences

The team's leadership skills were developed which helped them to be even more effective when they were working in partnership with staff in schools. Spending the time to work towards everyone being competent and confident in their role and responsibilities as well as being reflective practitioners has to be a priority if staff are going to improve outcomes for children.

The conscious competence model which we became more aware of from leadership training and the NPSLBA reinforced that it takes time to build new skills and learn new

Table 3.2 The learning experiences of the Primary Inclusion Development Service

Learning experiences	What it included
Observations	• Whole class observations • Focused observations of individual children • Focused observations of groups of children • Focused observations of children's learning behaviours • Observations of the strategies used by adults to promote learning behaviours in the classroom • Joint observations with early years practitioners • Joint observations with an Education Psychologist focused on learning behaviours • Joint observations with headteachers • Joint observations with SENCOs • Joint observations with LA Inspectors
Use of videoing	• Staff organising their own videos and reflecting on their practice with a member of the PIDS • Staff observing strategies used by other members of staff which promoted learning behaviours of children, individuals and small groups • Observing good practice of Behaviour for Learning with different staff in class, out of class, at breakfast club and at assembly
Solution-focused approaches	• Training on Solution brief therapy – miracle question, scaling • Training on solution-focused approaches in leadership – miracle question, scaling • Using solution-focused model in training • Using solution-focused model in request for intervention process
Working collaboratively	• Working on all stages of the request for intervention in pairs • Head of service attending all initial requests for the first term to support process and establish a new way of working • Head of service attending all reviews to oversee the impact of the interventions

Learning experiences	What it included
Coaching	• Working alongside colleagues to help them to develop their practice • Supporting the development of new approaches/strategies identified by the coachee
Case Studies	• All staff having an opportunity to share an intervention with the team that they have been involved in, for example, an individual, group, parent/carer or a project, for example, playground • Case studies focused on Behaviour for Learning
Drop in	• An opportunity for staff to get support from a member of SLT with an intervention, especially where they felt they needed specific support
Peer Supervision	• A structured approach to sharing interventions • Opportunities to problem solve and be supported • Opportunities to get feedback and for learning to take place

things. Even though we worked with very experienced teachers we realised very quickly that learning a new approach to how we were going to implement Behaviour for Learning was not a quick process. The training that we received on the five stages of learning competencies helped us to develop our learning programme for staff. It was particularly important when new staff were appointed either to the Primary Inclusion Development Service or Courtyard AP Academy.

How did we induct new staff?

One of the key questions that arose early on was how do we induct new staff into the Behaviour for Learning approaches that we were using. The stages of learning competencies were helpful in providing an approach to support staff, some of whom were very experienced. In their previous schools the emphasis was on 'managing behaviour.' The stages and explanation of each stage can be seen in Table 3.3.

Five stages of learning competence

This model provided a good basis for discussion, for identifying staff needs and personalising our staff training programme. It was especially helpful for new staff joining the service. The majority of staff who joined the team were experienced teachers coming from mainstream schools. They were often very confident when it came to 'managing behaviour' in their school and it was evident in their practice. Some staff had come from the outreach service of another borough and so had experience of supporting schools. Our vision at the Primary Inclusion Development Service was different and the fundamental difference was that Behaviour for Learning was underpinning the approach that we were using across schools and in the Courtyard AP Academy. It was interesting that some staff did talk about having a knowledge of Behaviour for Learning; in fact, that was a usual response from schools when we started to share our focus was 'yes we do Behaviour for Learning here.' However, the model that we were using was different and this became clear when it was shared. When the model and theory was shared with new staff, they had the opportunity to shadow staff who were already experienced in using the Behaviour for Learning model that we had implemented. They were able to identify areas that they needed to learn, develop

Table 3.3 Five stages of learning competence

Stages of Learning Competence	Explanation
Unconscious Incompetence	• The learner is unaware of how much they know. • You don't know what you don't know. • The learner does not know there is a better way to do things. • This can be a challenging stage as you are not aware that there are things that you need to learn.
Conscious Incompetence	• The learner becomes more aware that there are things that they do not know. • The learner knows there is a better way but does not know how to get there. • The learner is not clear where to look for information or resources to support them.
Conscious Competence	• The learner can do it and understands it. • The learner is developing a level of competency by learning and practicing. • It is in the leaner's mind, and they have to think about it and therefore the task can take more time than for someone who is skilled.
Unconscious Competence	• The learner is able to do the tasks without thinking about it. • The learner has the knowledge and skills to perform the task. • At this stage, the learner could coach and mentor learners at earlier stages of their development.
Reflective Competence	• The learner is learning from what they are doing. • The learner is able to adapt and change as and when needed. • Reflection is a core part of what you do. • You reflect during and after a task, you can change and adapt.

and practice. The most important stage for all staff was to be a reflective practitioner. The five stages of learning competencies model was useful to share with experienced teachers as they moved to the PPRU/Courtyard. Staff became more aware of the Behaviour for Learning approaches as they observed classroom practice where it was modelled. Feedback, reflections and coaching supported staff to believe that they had a good grasp of Behaviour for Learning not only in their knowledge and understanding but also in practice.

While the five-stage learning competencies model gave us an understanding of where staff might be in relation to their learning of Behaviour for Learning, it was the situational leadership model that helped us to look at how to respond. Situational leadership was devised by Ken Blanchard and Paul Hersey Hersey, P., and Blanchard, K.H. (1977) and our approach to leadership was influenced by Ken Blanchard (Blanchard et al., 1985). In this model the focus is on the balance between the amount of direction and the amount of support that a leader or manager provides to staff. From an induction perspective, staff will be at different stages in their knowledge and understanding and therefore the amount of support required will differ. One cannot make assumptions about where a person is or how quickly they may move to another stage. A discussion with experienced staff was also helpful; for example, we had staff in the PIDS team who were experienced in providing support to schools on behaviour management. They requested shadowing and then being observed with feedback. Staff in the PPRU/Courtyard AP Academy requested observing Behaviour for Learning in practice so that they could incorporate it into their work and requested feedback. In both these situations staff would also request specific training.

These were the key areas covered in an induction programme:

- The vision of the service and theory of Behaviour for Learning was shared.
- An opportunity for the member of staff to reflect and review their own practice.
- The theory of Behaviour for Learning and the opportunities to look at that in practice by shadowing a member of staff using Behaviour for Learning at different stages of the process.
- An opportunity was provided to observe Behaviour for Learning in practice.
- Identifying professional development and learning needs based on observations and discussions.
- Writing a personalised action plan, which included targets, objectives, specific action to be taken and success criteria. This was completed by the member of staff.
- Working alongside an experienced member of staff to lead an intervention with support and feedback.
- Completing a review using the following headings: Work completed, Progress against outcomes, barriers and Next steps.
- To ensure that the programme was effectively implemented, regular line management meetings were held to review and reflect on the programme and identify any support needed.

This programme fitted in well with the structured approach adopted by the local authority for inducting staff new to alternative provision.

Tables 3.4 and 3.5 are an example of an action plan and review completed by a member of staff who joined the Primary Inclusion Development Service.

Table 3.4 An example of an action plan completed by a member of staff shortly after joining PIDS

Action Plan for Specific Responsibility Area

Target
What are you aiming to achieve by the end of the academic year?
- To build good working relationships with schools and class teachers.
- To reduce and prevent exclusions from primary cchools in LA by providing successful targeted support to children being reintegrated into mainstream settings and then undertaking a 'managed move' in lieu of exclusion.
- To help reintegrate selected children in the PPRU and mainstream schools.

Success Criteria
How will you know if you have been successful? What will you see? What will be happening? What will the changes look like?
- I will have made positive links with schools.
- Schools will understand the purpose of the PIDS service and make appropriate referrals.
- Schools will cooperate in working towards reintegrating children into mainstream settings, as well as supporting at risk children to avoid exclusions.
- Positive feedback on the impact of interventions will be received from parents and children.
- Children will have been successfully reintegrated or kept in mainstream settings with improved behaviour and attendance, which is being managed effectively by the school.
- There will be a reduction in fixed term and permanent exclusions from primary schools across the borough.

(Continued)

Table 3.4 (Continued)

Actions/Strategies and Timescale

What do you need to do to meet target?

List all the things you need to do including contacts.

Training

- To understand my role and attend appropriate training (TA training, team teach – ongoing).
- To be aware of continuing training needs and seek out relevant courses (ongoing).

Shadowing/Observations:

- Shadow other team members in order to be introduced to schools and reinforce link with those previously supported.
- Shadow x (development worker) at 1 school and attend MDA meeting about a child there.
- Attend Family Group sessions with H on Friday morning.
- Set up visits/observation sessions in schools with specialist provisions, e.g., School Q, Z, Y.
- Set up observation of a lead teacher within the borough.
- Conduct joint observations of individuals/groups of pupils with another team member.
- Attend 'Peer Massage' sessions with T to observe children.
- Assist in PPRU and Courtyard classes and Breakfast Club/playtimes/lunch times.

Administration

- Keep records of information relevant to my role and the children I am working with in order to measure progress made (ongoing).
- Familiarise myself with the resources used in the department and compile a collection of those relevant to my role.
- Familiarise myself with department/PPRU procedures.

Role Specific

- Begin to build relationships with children and families I will be supporting (Oct '09 and ongoing).
- Attend meetings about those children I will be supporting (attend scheduled CIN meeting in October 09).
- To accompany selected PPRU children when reintegrating into mainstream schools (ongoing).
- To provide short-term classroom support to pupils at risk of exclusion or undertaking a 'managed move' (ongoing).

Table 3.5 Term 1 review completed by a member of staff who completed the action plan (3.4)

Review completed by a Development worker new to the service

Specific area of responsibility

Work completed

- ✓ Have begun to build up relationships with schools and class teachers
- ✓ Have shadowed team members
- ✓ Have started to build relationship with PPRU child I will be supporting
- ✓ Have drawn up a timetable of when I will be supporting in PPRU class
- ✓ Have attended CIN and CP meetings
- ✓ Have been involved in schools audits, joint observations and PIDS panel
- ✓ Have started to keep records of information
- ✓ Have begun I day placement at M school
- ✓ Have completed 'team teach' and promoting 'Positive Behaviour' training
- ✓ Helped prepare and attended PIDS launch

Progress against outcomes

- ✓ Positive links with schools have been formed
- ✓ Schools understand the purpose of the PIDS service and the referral process
- ✓ I have developed a good understanding of the PIDS service, the processes in place and the resources used
- ✓ I have/am developing a more in depth understanding of the education provision in the borough
- ✓ Training has developed my understanding of my role and how to carry it out effectively

---

Barriers

- ✓ It has been difficult to find a mainstream school place for this child, therefore reintegration work has not started
- ✓ Waiting for more referrals

Next steps

- ✓ To begin supporting in KS2 PPRU class
- ✓ Continue placement at 'M' school
- ✓ Once a school has been found for Y2 PPRU child, begin reintegration work
- ✓ Attend family group once it is up and running
- ✓ Continue to shadow team members
- ✓ To carry out more joint observations with other team members
- ✓ Meet with Educational Psychology Team
- ✓ Attend further training relevant to my role, including NPSLBA

Changing the culture

The strong belief that we held as a senior leadership team that its impact was transformational was the basis for the continued growth and change that occurred within staff and the Courtyard AP Academy.

These are some of the ways that we continued to change the culture and ethos of the school.

A major focus for us was to immerse new staff into our ethos, language and expectations. We worked hard to highlight the distinctive aspects of our work and in particular, the way in which we operated within the Behaviour for Learning framework.

In order to learn and adapt to the norms of the framework, it was essential to recognise and understand them first and we found the best way to achieve this was to dedicate a significant proportion of time to learning about the key elements that contributed and that had an impact on learners and their achievement.

It was important for us to provide a more immersive experience, essentially 'a day in the life of' so that new staff could experience the reality of our school. In order to do this, and to provide an understanding of how interactions, systems, structures, and rules and routines influenced the learning environment, we found shadowing key members of staff to be highly effective. To support the induction process, new staff members were also assigned a buddy who was an experienced member of staff with whom they were encouraged to discuss any questions that would arise, particularly in relation to the Behaviour for Learning framework.

A shared language

A shared or common language is more than just about words, it is also a belief system that requires a whole school to contribute in order for it to be effective. It is important for school leaders to create the right conditions within a school community so that outcomes for children are improved (Garner, 2011). For us, it was one of the most crucial elements of operating within the Behaviour for Learning framework with success. The range of language used in schools when referring to learning and behaviour can vary to a huge degree which can lead to ambiguity. For this reason, it was crucial to have a shared language when referring to learning behaviours so that children were clear about what they were striving for and working towards.

Additionally, having a common language supported staff to have meaningful, professional conversations and its use improved overall communication. At Courtyard AP Academy it was implemented consistently: with learners, staff, when feeding back to parents and other agencies, when reporting to the board and when having discussions with external services. Feedback showed that it was accessible and unambiguous and when presented, provided a clear picture of the child, their progress and their next steps. We also found that adults outside the school community, who were working with the same families, would adopt the terminology during discussions which was a result of its consistency and effectiveness.

Developing a shared language was an ongoing and perpetual process that required intention, time and perseverance. Without these things, it would not have become fully embedded or as purposeful as it did. The language used was in direct correlation with one of our key tools, the Behaviour for Learning assessment, and targets set for individual learners were taken directly from this. In order to develop its systematic use, we were required to know and understand the Behaviour for Learning framework and assessment inside out. It needed to be internalised by adults in order for them to confidently and regularly use the language and there were several ways in which this was achieved.

The language was displayed in every corner of the school, including a display dedicated to our specific learning behaviours in each classroom. It was used and modelled at all times ranging from formal learning to more unstructured times. It was captured and highlighted during learning walks, used in professional discussions and target setting was rooted in it.

Where language can be open to interpretation, ongoing and targeted work was done with both learners and staff in order to define each of the learning behaviours by asking and answering the question 'what does that look like?' We worked tirelessly to achieve consistency when moving from class to class or adult to adult and as a result, a lot of worry and anxiety for the children was removed and expectations were clear.

Everyone understood the behaviours, they understood what the behaviours looked like in practice and they understood how they contributed to being a successful learner. The language became a vital thread that was woven throughout the school; it was in its reports and policies, it held a space in the curriculum, it was everywhere and brought about a deep consistency.

Recognition and reinforcement

It can be a challenge to recognise staff effort and achievement as frequently as it probably should be; however, there were several ways in which we celebrated positive staff behaviours which helped to reinforce the culture of Behaviour for Learning. Much in the same way that learner rewards were driven by the acknowledgement of positive learning behaviours, so too were the ways in which adults were recognised. Individualised praise for demonstrating positive adult behaviours and strategies that facilitated Behaviour for Learning progress was most effective and was a fantastic way to create a positive climate where people felt valued for their contributions. Creating a recognition rich environment is the ideal case scenario with praise coming from different angles and at regular intervals to highlight positive teacher behaviours and by introducing several ways to feedback, staff were receiving reinforcement but also expected to identify and acknowledge this in others.

A 'peer recognition' system was developed which was named the 'Lollipop Challenge.' This was aimed at staff noticing the good in each other. On a Monday each week, a lollipop stick would be selected which would reveal the name of a colleague who was to be focused on for the remainder of that week. The aim was to recognise something that the adult had done well and this was recorded on a post it note and displayed on a giant lollipop in the staff room. The comments recorded were always astute and based on having observed a positive behaviour or strategy that had had an impact on learners and some examples include: 'Miss G, the positive language that you use with the learners is such a good example to them and helps them feel confident,' 'Mrs N I like how you gave C space to attempt the challenge and intervened at the right time so that he kept going,' 'Mr B I loved the way you were able to listen to M in the morning and remain calm as she was so angry. She did feel happier when she left.' 'Miss V, your enthusiasm in phonics was infectious, the learners couldn't wait to get started!, 'Mr X that was a very inspiring way of explaining how sound travels to the children. They were so engaged,'Mr W, you are as cool as a cucumber, even in the most stressful situations. Your de-escalation skills are bang on!' Staff were encouraged to read their note before leaving on a Friday afternoon and feedback showed that it was a lovely way to end the week. Over the term, the post it notes were collated in a scrap book and when the going got tough, staff could receive a boost by glancing at some of the positive things that colleagues had identified about them.

In addition to the 'Lollipop Challenge,' staff exchanged compliments during assembly. This was an excellent way to model to learners, to reinforce the Behaviour for Learning language and to provide public recognition. Some examples include 'Miss F, you showed excellent resilience when planning this week despite finding it a challenge 'Miss R, you are always able to independently solve problems and it's always with a positive attitude 'Mr A, you went over and above this week and took risks in your lessons by introducing hands on tasks. The learners REALLY enjoyed that!'

Some other vehicles to recognise effort was through internal communications such as emails, which allowed leaders to highlight and honour behaviours and qualities that we valued most, during briefings where good news and examples of exemplary practice were shared and personalised cards written to highlight strengths and achievements.

Capturing good practice and successful strategies in case studies was another excellent way to demonstrate the impact of the work of adults and the systems and structures that they put in place.

We talk a lot in education about emotional currency for learners or discuss how 'full their cup is' but this also applies to adults and receiving sincere acknowledgement in a range of ways as discussed previously goes a long way to help people feel valued and motivated.

Peer supervision

Peer Supervision was one of the key approaches that we used to build capacity across the team. It provided an opportunity for people to learn from their peers. It was a process where people learnt from each other in an equal relationship focusing on the interventions with the aim of providing the best quality service for schools.

Peer Supervision was initially led by the Education Psychologist attached to the Primary Inclusion Development Service and then by other members of the local authority Education Psychology team. Peer Supervision gave staff the opportunity to share the interventions that they were involved in within a safe and secure environment, and they deepened their knowledge and understanding of Behaviour for Learning as a result.

This was evident in the school-based interventions and reflected in the review process that took place regularly. The Education Psychologist (EP) introduced the model based on Stringer et al. (1992) and provided a structure and a process that the group worked through. The Education Psychologist took on the role of the facilitator and modelled the process with the team. Once the team had grasped the process, different members of the team took on the role of facilitator.

This was the process that was followed:

1. A member of the team is the facilitator who ensures that the process is followed with an agreed time. All team members are clear about the ground rules which have been agreed to prior to the meeting. There is a confidentiality agreement and feedback which is non-judgemental. This role proved to be vital to the success of the Peer Supervision process.
2. One person brings an issue or problem from the intervention they are involved in to the meeting and explains it in detail. This could be any aspect of the intervention. When the person is sharing, everyone in the group listens to what is being shared, there are no comments or interruptions. All staff did have an opportunity to bring and share an issue or problem.
3. Members of the team now have the opportunity to ask questions or for more information for clarification so that they are clearer about what is shared. The person sharing can elaborate on what they have said.
4. Each person in the group can affirm the member of staff presenting the issue, pointing out what has gone well or the strengths.
5. Each member of the group can offer advice, a comment or point out similarities that they believe will help the person to solve the issue or the problem. The aim is to help identify the potential way forward.
6. Finally, the person who has brought the issue decides what they are going to do to move forward; this could mean taking one idea or more. It is always the person who has brought the problem who decides what action to take.
7. The session always ended with a review of the process, what went well, even better if.

Everyone benefited from the process, everyone shared and learnt from each other across professional boundaries. This process supported the learning and development of all staff which in turn impacted the interventions work with staff in school.

Bank of expertise

We recognised as we embarked on our professional learning programme and staff took part in the NPSLBA and were involved in partnership on interventions that we had a wide range of expertise that we could build on. This was a chance for staff to gain opportunities to share their skills, knowledge and understanding to enrich the service that we were providing for schools. We had staff who had led playground projects, nurture groups, parents support groups and had expertise in early years provision. This skillset widened as the PIDS developed over time.

Impact of peer supervision on staff learning and development

Peer Supervision created a climate and ethos where staff supported each other. A reflective learning culture was developed where staff shared their knowledge, expertise and learnt from each other. They also shared their experience of using Behaviour for Learning in school-based interventions. Staff were open to feedback from each other and developed confidence in their role. This was reinforced as staff initially worked on interventions collaboratively so that they gained confidence in the new approach, Behaviour for Learning and capacity building. The Peer Supervision structure provided a way of generating practical strategies to problem solve the situation, so staff were able to address problems that arose or raise concerns. Sharing of strategies in the team enabled staff to identify further training they needed but also helped them to develop strategies for themselves.

As the group sessions were working so well we introduced individual sessions for the Development workers with the Educational Psychologist so that they became even more confident in their role and responsibilities.

Solution-focused approaches

All staff in the team were trained in solution-focused brief therapy and solution-focused approaches with opportunities to look at video and practice. Solution-focused approaches was originally developed in the United States in 1989 and the 1990s and has its roots in the therapeutic world. The ideas can be used in many different settings and applied in different ways. De Shazer and Berghave played an important role in the development of solution-focused approaches and in 1986, de Shazer described the technique of the scaling question. The scaling question is simple, effective, and easy to use with adults and children (De Shazer, 1982). It has informed our practice and has been very effective in helping children and adults to look ahead.

A solution-focused approach is focused on helping people move towards the future that they want, envisioning what can be different by using existing skills strategies and ideas rather than focusing on the problem (George et al., 2011). Scaling is a powerful technique which was used in PIDS and at CAPA. The advantage is that the focus is on what has been achieved and then the next steps. The approach was motivating for children with a positive belief that they would be able to achieve what they were working towards. Visser (2013) describes clients as becoming more optimistic and hopeful when they use the scaling technique.

Solution-focused approaches in the Primary Inclusion Development Service

We included a solution-focused approach in our forms, for example, the action plans adopted this approach including questions which formed the basis for discussions. In the following questions we are creating an expectation of change in the intervention.

- What are the anticipated outcomes of the intervention?
- What changes will you be looking for?

Solution-focused coaching was a way of staff identifying the areas in their practice that were working well. This is referred to as the concept of exceptions and refers to the fact that problems fluctuate and there are times when the problem is less severe or even absent. This was evident when we carried out observations that there would be exceptions to the behaviour that was described. On a number of occasions, the behaviour which was causing concern would not be evident and there would be a strategy that the adult had used which they may not have been aware of. This provided an opportunity for the adult to discuss from the feedback what they did that impacted the child's learning behaviour. There would always be areas that were going well and where the member of staff was having an impact. This was confirmed by classroom observations. It was helpful to highlight the strengths, skills and strategies of the member of staff and have specific feedback on the impact they were having on either the individual child or class. The focus always remained on the positive – what was working well and what the member of staff could do more of. This was always acknowledged in the review process.

Scaling was an effective way of enabling children to evaluate different aspects of their learning. It was a way of helping children to assess their progress in their learning behaviours. In the process there is the assumption that the child is the expert on their own learning.

Solution-focused approaches at Courtyard AP Academy

Chapter 5 provides further detail about Behaviour for Learning at Courtyard AP Academy which includes how solution-focused approaches were instrumental in helping children to reflect on their academic progress, attendance and learning behaviours. This was one of the most effective strategies used at Courtyard AP Academy to get children to openly reflect and set new targets/goals of what they wanted to achieve. The culture was such that children could share this openly in a safe and secure environment without feeling that they were going to be judged or criticised.

SEAL

SEAL was implemented to 'promote the development and application to learning of social and emotional skills' that were classified under the five domains proposed in Goleman's (1995) model of 'emotional intelligence' (DCSF, 2007b).

The five domains:

- Self-awareness
- Self-regulation (managing feelings)
- Motivation
- Empathy
- Social skills

In addition, SEAL was recognised as the process through which children and adults could acquire the knowledge, attitudes and skills to recognise and manage their emotions and set and achieve positive goals. They were able to deomonstrate care and concern for others, establish positive relationships, make responsible decisions and be able to handle interpersonal situations effectively.

Securing good or better – a focus on SEAL

This successful programme developed by the learning trust in Hackney (2010) had a significant impact on the work that we were doing as a service. The purpose of the programme was to improve the quality of teaching by focusing on the Social and Emotional Aspects of Learning (SEAL). The 5 domains in SEAL were Motivation; Social skills; Managing Feelings; Empathy; Self Awareness.

In collaboration with the SEAL coordinator for the local authority we implemented the programme in some of our primary schools. The process that we used involved teachers filming themselves, reflecting on their own practice, identifying the teacher behaviours and classroom structures and then identifying areas for development, referred to as Development goals in the project. Staff would then plan to implement their goal and use filming to track their progress. Solution-focused coaching was used to support staff to reflect and then continue to build on their success. Figure 3.2 is a case study of one of the schools where the project was implemented.

Case Study Focus: Learning Project – *'Securing Good or Better'*

Reason for Request:
The Senior Leadership Team (SLT) in a local primary school was introduced to the learning project by the head of service. The SLT felt that the focus of the project would impact the learning in the classrooms and asked PIDS to implement the programme during the 2011–2012 academic year.

Context/Process
Eight teachers were identified to participate in the project along with two senior leaders in the school. The project ran during the autumn term 2011 and the spring term 2012 with a focus on quality first teaching through developing teacher behaviours and classroom structures.

Targets set
The individual teachers set their own development goals to work towards.

Intervention strategies implemented
Fortnightly group meetings, initially through large group sessions and then working in small groups of two or three teachers, each supported by a member of the PIDS.

Whole group discussions began with developing an understanding of a solution-focused approach.

Video footage was used to capture the practice of teachers in their classrooms.

Opportunities were given in the small group sessions for the teachers to reflect on their behaviours and classroom structures and to identify positive aspects of both.

Small groups provided opportunities to give positive feedback to each other as well as reflection time.

A structured set of questions were followed during the small group sessions which enabled the discussions to remain on solution-focused thinking and identifying progress made.

Impact of intervention
Participants and SLT gave the following feedback on the process of the project itself and how it impacted their own practice:

Good to reflect on my practice and learn from each other. Talk through and learn to focus on positives.

Figure 3.2 Case study on school-based learning project securing good to better

Highlighted areas that although I knew already, it was beneficial to be reminded.

Reflective on own teaching. Would like to have seen others teach to share their ideas.

Conscious of myself and impact. Able to analyse the positive response from the children.

Helpful to see my practice and discuss and share ideas in confidence. I felt the conversations were a little repetitive.

Being reflective about 'what I am doing?' rather than 'what are they doing?'

Differentiating questions and empathy with those who, for example, cannot speak English.

More positive about my practice.

Changed practice in morning greetings and so on. SEAL focus encourages learning, for example, making mistakes.

Making the most of time and pace of learning and challenging children but differentiating so they can access it.

Being varied in approach.

Figure 3.2 (Continued)

Working through this project with schools was excellent groundwork when looking at how we could implement Behaviour for Learning across schools, focusing on the three relationships. The use of observations, videos, reflecting on one's own practice with opportunities for feedback reflection and identifying the adult behaviours and structures in place which promote the learning behaviours were instrumental. Most of all we had the evidence to show that the tools used in this project was effective with the staff who took part in the project.

SEAL at the Courtyard AP Academy

Teaching at the Courtyard AP Academy was underpinned by Social and Emotional Aspects of Learning (SEAL). This was a comprehensive, whole-school approach that was adopted to encourage the development of social and emotional skills, in turn promoting effective learning, positive behaviour, staff effectiveness and emotional health.

At Courtyard AP Academy, a strong commitment was made to promoting SEAL across all areas of the school and learners were provided with planned opportunities to enhance these skills. Similarly, staff recognised the significance of social and emotional skills on effective learning and on the emotional well-being of the children. Efforts were directed at supporting both learners and staff to develop competence in the key domains. The development of the Behaviour for Learning programme linked to the personal social and health education programme provided the opportunity for the lead learning support professional at the Courtyard AP Academy to implement a programme for all children which included relationship with self, promoting the children's learning behaviours associated with self, that is, their emotional well-being. We believe that all staff have a role to play in enabling children to have good mental health. This is reinforced in government guidance on promoting children's and young people's mental health and well-being (DFE, 2017, 2018; Public Health England, 2021).

Was it important for the children to learn about learning behaviours?

Definitely. We knew that from our work across schools and at Courtyard AP Academy. In the same way that it was important for the adults to have a professional learning programme where they gained a good knowledge and understanding of Behaviour for Learning, it was just as important for the children. They had to know and understand the learning behaviours so that they could put them into practice and reflect on their own development. In the PIDS team this was incorporated into the interventions and an example of Peer Support is given in Chapter 4. At Courtyard AP Academy, the implementation of Behaviour for Learning meant that children became very confident in being able to identify their own learning behaviours and know what they had to do to improve. In the same way that they would have an academic target, there was one for Behaviour for Learning. The teaching of Behaviour for Learning at Courtyard AP Academy is discussed further in Chapter 5. One of the six recommendations cited in the report: Improving Behaviours in School by the Education Endowment Foundation (EEF, 2019) is that learning behaviours should be taught alongside managing misbehaviour to improve behaviour.

Training opportunities at Courtyard AP Academy

We had evidence of very strong Behaviour for Learning practice taking place across the school where staff were successfully using Behaviour for Learning strategies to support and nurture learners. We decided to capitalise on this by timetabling staff to spend time in each other's classrooms so that they could see what this actually looked like in practice, a very powerful learning experience. As the observations were a developmental tool, a focus for a specific strategy was usually given such as 'positive feedback' or 'use of Behaviour for Learning language' and this would be central to the visit. The staff would meet at a convenient time following the observation to discuss the impactful strategies that had been observed and how this might be implemented or used more effectively within their classroom. These discussions gave staff a deeper understanding of strategies being used, the decisions being made as well as the impact. The length of the visits was flexible, and the focus also changed; however, what remained the same was that staff would generate a target or a goal for themselves following the visit. The observer would keep notes or a record of their findings/observations so that they could revisit the points recorded. Feedback was positive where staff found the sessions valuable and felt they gained good insight into the practice of others which allowed them to develop their own practice. Adult self-awareness and self-reflectiveness were also developed significantly which allowed staff to take responsibility for their growth – staff entered with a 'I'm here to learn' attitude creating a supportive atmosphere. These observations became a powerful motivator and contributed significantly to a culture of collaboration. Most importantly of all, the effective practices across the school were becoming more far reaching, widespread and therefore impactful.

> Super duper! You listened so carefully and you worked with a super attitude towards your learning. You have included some excellent safety advice in your learning and I will certainly be taking this on board. I really like how you used sub-headings today.

Sharing experiences: Cascading ideas by sharing with others can help to highlight positive teaching behaviours and strategies and to promote their implementation. It can also contribute to adults evolving their practice as a result which was certainly the case at Courtyard AP Academy. The culture of collaboration and the sharing of ideas was supported by the ten- minute 'Catch up time' (see Chapter 5) that was built into the school day where class teams could discuss the day's events, talk through any issues arising and any strategies used that had a significant impact. Creating this dialogue was an informal opportunity to discuss successes and difficulties and had a positive impact on staff personal growth. Staff experienced increased confidence as a result of trialling new approaches suggested and a by-product of this was that it also helped to build the reputation of the staff sharing and using effective strategies. Sharing in itself was not enough, however. Building capacity helped to embed and transfer the ideas and practices so following catch up sessions, staff would go on to support one another to implement what had been discussed. The impact of sharing ideas and working alongside one another was that there were small and incremental changes to practice across the school. By trying new things and tweaking practice, adults were building up a wider repertoire of strategies, essentially creating a tool kit of ideas which could be dipped in and out of. More formally, and to support the catch up sessions, staff created a short bullet point working document which included the ideas about the strategies discussed and employed. This was a great way to record what worked with individuals and groups and could be used during new staff induction and for anyone who would be working in that class or just as a refresher and reference point for any staff member.

Bank of expertise: As with the PIDS team there were staff at Courtyard AP Academy with strengths and expertise who contributed to the outstanding progress that children made. The question is how could we develop a culture which built on the strengths and expertise that different staff had. Using this approach provided an amazing opportunity for improving practice at Courtyard AP Academy and achieving sustainable change. Identifying the specific behaviours displayed by these adults and being able to observe and share it is important. The great thing about this it is based on the discovery of what is already happening successfully in the school. Essentially, we were using the most powerful resource available, the staff who are working in the school. There were several ways in which this was captured at Courtyard AP Academy.

Here are some examples:

- Classroom observation
- Observations of specific sessions – enrichment time
- Learning walks
- Scrutiny of children's work
- Drop down days
- School visits

Positive handling

What do you do when you are faced with a crisis, a child is out of control and there is an 'explosion' – the child is so angry that they lose control? The anger can be shown in different ways – physically assaulting another child, throwing chairs, tearing down the classroom display and loads of verbal abuse and sometimes racist abuse. If the child is young then you might get kicked, spat at, sworn at, or bitten. The child loses control; they have difficulty managing their emotions. This kind of behaviour often leads to a fixed term and in some cases a permanent exclusion from a school. We witnessed these behaviours in some of our PIDS interventions and certainly at the PPRU and Courtyard AP Academy.

The DFE guidance (DFE, 2013) on the use of reasonable force gives advice for head-teachers, staff and governing bodies. It is quite clear from the guidance that staff can use reasonable force that involves a degree of physical contact with pupils and all staff have a legal power to do so. In the guidance it also states that this power applies to any member of staff at the school. It can also apply to people whom the headteacher has temporarily put in charge of pupils such as unpaid volunteers or parents accompanying students on a school organised visit (DFE, 2013, p. 4).

The guidance does provide a degree of protection for staff by stating that:

- School staff have a power to use force and lawful use of the power will provide a defence to any related criminal prosecution or other legal action.
- Suspension should not be used as an automatic response when a member of staff has been accused of using excessive force.
- Senior leaders should support their staff when they use this power.

DFE, 2013, p. 3

DFE refers to reasonable force and uses it to describe physical contact between staff and pupils. The examples they give range from guiding a child safely by the arm or a more extreme case such as breaking up a fight where a child needs to be restrained to prevent violence or injury.

We knew that children whose behaviour was more challenging might need physical intervention following the form completed by the school. All staff, especially those in the PPRU and Courtyard AP Academy, were trained in team teach (Allen and Matthews, 2013). Team teach was not just about restraint but about adopting a holistic approach, the emphasis being 95% on preventative measures, environmental management, and included personal behaviour diversion, defusion and de-escalation; in fact, restraint was a small part of the framework. Interventions started as those which were least intrusive to those most restrictive. Team teach (Allen and Matthews, 2013) staff were observed and had to complete an assessment as part of the training and were given a certificate which was renewed yearly. It was important that staff were properly trained so that they could respond using correct and recommended holds for a primary child. The training was an advantage as staff became more aware of the preventative measures that could be used when a child had an emotional outburst. We also had a member of the team who was a trainer of team teach and modelled the correct way of any physical interventions that we used. Even though the guidance does say the power of restraint can apply to anyone the headteacher has put temporarily in charge of pupils, it was very clear to the leadership team at the PPRU/Courtyard that there was a significant difference between staff who had been trained to physically intervene using team teach and those who had not. Those who had not been trained were not aware of the range of de-escalation strategies or the correct restraint holds to use.

As part of our work across schools we promoted schools having a member of staff trained in team teach, and some schools decided to train all their staff. This was in line with the recommendation which came through in the document produced by the DCSF 2010 on the use of force to control and restrain pupils. The recommendation is that as part of staff training schools should consider suitable accredited training and it refers to organisations who offer training in the use of de-escalation which introduce the use of force at appropriate times based on a consideration of other options (DCSF, 2010, p. 17). It also stated that it is good practice for schools to set out their approach to relevant training in their policy on use of force. In the Guidance 2013 it is the headteacher who has the responsibility to consider whether staff require any additional training (DFE, 2013).

All schools do have to have a behaviour policy and as a service we encouraged schools to be explicit about when they may use physical intervention and how they are going to respond if they have to use reasonable force. This should be made clear to staff, pupils and parents/carers. The guidance is clear that schools should not have a no contact policy. Any policy that the school uses that includes reasonable force will also have to be explicit about the school's legal duty to make reasonable adjustments for disabled children and children with special education needs.

The effectiveness of positive handling was also down to the relationships, children needed to know that staff wanted to help them and not hurt them and the physical techniques had to be devised to protect children from being hurt. It was also important for children to feel safe and secure. Parents did struggle when they knew that the only option left was for the child to be restrained, but it did help when they knew and understood what it looked like so at Courtyard AP Academy we showed them the physical interventions, which is the holds that the staff would do as a last resort. The implementation of a positive behaviour support plan for each child helped to reduce and stop the number of physical restraints which took place. The identification of positive strategies that are effective and included any triggers helps to provide an early intervention. Staff in the team were trained regularly and we would emphasize that all staff should be trained so that they can use positive handling to keep themselves and children safe.

One of the key areas in the Behaviour for Learning framework is 'children being able to manage their emotions and schools identifying strategies, behaviours, and approaches to support children to manage their emotions.' Chapter 6 shares strategies that supported children to manage their emotions which had a positive impact.

Parenting Programme

A member of staff took responsibility for families alongside parents and families of children in the PPRU. We decided to implement the Strengthening Families, Strengthening Communities (SFSC) parenting programme (Steele and Marigna, 1994) for the PPRU and parents of children who were part of a PIDS intervention. The programme, which was initially developed in the United States, was adapted for use by the United Kingdom by the Race Equality Foundation. SFSC stresses the importance of ethnic, cultural and spiritual roots. The programme is presented within a cultural framework and covered the following areas: cultural, spiritual, rites of passage, positive discipline, enhancing relationships, violence prevention and community involvement.

This was a highly successful programme and relevant to the diverse community that we worked in. The programme, which included talks, information, discussion and activities which reflected different learning styles, meant that parents actively engaged and shared their own experiences. As they did, relationships amongst parents developed and were positive, parents were learning from each other. We received extremely positive feedback from the parents who were involved in the programme. Parents were particularly interested in the 'Rites of Passage' and the areas that they covered: personal rite of passage,

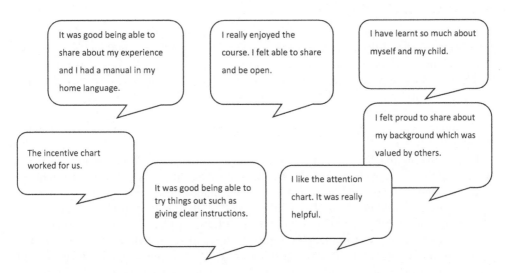

Figure 3.3 Parental feedback from course participants on SFSC course

spiritual rite of passage, physical rite of passage, mental rite of passage, cultural rite of passage, historical rite of passage, emotional rite of passage, economic rite of passage, social rite of passage and political rite of passage.

Parents enjoyed the programme which helped them to engage in the school and supported them with their children at home. It was a 12-week programme, each session lasting 3 hours. Figure 3.3 shows feedback from some of the participants in the programme.

The parents planned their certificate ceremony. What a celebration! We are reminded of the belief quoted in the SFSC programme:

> when people feel good about who they are and where they have come from, when they feel a sense of connection to the past and the future, when they share their values and experiences, they are more open to understand others and they will find that we are all more alike that we are different.
>
> SFSC Facilitator Manual, 2009, p. 13

Restorative approaches

On the original staffing structure for the PIDS there was a post for a development worker to lead on restorative justice; however, we made the decision to train all staff in restorative practice. (Restorative Solutions, 2007). Restorative practice was seen as an important approach to be used to provide an alternative way for schools to work with pupils who were engaged in conflict, fighting, violent or aggressive behaviour which would lead to an exclusion. The evidence from schools who were using this approach was that there was a reduction in exclusions and young people were able to resolve conflicts not only with the support of an adult but in some schools, children led restorative conferences with children (Clarke, 2012). All staff were trained in level 1 and 2 restorative practice so that they could use their knowledge and skills developed from the training to support and advise schools.

Why restorative approaches?

Restorative justice is a process where all the parties with a stake in a particular offence come together to resolve collectively how to deal with the aftermath of the offence and showed us that the use of restorative practice reduces its implications for the future (Marshall, 1999).

The key purpose of restorative approaches is to repair harm; in fact, it is a harm reduction process and reduces the effects of harm on people and in many cases stops the person who caused the harm from repeating the behaviour. It is an additional tool that can be used when responding to conflict rather than adopting a punitive approach to incidents (Clarke, 2012).

Restorative approaches was implemented at the Courtyard AP Academy and was based on the training and resources provided by Restorative Solutions. A structured set of questions are used to help children to express their feelings, needs and wants. This was an opportunity for children to resolve conflict and be fully involved in the process and to understand other children's feelings. Staff in the PIDS who had been trained shared the training with schools and modelled the process for staff so that they could observe the impact. Some schools chose to develop this approach further and trained primary school children so that they were involved in leading restorative conferences for their peers.

Summary

To implement change so that it permeates throughout the school, it starts with the school/service improvement plan. We describe the learning journey that all our staff took part in with an emphasis on the strategies that were the most effective.

We include the five-stage learning model and five stages of learning competence and how an understanding of these can support new staff and inform the planning of your staff professional development learning programme.

Situational leadership is a model that can be used by leaders to focus on support for members of staff so that they can be unconsciously competent. It also provides an approach where you can decide on how much direction and support will be needed by staff.

The most significant strategies to develop an open and trusting culture where staff developed was peer supervision. To enable and support everyone to focus on solutions rather than problems and blame, everyone was trained in solution-focused approaches, and these were incorporated into some of the processes we adopted.

Takeaways

☞ Implementation of 'the five-stage learning model' will empower staff and help to create a learning environment.

☞ Training the whole school staff community will ensure consistency of approach.

☞ Peer supervision is an effective strategy to enable staff to support each other to problem solve and learn from each other.

☞ Implementation of restorative approaches will help children to deal with conflict and reduce exclusions.

Reflective questions

How do you use your bank of expertise to enhance the quality of provision at your school/provision?

How can you use the five stages of learning competence to support the induction and development of all staff?

In what ways can you support parents so that they are empowered and feel valued?

Which learning strategies have been the most effective in transforming the culture in your school? What else could you do?

References

Allen, B. and Matthews, G. (2013). *Team Teach Workbook v.2013.1*. London: Team Teach.

Blanchard, K., Zigarmi, P. and Zigarmi, D. (1985). *Leadership and the One Minute Manager*. London: Harper Collins.

Bubb, S. and Earley, P. (2007). *Leading and Managing Continuing Professional Development* (2nd ed.). London: Paul Chapman.

Bullock, K. (2009). *The Importance of Emotional Intelligence to Effective School Leadership, Research Associate Summary Report*. Nottingham: National College. NCSL3. Autumn.

Clarke, J. (2012). *Restorative Schools, Restorative Communities*. Great Britain: Taylor and Francis.

De Shazer, S. (1982). *Patterns of Brief Family Therapy: An Ecosystem Approach*. New York Guilford Key to Solution in Brief Therapy. New York: Norton.

Department for Children, Schools and Families (DCSF). (2007a). *NPSLBA The National Programme for Specialist Leaders of Behaviour and Attendance: The Role of Senior Leadership in Behaviour and Attendance*. https://dera.ioe.ac.uk/8687/1/5614a0a07b35847e5384f0f591ef0e26.pdf (accessed 29/07/22).

Department for Children, Schools and Families (DCSF). (2007b). *Social and Emotional Aspects of Learning for Secondary Schools*. Nottingham: DCSF Publications.

Department for Children, Schools and Families (DCSF). (2010). *The Use of Force to Control or Restrain Pupils. Guidance for Schools in England*. Nottingham: DCSF.

Department for Education (DFE). (2011). *The National Strategies 1997–2011: A Brief Summary of the Impact and Effectiveness of the National Strategies*. London: DFE.

Department for Education (DFE). (2013). *Use of Reasonable Force. Advice for Headteachers, Staff and Governing Bodies*. London: DFE.

Department for Education (DFE). (2017). *Transforming Children and Young People's Mental Health Provision: A Green Paper*. London: DFE.

Department for Education (DFE). (2018). *Mental Health and Behaviour in Schools: Departmental Advice for School Staff*. London: DFE.

Department for Education and Science (DFES). (2004). *Primary National Strategy: Behaviour and Attendance Materials*. London: DFES.

Ellis, S. and Tod, J. (2009). *Behaviour for Learning: Proactive Approaches to Behaviour Management*. Abingdon: Routledge.

Education Endowment Foundation (EEF). (2019). *Improving Behaviour in Schools*. https://d2tic4wvo1iusb.cloudfront.net/eef-guidance-reports/behaviour/EEF_Improving_behaviour_in_schools_Report.pdf?v=1635355216 (accessed 29/07/22).

Garner, P. (2011). *Promoting the Conditions for Positive Behaviour, to Help Every Child Succeed: Review of the Landscape*. Nottingham: National College for School Leadership.

George, E., Iveson, C., and Ratner, H. (2011). *Briefer, a Solution Focused Practice Manual*. London: Brief.

Goleman, D. (1995). *Emotional Intelligence*. New York: Bentam Books.

Goleman, D. (1998). *Working with Emotional Intelligence*. London: Bloomsbury Publishing.

Goleman, D., Boyatzis, R., and McKee, A. (2002). *Primal Leadership: Realizing the Power of Emotional Intelligence*. Boston: Harvard Business School Press.

Gomez-Leal, R., Holzer Allison, A., Bradley, C., Fernandez-Berrocal, P., and Patti, J. (2021). The relationship between emotional intelligence and leadership in school leaders: A systematic review. *Cambridge Journal of Education*, 52(10), 1–21.

Gray, D. (2009). Emotional intelligence and school leadership. *International Journal of Educational Leadership*, 4(4), October–December.

Hersey, P. and Blanchard, K.H. (1977). *Management of Organisational Behaviour - Utilising Human Resources*. New Jersey: Prentice Hall.

Joyce, B. and Showers, B. (1980). Improving service training: The message of research. *Educational Leadership*, 37(5), 379–385.

Marshall, T.F. (1999). *Restorative Justice an Overview*. London: Home Office.

OFSTED. (2009). *Inspecting Behaviour: Supplementary Guidance for Section 5 Inspection*. September. London: OFSTED.

Public Health England. (2021). *Promoting Children and Young People's Mental Health and Wellbeing. A Whole School or College Approach*. London.

Restorative Solutions. (2007). *Restorative Practice Pack*. Preston: Restorative Solutions CIC.

Steele, M. and Marigna, M. (1994). *Strengthening Families, Strengthening Communities: An Inclusive Parent Programme*. London: Race Equality Foundation.

Stoll, L., Harris, A., and Handscomb, G. (2012). *Great Professional Development Which Leads to Great Pedagogy: Nine Claims from Research*. Nottingham: National College for School Leadership.

Stringer, P., Stow, L., Hibbert, K., Powell, J., and Louw, E. (1992). Establishing Staff Consultation Groups in Schools: A programme to train facilitators of school based staff support groups in consultancy. *Educational Psychology in Practice*, 8(2), July.

The Learning Trust. (2010). *Securing Good or Better: Improving Quality First Teaching Through Social and Emotional Aspects of Learning (SEAL)*. Hackney: Hackney Education.

Visser, C.F. (2013). The origins of the solution – focused approach. *International Journal of Solution – Focused Practices,* (1), 10–17.

4 Developing our assessment tool

Introduction

This chapter focuses on the assessment tools that we implemented based on the three relationships: 'Relationship with self,' 'Relationship with others' and 'Relationship with the curriculum' of the Behaviour for Learning framework. We explain the assessment procedure that we used and how we analysed the learning behaviours to show an individual child's progress. We worked with other professionals across the service to review a child's assessment regularly and include how we used it to identify children's needs, set targets and track pupil progress. Readers will be interested to see how the analysis of the assessments can be used effectively to track a child's learning behaviours and see the relationship between them.

Using a Behaviour for Learning perspective

According to Ellis and Tod (2009), 'Behaviour for Learning encourages the use of a range of existing positive behaviour management strategies and approaches but requires that they are evaluated against the extent to which they promote learning behaviour.'

Using this perspective encouraged us to take the opportunity to consider the *why* behind a particular chosen approach and the impact that it had on learning.

The Behaviour for Learning conceptual framework enabled us to move on from traditional behaviour management systems of simply managing perceived 'misbehaviour,' to creating environments where children could be successful in developing learning behaviours. The environment, including interactions with and the perspective of the adults, was a key element in enabling this to happen.

The complexity of the variables which can affect learning behaviours is considerable. Therefore, it was important for our approach to put these three relationships at the heart of our interventions and use them as a focus to further develop our provision. We aimed to support school staff to teach positive learning behaviours alongside developing positive classroom management approaches.

Behaviour for Learning assessment tool that we developed and used

The assessment tool (see Chapter 1, Table 1.1), was devised using key elements of learning behaviours identified in the Behaviour for Learning conceptual framework (Ellis and Tod, 2009). It was developed with input from local headteachers, Educational Psychologists and a local authority inspector. It was piloted in a small number of schools and received positive feedback.

DOI: 10.4324/9781003166672-5

Having reviewed the QCA Behaviour Assessment tool that was commonly used in schools at the time, we decided to develop our own assessment tool that more accurately reflected the three relationships at the heart of enhancing learning behaviours.

The list of learning behaviours included was not exhaustive, as due to the complexity of the interconnecting relationships, it was difficult to define exact learning behaviours.

However Ellis and Tod (2009) described the following key aspects of learning behaviours: 'engagement; collaboration; participation; communication; motivation; independent activity; responsiveness; self-regard; self-esteem; responsibility; disruptiveness; disaffection and problems.' We then incorporated these into our assessment.

The assessment tool maintains a focus on the three relationships detailed in the conceptual framework: relationship with self, others and the curriculum. This tool has been used effectively as a starting point for interventions in the Primary Inclusion Development Service (PIDS) and reflects the perception of individual teachers regarding the learning behaviours of identified learners. The focus on relationships meant that the same tool could be completed in very different ways by different individuals. This is an important factor to consider when devising interventions. As relationships are a key element in promoting positive learning behaviours, the strength of those relationships often determines what is observed by the adults working most closely with the children. As the initial assessment was based on the perception of the adult completing it and based on their own observations, it was important that the same person completed subsequent assessments in order to measure progress and plan next steps.

A version of the assessment tool was also devised for completion by the child and their parents/carers. On completing the form, they were asked to scale how regularly a particular learning behaviour occurred. The responses to each were from the unique perspective of the individual completing the form. This in itself provided valuable information for us regarding the experience and starting point of the child or adult's perspective.

The three relationships – what are they and why they are important

This approach is best conceptualised as a set of three key relationships experienced by learners. These relate to their:

- **Relationship with Self:** Being willing to, and able to, include themselves in the learning opportunities and relationships on offer in the classroom and school context. Included in this is how the learner feels about themselves – their self-esteem, self-efficacy and their perceptions of how important or relevant school learning is to them.
- **Relationship with Others:** Being able to take part in play and learning opportunities that involve others and participate in aspects of school life as a member of the school community. This involves being willing and able to interact socially and academically with others, including the teacher and other adults.
- **Relationship with the Curriculum:** The dynamic interactions that make up the reciprocal activity between the learner and the curriculum. This involves being able and willing to access, process and respond to information available through the curriculum.

Enabling children to establish and develop these relationships was key to developing positive learning behaviours. With an emphasis on learning behaviours, the focus was shifted onto those elements of the learning experience that learners could have a sense of ownership over and that the teachers could have a positive influence on.

Relationship with Self (Engagement)

This is the predominantly emotional aspect of the Behaviour for Learning model and relates to children's engagement in the learning process. It refers to intrapersonal skills, mindset, regulations and managing emotions.

For some of our young learners, due to past experiences of trauma, Adverse Childhood Experiences (ACE) or other unmet needs, they were often operating in a state of hyperarousal and reacting to their learning environment, and those within it, with a fight/flight/freeze response. Bruce Perry's Neurosequential Model (2008) further supported our understanding of how some of this may manifest itself in classroom behaviour and its impact on how children might engage with and process their environment.

Our aim was to enable the children we worked with to have the tools to be able to regulate, so that they were in an emotional state to be ready to learn. When the children had a more positive relationship with self, they were able to engage in the learning process and the learning environment in a more meaningful and productive way.

However, there were also many children for whom the context of their particular learning environment did not meet their specific learning and emotional needs. This often resulted in behaviours that challenged those who were teaching these children.

Our data showed us that the same children who were being excluded from school were also most likely those who were experiencing barriers to engaging in learning, and as a result were often underachieving. Thus, children who are emotionally secure were better able to concentrate on their learning and on developing effective social relationships. As a team we worked towards helping school staff to recognise the ways in which they had influence over creating an emotionally secure classroom/school environment. Integral to this was beginning to build habits in reframing a view of observed behaviour, to empower adults to respond in new ways to support children to achieve improved outcomes.

Table 4.1 gives examples of reframing how we viewed behaviour.

Table 4.1 Reframing behaviour

Interpretation of Language	Reframing
'She is always seeking attention in class'	She is seeking connection/attention needing.
'He doesn't try to take part in lessons.'	He does not yet feel ready to join in.
'He is always calling out his answer.'	He has some ideas that he is trying to share.

Relationship with Others (Participation)

This is the predominantly social aspect of the model and relates to how learners participate within the learning environment. It is a key element that heavily influences how individuals behave within a given context. This behaviour can be impacted by many factors, including how well you perceive others know you, the trust that you have in others and your experience within friendship and learning groups, which all contribute to effective participation. The success of this participation is also likely to be influenced by the skills and aptitudes that an individual has that enable them to function effectively within a group. The relationship with the adults in the classroom were also a determinant of how successful a learner's participation can be. Those children who did not feel that sense of belonging or had underdeveloped skills in speaking, listening and turn taking were more likely to be unwilling or unable to participate as a member of a team within a class or school. They needed to feel seen and valued by both their peers and the adults around them.

Examples of some ways that this was facilitated follow.

Peer assessments through learner peer observations

Children were given the opportunity to observe and give feedback to their peers. A specific learning behaviour was the focus of each observation and there were clear but simple parameters around what they recorded and gave feedback on. For example, if the child was observing another group of children cooperating and collaborating in a group, they were not to name individuals but rather the behaviours seen. There were three things they had to record and then report on:

1. Draw or write about all aspects of the focus learning behaviour, that they could observe or hear happening during the 10-minute observation.
2. Identify one aspect that the child/group were doing really well.
3. Suggest one aspect that they could improve on next time.

There were many benefits to this approach, including allowing children who needed to develop a particular learning behaviour the opportunity to observe it being modelled well by peers and see the impact of that. This approach also supported the children to develop their language around learning behaviours and over time becoming able to confidently articulate what they could see that was making learning possible. The process resulted in children devising a short set of 'even better if' outcomes to work towards. When displayed in the classroom, it also served as a reminder to the teacher about which learning behaviours to recognise the children participating in and give them feedback accordingly.

Peer support groups

This was an opportunity for children to work collaboratively to solve problems. We used a 'Circle of Friends' approach where children asked for support from their peers to improve particular learning behaviours related to self, others and the curriculum. The child had a focus behaviour to work on and scaled themselves accordingly on a scale from 0–10, with 10 being the best it could be.

They met weekly for 20 minutes, along with an adult overseeing the project, to reflect on their progress over the week, using the scaling method to record progress. The child reflected on positive aspects and would hear from their peers about positive behaviours they too had noticed. The group would agree on some 'even better if' suggestions and set a focus for the week ahead.

The outcomes were that the peers were focused on the positive contributions that the child had made during that week and were able to listen to the feedback from their peers. That innate need to feel a sense of belonging was very powerfully met by the collective support given by the group to the child.

Relationship with Curriculum (Access)

This is the predominantly cognitive aspect of the model and relates to how well children are able to access the learning curriculum. It refers to the child's previous experiences of learning and specific learning needs, how learning is presented and differentiated and the importance of being able to make mistakes and learn from them. The reasons that there were barriers to access for some of our children were complex and varied. For some children there were gaps in their learning as they may have had low school attendance or previous negative experiences of accessing learning opportunities. In any average classroom there are sure to be a range of needs and access requirements; therefore, creating a calm and purposeful environment is an important start in protecting and enhancing a positive relationship to the curriculum. However, that is only part of the picture. For children who were easily distracted or had difficulty in directing their own learning, they could quickly become disengaged, so thinking carefully about what they needed to access and engage in lessons was vital.

When there were potential difficulties with accessing the curriculum for some children, they were more likely to engage in behaviours that deflected from the learning tasks. In turn this impacted their likelihood of being able to collaborate effectively with peers and participate in group discussions or tasks. With less participation there was the potential to continue to reinforce a negative self-image of themselves as a learner and that their role within the class dynamic is less important or that they are failing at learning.

In order to create the climate of a positive learning environment it was crucial to recognise the importance of engagement, participation and access and find creative ways to ensure that they were developed. Central to this was the contribution of the adults, including a willingness to reflect on the systems, practices and culture of the classroom. Some of the most important approaches we implemented included:

- Enabling children to recognise how their effort and resilience translated into making progress with various learning behaviours.
- Personalising the curriculum to meet a diverse range of needs.
- Encouraging active engagement in multi-sensory learning to help reinforce prior learning and embed new skills and concepts.
- Adults using language that encouraged, motivated and enhanced emotional well-being within the learning and teaching environment.
- Ensuring that anticipated learning outcomes were made explicit so that children were clear on what they were learning about and how it was structured to build on their existing knowledge.

Challenge linking learning with behaviour

Learning and behaviour were often seen as two separate aspects and approached as such.

However, it was evident from our experiences that progress with the curriculum and learner behaviours are inextricably linked. Providing meaningful curriculum progress is more likely to create an environment that promotes an interest in learning, motivation, collaboration and valuing making mistakes within the learning process.

All too often when we react rather than respond to the behaviour that challenges us, we do not move past the behaviour to reach the unmet need. We can easily become stuck in a repetitive cycle of consequences and 'fire-fighting' situations and lose sight of the importance of the child's relationship with the curriculum.

Assessment – interpretation of model

We wanted to be able to reflect the progress made by children in terms of developing their relationships with themselves, others and the curriculum. When carrying out observations of children in the school environment, we set about looking for small increases in learning behaviours as opposed to a focus on a reduction in behaviours that were a barrier to learning. The skill was in noticing and recording such increases in a way that could be built upon. Having anticipated outcomes that reflected such increases helped to maintain a focus on the progress we were working towards.

From the outset, we acknowledged the importance of teaching learning behaviours and the social and emotional aspects of learning and how the school ethos would impact this.

We also understood the significance of the other aspects that underpinned this, that is, family, culture and community, policies and services. Childrens' behaviour and learning are heavily influenced by language and culture. Being responsive to the child's identity, beliefs and norms serves to enhance a positive teacher/pupil relationship. Throughout interventions it was appropriate to encourage school staff to understand that although some of the behaviour shown by a particular child may not be regarded as appropriate in the classroom/school context, it may be very *normal* in the child's home life. This was especially important to be aware of in trying to understand the concerns of the child's parents/carers, that is, that the behaviours described in school were not what they had seen at home. Recognition of this created teaching points for development of learning behaviours.

When using a solution-focused approach to Behaviour for Learning, it is crucial to notice when effective learning behaviour was happening and therefore record even the smallest examples of positive learning behaviour.

Developing the five-point scale for assessment

When developing the Likert scale used in the assessment tool, we had originally included a section under the heading 'not at all' as the first point on the scale rather than 'rarely' as the first point on the scale. This proved problematic and unrealistic as we were finding that completed assessments indicated a high prevalence of learning behaviours that were described as occurring 'not at all' by school staff. However, following many observations it was clear that certain behaviours were indeed happening but were not always noticed.

For example, one child was described in the initial assessment by the class teacher as 'not at all' cooperating and collaborating with peers when working and playing together. However, when observed by a member of the team and the school SENCO, this child was observed turn-taking in a small group reading session, participating with success and cooperation with peers in a game of 'champ' at playtime and playing a game of number pairs with a partner during a maths lesson. So, whilst such interactions may have been rare, they were not in fact completely absent from the child's experience. As a strength-based observational/assessment tool we aimed to seek out even the smallest examples of where positive learning behaviours were occurring as a basis for building on these skills.

Appendix 1 shows the scale that we used. The rate of occurrence of behaviour is represented in the following way on the assessment tool:

- *Rarely* equates to approximately 5% of time
- *Sometimes* equates to approximately 25% of time
- *Fairly Often* equates to approximately 50% of time
- *Often* equates to approximately 75% of time
- *Always* equates to above 95% of time

If this is considered across a typical school week of 30 hours, 5% of time is equivalent to 1.5 hours. To say that a learner engages rarely in any particular behaviour would mean that they do so for around 20–25 minutes in an average day.

When completing the assessment, practitioners were encouraged to think of examples when the learner had engaged in such behaviour throughout the week as a way of gaining perspective on the frequency of occurrence. Other more common methods of observation and collection of evidence were used to feed into this. Completion of the assessment was then followed up by a focused observation of these learning behaviours.

Table 4.2 gives some examples of what might be considered when completing the assessment.

Table 4.2 Examples of learning behaviours which may be observed (list not exhaustive)

Relationship with Self	Relationship with Others	Relationship with the Curriculum
Is Interested in Learning – asking and answering questions – makes links to previous learning	**Is willing to work Independently as appropriate** – can maintain an appropriate noise level for concentration and manage distractions – generally able to commence a task without additional adult support	**Is willing to engage with the curriculum** – Can maintain focus on tasks and is willing to participate using a range of resources and learning contexts
Has a Positive Opinion of him/herself – Accepting compliments		**Can Take Responsibility for Own Learning** – Is aware of their own strengths and uses these to make progress – Avails of classroom resources
Can Manage Strong Emotions Such as Anger and/or Sadness – able to self-regulate – can express their feelings – have strategies that they use to help themselves	**Is socially aware of what is going on around him/her** – can read the behaviour cues of the environment they are in	**Is able to access the curriculum** – able to access the learning that is set at an appropriately differentiated level
Has a Belief That they are capable of being successful – positive comments and actions regarding their ability to participate and succeed	**Is willing and able to empathise with others** – can understand the point of view of others – can recognize emotions displayed by others	**Is willing to try new things and take risks** – embraces new challenges, not giving up easily
Can independently Make Choices and Try to Solve Problems – can use previous learning – able to make decisions without frequently seeking reassurance	**Is willing to ask for help** – will seek out help and support when needed in a way that is appropriate to the context	**Can make mistakes and move on** – using mistakes as learning opportunities
Can accept responsibility for own behaviour – can accept correction or redirection from an adult – honest in their interpretation of events	**Is willing to behave respectfully towards peers** – considers how they speak to adults, following instructions and take advice	**Is self-aware and knows how and when to get help** – uses all systems in place to seek help when required, e.g., 'brain, book.' board, buddy, before asking the teacher
	Is able to listen to others and be attentive – able to listen attentively in peer, small group and whole class discussions – shows attentive listening through asking and answering questions appropriately	**Motivated to complete tasks** – begins tasks promptly and remains on task until completion
Shows Good Self-Control – can wait for their turn	**Can cooperate and collaborate when working and playing in a group** – Can take turns, share resources and ideas – Follows rules of games and enjoys participating	**Able to work unaided** – confident in own ability and does not always need support
		Follow classroom rules and routines – understands classroom systems and procedures and is able to operate within the boundaries set

Coupled with the assessment tool and perspectives from child, parent and teachers, the classroom observations helped to identify the focus learning behaviour to be developed.

How were the Behaviour for Learning assessments analysed?

The Behaviour for Learning approach evaluates in terms of an increase or presence of behaviour. This is a reflection of solution focus practice which was integral to our approach. Following input from an inspector with responsibility for assessment and use of data, he showed how we could set about depicting increases in a way that could quickly be understood visually. Data from initial assessments were put into our database and were represented pictorially using a light grey colour, as shown in the diagram Figure 4.1. The key to the learning behaviours used on the assessment included on the graphic assessment however for the purpose of this book we have identified them separately in Table 4.3.

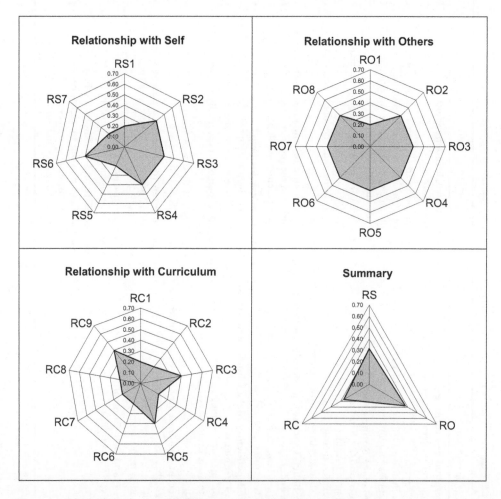

Figure 4.1 Initial BFL assessment of Child AB completed by class teacher

Table 4.3 Learning behaviours used on the assessments for each of the three relationships

Relationship with Self	Relationship with Others	Relationship with the Curriculum
RS1. is interested in learning	RO1. is willing to work independently as appropriate	RC1. is willing to engage with the curriculum
RS2. has a positive opinion of her/himself	RO2. socially aware of what is going on around him/her	RC2. can take responsibility for own learning
RS3. can manage strong emotions such as anger and/ or sadness	RO3. is willing and able to empathise with others	RC3. is able to access the curriculum
RS4. has a belief that she/he is capable of being successful	RO4. is willing to ask for help	RC4. is willing to try new things and take risks
RS5. can independently make choices and try to solve problems	RO5. is willing to behave respectfully towards adults in school	RC5. can make mistakes and move on
RS6. can accept responsibility for own behaviour	RO6. is willing to behave respectfully towards peers	RC6. is self-aware, knows how and when to get help
RS7. shows good self-control	RO7. is able to listen to others and be attentive	RC7. motivated to complete tasks
		RC8. able to work unaided
		RC9. follows classroom rules and routines

From this example you can see that aspects of the child's relationship with self and curriculum may be initial areas to focus on for development. The observations undertaken also helped to inform the starting point. The assessment tool was completed again by the same person 6–8 weeks later and data from this assessment was input and represented using a darker colour as shown in Figure 4.2 and described in Table 4.4.

The progress made was evidenced by observations from teachers, records of the child's participations in activities, samples of the child's work and feedback given.

As the three relationships are all so interconnected, they potentially had a circular nature to them in that improvements in the relationship with curriculum had a positive impact on the relationship with self and others and vice versa. Having a focus learning behaviour and recognising the emergence of other learning behaviours indicated improvements in the overall focus relationship.

Figure 4.3 is an example of a graphical analysis for a child who attended the Courtyard AP Academy following a school-based intervention. The analysis shows the progress made within the timeframe and the areas where the child needs to develop.

Table 4.5 shows key behaviours observed within each of the three relationships.

The next example which we expand on is from a school-based intervention. Figure 4.4 shows an analysis of a Behaviour for Learning assessment completed by the same member of staff. The light grey shows the initial assessment and the dark grey shows the progress that was made and the impact of the strategies implemented by the class teacher.

The next step was the important discussion between the class teacher/SENCO and team member picking out relevant themes.

From the previous information we can see that from the class teacher's perspective, the learner had an interest in learning, was able to access the curriculum and was willing to work independently as appropriate. Seen through an age-appropriate level, however, he

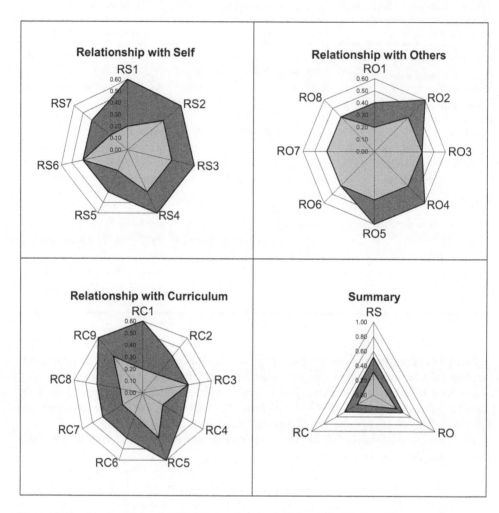

Figure 4.2 Graphical analysis of child AB showing the initial and final BFL assessment completed by class teacher

Table 4.4 Learning behaviours for each of the three relationships

Relationship with Self	Relationship with Others	Relationship with the Curriculum
RS1. is interested in learning	RO1. is willing to work independently as appropriate	RC1. is willing to engage with the curriculum
RS2. has a positive opinion of her/himself	RO2. socially aware of what is going on around him/her	RC2. can take responsibility for own learning
RS3. can manage strong emotions such as anger and/or sadness	RO3. is willing and able to empathise with others	RC3. is able to access the curriculum
RS4. has a belief that she/he is capable of being successful	RO4. is willing to ask for help	RC4. is willing to try new things and take risks
RS5. can independently make choices and try to solve problems	RO5. is willing to behave respectfully towards adults in school	RC5. can make mistakes and move on

Relationship with Self	Relationship with Others	Relationship with the Curriculum
RS6. can accept responsibility for own behaviour	RO6. is willing to behave respectfully towards peers	RC6. is self-aware, knows how and when to get help
RS7. shows good self-control	RO7. is able to listen to others and be attentive	RC7. motivated to complete tasks
		RC8. able to work unaided
		RC9. follows classroom rules and routines

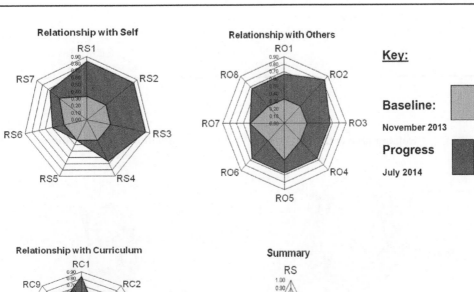

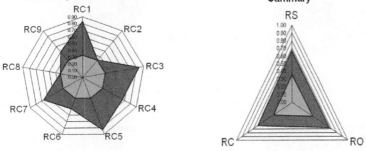

Figure 4.3 Graphical analysis showing progress of a child's Behaviour for Learning from November 2013 to July 2014

Table 4.5 Learning behaviours for each of the three relationships

Relationship with Self	Relationship with Others	Relationship with the Curriculum
RS1. is interested in learning	RO1. is willing to work independently as appropriate	RC1. is willing to engage with the curriculum
RS2. has a positive opinion of her/himself	RO2. socially aware of what is going on around him/her	RC2. can take responsibility for own learning
RS3. can manage strong emotions such as anger and/ or sadness	RO3. is willing and able to empathise with others	RC3. is able to access the curriculum
RS4. has a belief that she/he is capable of being successful	RO4. is willing to ask for help	RC4. is willing to try new things and take risks

(Continued)

Table 4.5 (Continued)

Relationship with Self	Relationship with Others	Relationship with the Curriculum
RS5. can independently make choices and try to solve problems	RO5. is willing to behave respectfully towards adults in school	RC5. can make mistakes and move on
RS6. can accept responsibility for own behaviour	RO6. is willing to behave respectfully towards peers	RC6. is self-aware, knows how and when to get help
RS7. shows good self-control	RO7. is able to listen to others and be attentive	RC7. motivated to complete tasks
		RC8. able to work unaided
		RC9. follows classroom rules and routines

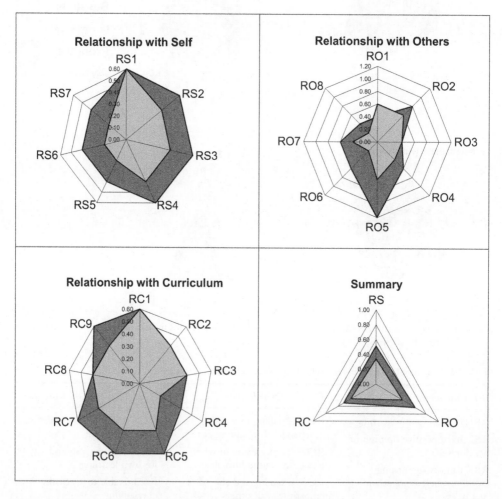

Figure 4.4 Graphical analysis showing progress of child CD's BFL

was not yet at a stage where he showed good self-control and found it difficult to accept responsibility for his own behaviour. He found it difficult to interact effectively with peers or cooperate and collaborate when working or playing in a group. He was not sure how and when to get help when needed.

At the beginning of the intervention, the learner shared that when he was 'out of control' it was too difficult for him to come back from it and he described that 'it all happened too quickly and I go over the top.'

This was also reflective of his teacher's experience, with her description being that he went from 0–100 in seconds, without any identifiable warning signs. In some ways there was a communication barrier between the two that needed to be broken. Using the child's own language and scaffolding the conversation to ensure that he was able to articulate his thoughts and feelings resulted in him also being able to identify some observable behaviours that would enable his teacher to intervene in a timely way to support him with regulating these big emotions. His progress was reviewed following the review process described in Chapter 2. This was a collaborative forum between mainstream school staff and the Primary Inclusion Development Service team.

In reviewing progress made towards anticipated outcomes it was important to maintain a focus on the aspects of learning behaviour identified at the start of the intervention, on the action plan. There were always aspects that child and teacher would continue to work on, and those sometimes small steps of progress were always significant to build upon.

The pupil's voice was highly valued in the process as our approach always had to start where the child was at in their developmental and learning journey. They needed to be an integral part of taking that journey forward and understanding their own next steps. Their perspective was very insightful in contributing to planning learning opportunities and building positive relationships. An example template of a learning behaviour plan can be seen in Table 4.6.

Table 4.6 Learning behaviour plan

My Learning Behaviour Plan (include image) **I would like to be even better at:** **When I am making progress we will notice:** **What might make this a challenge for me?** **Who/what might help?**

Case study

The case study of Child A in Table 4.7 shows how the assessment tool is used to inform the intervention and measure the impact of the strategies.

Figure 4.5 shows the Behaviour for Learning assessment for a child, the baseline and then the progress the child makes

Table 4.7 Case study of child A

Case study

BUILDING CAPACITY
Case Study

Reason for Request:

The school initially made a request for intervention in May 2012 when Child A was in Year 3. The school's main concerns at the time were that Child A was 'seeking attention' in class through what they described as negative behaviour. This included disrupting others by calling out and finding it difficult to accept responsibility for his behaviour by blaming others. This was particularly evident to them when Child A was in situations where he had to work collaboratively with his peers. He also found it difficult to manage strong emotions. The school's SENCO also described that Child A had difficulty accessing the curriculum and that he often arrived to school late in the morning.

Context/Process:

The intervention involved using assessments by Child A and his class teacher, to gauge their perception of his independent learning skills. At the beginning of the 2012–2013 academic year, Child A joined his existing class from another one within the school, where he had been since Year 1. From observations of Child A in class and from the Behaviour for Learning initial assessments completed by his teacher, there was evidence to suggest that Child A did not feel a sense of belonging within his new class. Throughout the intervention, support was provided for the class teacher to implement new strategies through weekly feedback and planning meetings and modelling strategies and approaches.

Anticipated outcomes:
- To increase Child A's engagement and interest in learning
- For Child A to be able to participate in collaborative problem solving with peers

Intervention strategies implemented
- Self-assessment with Child A to gauge his perception of his independent learning skills, and in-class support
- Set up the 5Bs system in class which supported children to plan how they access support for their learning in order to develop their independence
- Child A responded well to a high level of carefully targeted praise, including non-verbal signals, such as smiling and 'thumbs up'; verbal praise, continued encouragement for the children to praise each other and also themselves, through self-evaluation, for example, 'How do you feel you did during that activity?' which helped Child A to self-reflect upon his own success. This also helped to reduce the frequency of his name being used in a negative context.
- Child A benefited from developing trusting relationships with support staff in his classroom and the playground, his class teacher, the school's learning mentor, which provided him with safe boundaries to function within
- Using language that was clear and concise helped Child A to follow instructions and to engage in activities. For example, the use of one-word instructions in the form of imperative verbs, such as, 'Wait, Go or Stop,' were effective in giving Child A simple direction without overwhelming him
- Using peers as a means of positive support and encouragement was an effective method in helping Child A and was beginning to encourage him to take more ownership over his responses, where possible. Opportunity was provided to participate in a weekly peer support group
- Opportunities for Child A to receive and give feedback through a solution- focused peer observation format
- Rewarding for effort to overcome fear of making mistakes as he often viewed things in absolute terms, e.g., right/wrong, good/bad. Noticing the impact of his effort supported the development of a growth mind set
- Ensuring that Child A understood how to complete his set work, the time he had to complete his work and the standard of work expected

Impact of intervention
- Through the self-assessment tool Child A recognised progress he had made in terms of being a more independent learner and having the confidence to try new things himself. For example, in relation to this, on a scale of 0–10 with 10 being the best it could be and 0 being the opposite, Child A assessed himself as moving from 0 to 8 between October 3rd and November 16th, 2012

- The class teacher has been able to use the 5Bs strategy with the whole class and has shared this practice with other members of staff across KS2
- The positive relationship that had developed between the class teacher and Child A's mother helped to keep lines of communication open and support Child A in making progress
- The class teacher described Child A as now being able to take more responsibility for his own learning and behaviour as he seemed more confident to do so
- Behaviour for Learning assessments have shown that Child A has made some progress in many aspects related to his relationships with self, others and the curriculum.
- At the beginning of the intervention Child A described himself as being quite angry and bad tempered. For example, he explained that some children often laughed at him saying that he is not good at football. He stated that his usual reaction to such a situation was, 'get angry, run after them and hit them.' By the end of the intervention, when reviewing his progress Child A said he had learnt 'how to work as a team, consequences of your actions and how to calm down when I ended up in fights.' These developing social and emotional skills were reflected in his increased participation in learning as observed by his class teacher.

Next Steps
- Class teacher to continue to receive support for whole-class strategies to further develop her practice
- Continue to involve Child A as much as possible in planning ways to overcome barriers that arise
- Implement new peer learning partners approach so that Child A can give and receive feedback from peers on learning progress and next steps.

Key: 5Bs Brain, Board, Book Buddy, Boss to promote independent learning

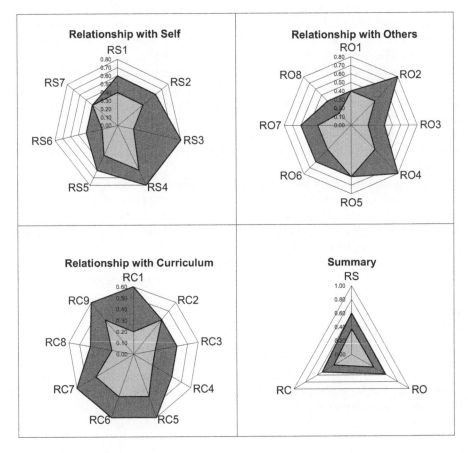

Figure 4.5 Graphical analysis showing progress of Child A's BFL

Recognising children's progress

Considering where our focus lay was crucial in enabling children to access, engage and participate in all learning experiences. It required an approach in recognising each individual child's starting point and paying close attention to small steps in development.

Our assessment tool did not seek to provide all the answers but rather acted as a starting point in considering specific interventions for individual children. It provided an opportunity to consider the perspective of the child, parent/carer/family and the professionals working most closely with the learner.

One of Educational Psychologist, Rob Long's mantras claims, 'The problem is the problem, not the child' (Long, 2008). Indeed, all observed behaviour cannot be fully analysed without considering the context. Relationships with self, others and curriculum are at the heart of this but so much is influenced by the responses of adults and the classroom, the classroom and school ethos in which such relationships exist.

Behaviours observed in the classroom are often as a result of the interaction between emotional, social and cognitive factors. A Behaviour for Learning approach is positive and proactive. We had an underlining focus on enabling learners to understand the behaviour and interaction skills that would help them to maximise their learning opportunities.

Taking a solution-focused approach, we were always seeking to see where the positive learning behaviours were already happening. Classroom observations gave a great insight into when, where and how learners were engaging in such positive behaviours. However, this did not give the full picture and in order to plan interventions it was crucial to hear the voice and perspective of the learners themselves, their parents/carers and teachers. The focus was on recognising progress made by children. This does not dismiss their specific needs or the context they were operating in, but taking a solution-focused approach meant noticing where and when progress had been made, no matter how small. This was reflective in how specific behaviours were observed, recorded and reported on.

The observation itself is only a snapshot in time and the child's behaviour at that time can be influenced by so many factors, including the very presence of an unknown adult in the room.

The conversation that took place between team members and school staff, in various roles, was the crucial element in achieving agreement on the focus of interventions. Two observations were unusually undertaken. The first observation served to gain a better understanding and a shared approach with school staff and the second observation was an opportunity to help in refining the focus of an intervention.

Conducting joint observations with other members of the team, the school's SENCO, or other members of the school's leadership team, is an invaluable process for developing a range of perspectives that may differ from your own.

It is important to be aware of what you bring to the situation, in terms of your personal relationships to self, others and the curriculum as well as your own unconscious bias, as this can influence your observations.

Joint observations had the potential to draw parallels and highlight different perspectives as we each observe through our own frame of reference and experience. Frequently, approaching observations in this way created opportunities to engage in collaborative conversations that encouraged a sense of remaining open minded in our practice and reflecting on how the child's needs were communicated through their behaviour.

The Behaviour for Learning assessments were described by headteachers in the feedback that we received as a 'good tool for tracking progress.' As well as being an indication of the strategies that were impacting a child's learning behaviour, we also had an indication of strategies which were not effective.

Summary

In this chapter we have shared the Behaviour for Learning assessment that we developed based on the conceptual framework by Ellis and Tod.

We have stated why we believe the three relationships are important.

We have shown how the analysis of the Behaviour for Learning assessment can be used effectively to track the Behaviour for Learning of individual children. We also included how children can be actively involved in developing Behaviour for Learning amongst their peers.

Takeaways

- Get the balance right. Give equal attention to nurturing all three key relationships.
- Reframe your perspective to gather a broader view and help meet the child's underlying needs.
- Include the learner. Use pupil voice to empower the learner to be actively involved in their own progress.
- Join the dots. Make links across the key relationships, for example, how barriers to accessing the curriculum impacts the child/young person's image of themselves as a successful learner.

Reflective questions

1. Reflect on your current analysis of behaviour. What further information could the Behaviour for Learning assessments provide?
2. How does your own view of the world shape your practice and impact on outcomes?
3. In what ways does the involvement of children in Behaviour for Learning improve the behaviour of individuals, their class and the whole school?

References

Ellis, S. and Tod, J. (2009). *Behaviour for Learning: Proactive Approaches to Behaviour Management*. Abingdon: Routledge.

Long, R. (2008). *Rob Long's Intervention Toolbox: For Social, Emotional and Behavioural Difficulties*. London: SAGE Publications Ltd.

Perry, B. and Hambrick, E. (2008). The Neurosequential Model of Therapeutics (NMT). *Reclaiming Children and Youth*, 17(3), 38–43.

5 The golden thread

Introduction

In this chapter, we will begin by considering the importance of relationship building as the cornerstone of implementing the Behaviour for Learning framework successfully. We will look more specifically at ways in which to build these relationships and offer an insight into how they can be fostered to have far reaching effects. We will also examine the crucial elements of Behaviour for Learning in practice and provide a range of strategies and examples of how to promote positive learning behaviours.

In addition, we aim to look in detail at the power of Behaviour for Learning language as well as to consider the impact of an embedded, shared language on outcomes for learners. A substantial proportion of this chapter is written with a view to offer recommendations to enhance and develop the three relationships: self, others and curriculum and to present practical ideas of how to create a personalised approach and inspire a love for learning.

Building relationships

Relationships are everything! The be all and end all, the single most important place to start. They are what we as humans unanimously seek out in life and are a vital component in our sense of belonging. Great teachers become experts in creating environments that build, nurture and sustain them. The significance of positive relationships in schools is indisputable and widely recognised as the most crucial tool to support learner achievement. The impact that they have cannot be underestimated and ultimately lie in the hands of the adults; we must understand that it is our responsibility to create as many opportunities as possible to forge and maintain strong and meaningful relationships in order to draw the best out of our learners.

The ability to successfully work with an individual, group or class depends largely on the relationship that has been built and this in itself is a huge reason to invest the time to make it happen. By creating a connection that is based on trust, care and respect, a strong foundation can be formed upon which learning and behavioural progress can be made. In the first instance, it is the continuous and unwavering effort to notice the details of individual learners and to show care and compassion that begin the journey. We all have memories of teachers at school that made us feel confident and some quite to the contrary, but what was it that affected this? Inevitably, it would have been relationship. It could be the question you ask about the long-anticipated birthday party at the weekend, or the comment you make about the new trainers that go a long way to make a learner

DOI: 10.4324/9781003166672-6

feel valued. The kindness shown by an adult can be the difference between a learner engaging well or not, a child that makes a good choice or not, or even a crisis being escalated or de-escalated down the line – the payoff is worth it.

The adults who work most effectively with children consistently go out of their way to build emotional currency with them and to find as many small ways as possible to connect. It is not always an easy road to navigate but excellent relationship building is characterised by a steadfast and persistent effort to do so. Relationships with learners are not a 50:50 ratio; this can be a common misconception that can lead adults to back away when learners damage or undermine the relationship. It is vital, however, that we continue to give 100% regardless of what is thrown in our direction. At one time or another, learners will test and challenge us, they will put us through our paces, but these hard yards are where the relationships must be preserved and protected.

Many of the individuals who attended the Courtyard AP Academy had very little understanding of consistent and safe relationships; countless also had a significant lack of experience in forming secure attachments which affected the ways in which they behaved, communicated, learned and progressed. As we know, social and emotional health is key to the progress that children make and central to this are those unwavering, sustained and stable relationships. With a deeper and more meaningful bond comes a greater ease within the classroom, ultimately resulting in learners who are more willing to engage, contribute and take risks.

There are many ways in which to achieve these positive and productive relationships and every adult's approach will differ; however, here are some tried and tested methods used at the Courtyard AP Academy that helped learners gain a sense of belonging:

- **Kindness:** Kindness counts and can change everything (Dix, 2017). Adults who prioritise and practice kindness as a habit will have noticeably better relationships with learners than those who do not. Showing kindness to learners is one of the best strategies to build and maintain positive relationships and in the moment, can also turn someone's day around. The ways in which you can show kindness to a learner are endless, however, it will always amount to strengthening connections. We have all heard of 'random acts of kindness' and a version of this can be applied by adults in schools too. It refers to a selfless act resulting in happiness and joy in the other person. Kindness has so many benefits, including improved emotional well-being and helps us to develop more meaningful relationships with others. On a physical level, kindness can trigger the release of oxytocin which can help to reduce stress and can contribute to a greater sense of belonging and improved self-esteem. Some small ways to practice kindness on a day-to- day basis could be:
  - hold a door open
  - write a thank you note to a learner who, for example, helped you hand out resources
  - give a compliment
  - tell a joke
  - greet with a smile
  - make time to listen
  - give a high five
  - find something you have in common with a learner
  - ask about something that matters to them

- set aside some uninterrupted teacher/learner time
- verbally express appreciation
- give your full attention
- give positive feedback
- forgive/apologise
- give the benefit of the doubt
- show patience
- happily participate in something even when you don't want to
- be available

Kindness is infectious and has a great deal of impact, even on the most challenging individuals. It's hard to resist!

- **Envisioning language and positive naming:** This is an excellent way to address learners in an affectionate and motivating way. Giving a unique identity that is relevant between the two of you is a powerful way to build rapport. Here are some examples of positive naming used at the Courtyard AP Academy: Mr Excellent, Master Reliable, Magnificent Mango class. Positive names or descriptions can help learners to feel inspired and can encourage them to live up to your vision of them. The names or words chosen should reflect behaviours, skills or capabilities. Positive naming can lend a helping hand in learners developing a vision of themselves as capable individuals. This naming process allows you to pinpoint specific strengths or positive attributes that learners possess. The terms can also be used more generally with groups of learners such as 'well done problem solvers,' 'amazing learning today scholars.' These names or terms of affection not only help to build relationships between you and an individual/ group but also supports the process of building and strengthening self-concept.

- **Staying in control:** For learners who find it difficult to regulate their emotions, having an adult who is able to remain calm, consistent and in control is essential to being able to de-escalate a situation whilst keeping the relationship intact. Relationships can be destroyed in the space of a few seconds through negative reactions or an overreaction to poor behaviour. The adult showing concern for a learner's problem in a crisis can yield profound results. Not only does it demonstrate that you care about them, but it also helps to avoid an even more difficult situation. By remaining calm and in control and modelling self-regulation, learners see that you are not abandoning them but that you care enough about them to stick around. Emotional dysregulation can feel frightening for children and an unplanned reaction that is overly emotional can easily undo months of hard work that you have invested. It is practically impossible to reason with an individual who is dysregulated and so regulating with them in these moments is of utmost importance: listen, ask questions, show empathy. Offer a way out, a cold glass of water, a short stroll, be curious and help them to preserve their integrity. When a learner is 'standing on the ledge' the thing that they need most from you is for you to remain in control and to show them that you 'see them' but you are not going to join them.

- **Positive phone calls home:** This is a rather straightforward concept but one that can be overlooked or underestimated in terms of its impact. These conversations always started with something along the lines of 'It's great news!', or 'I want to tell you something positive about today' and the reason for this was that many parents/ carers of the learners at the Courtyard AP Academy had become so accustomed to receiving calls for some crisis or incident that had occurred that many had backed off completely and were difficult to reach, or if they were available, were not keen on having a discussion, so the phone call could be met with a long anxious silence. It was important that there was a shift away from the 'dreaded phone call' towards something more positive and rewarding and as a result, parental engagement improved. This is not to say that feedback was always positive; however, those calls that are specifically made just to say, 'I want to tell you how wonderful your child has been today!' are so powerful in boosting relationships. The effects can be felt by the learner too when the parent/carer recounts what they have been told and this reinforces that someone has gone out of their way to speak positively about them.

- **Greeting at the door/welcome to the day:** What better way to start the day/session than with a positive interaction? A pleasant exchange, a smile. Adults will have a wide variety of methods and ideas about what these greetings might look like depending on their style, for example, a high five, fist bump or a hand shake. Get creative with your greetings and watch the response from the learners. Setting an inviting tone for the day that screams, 'You are welcome here!' helps learners to feel valued. This is also an excellent opportunity to mention a recent achievement or ask about something that is important to them. These greetings do not only benefit the learner, but they are also a positive moment for the adult too. This is a low effort, high yield strategy that can be used and introduced very easily into the daily routine (Dix, 2017). The greeting not only promotes a sense of belonging but is also a proactive approach to managing a transition time which can reduce any problems or identify any issues coming into the classroom. An adult can pick up a great deal about a learner's mood at that time and it can provide an insight into a concern that has arisen, for example, which allows us to be on the front foot in tackling issues before they escalate.

- **Expressing joy and interest:** One of the simplest gestures an adult can make is expressing joy and interest in a learner and this is because the most powerful form of reward is relational. It can have a tremendous impact and can make an individual feel valued and held in mind. It can also reinforce their sense of self by being acknowledged and appreciated. Learners spend so much time with adults at school and what happens during these hours can have a deep and lasting effect on them. Expressing your delight at seeing them, at listening to their story about what happened over the weekend or just being in their company can be extremely nurturing. This time can also help to identify learner strengths, talents or personal goals that may not come to light otherwise.

- **Unexpected messages:** Leaving unexpected and motivational notes or messages for learners is always well received. These messages are a way of providing a personalised, hopeful and optimistic message to an individual, perhaps to congratulate them on an achievement, to let them know you are proud of them or simply to say, 'Good morning, let's have a great day!' A small gesture like this takes no time at all, but can go a long way in building a relationship.

- **Affirmations:** Dedicating time to affirming instances of positive learning behaviour is always to be encouraged and is a way of drawing attention to a learner's most positive choices and interactions. By noticing, pointing out and affirming these details, they receive reinforcement that they are doing the right thing. Using positive statements based on what you see in or from a learner can be very powerful and can help them build a positive sense of self. It can also contribute to challenging and overcoming perceptions that learners may already have of themselves. This small exercise in pointing out the good demonstrates to them that you are noticing their positive choices and that you value these. It is a win–win situation in that not only are you encouraging an increase in positive behaviours, but also showing an interest in them and valuing their contribution. Catch them being good at every opportunity!

- **Time and space:** Our time is so precious with 101 (or even more) things to do in a day but dedicating even a very small amount of time to have some fun can inject some positivity into your relationship with a learner. Perhaps spending five minutes at the start of break to play a quick card game, finding out the name of their pet hamster, sharing some personal anecdotes or inviting a few learners to join you for lunch one day. Over time, this investment can mean that connections are improved, and a learner may feel happier to participate or take a risk where they would not have otherwise. What you learn about the children in these times can be referred to later on: 'How is your new puppy settling in?,' 'Did you enjoy your trip to the beach at the week-end?' Children like to know that you are interested in them as a person and this can be achieved easily when you have taken the time to find out about them. Be sure to remember the details of what has been shared – this will mean a lot. Be a bit silly at times, let loose a little more than you would normally; it is not a weakness and won't leave you vulnerable, in fact it will help learners to see you in a different light, a light that they will inevitably enjoy very much. Many may think that this compromises their professional persona but in fact, it will contribute to more depth in your relationship where a learner may feel they know a different side of you. As a newly qualified teacher (NQT), I think we all receive the horrendous advice, 'Don't smile until Christmas!' which goes against everything that it is to build a positive relationship. The personal connection that is built up by sharing some of yourself and spending time with the learners can contribute to the development of intrinsic motivation. The investment that you make in an individual is usually reciprocated – your efforts won't go to waste.

- **Moving on after an incident:** This important element of relationship building and preservation can be a challenge for even the most seasoned adult. You may feel that a relationship has been damaged during an incident, however, being ready to reconnect with a learner even when the reparation process may not have taken place yet shows them that you are there for them. It demonstrates that despite the fact that you may not have liked the behaviour or the situation, you are not judging their character or rejecting them as a result. All learners will be 'difficult' or 'challenging' at one time or another, but it is crucial not to take it personally. These unwelcome behaviours will almost never be about you. Holding a grudge following an incident will reinforce the learner's negative sense of self and be detrimental to your relationship. Always make time, however, to reflect on the incident, whether that is through a restorative con-versation or a more informal discussion. You may find that the learner suddenly turns up at your door with a piece of work to show you – a peace offering so to speak. It may be their way of saying, 'I'm sorry for letting you down.' Would this need to be followed up by a formal apology? Not in my view. This is the golden opportunity to demonstrate that the relationship is not destroyed, that you still care and that the child is still valued. You may never receive the 'sorry' that you feel you deserve, and this may feel difficult; however, the important thing is possessing the ability to repair the relationship and prove that you are going to stick around. It is in the most dif-ficult moments that children need your kindness and care the most and they deserve someone who will never give up on them – that person can be you.

- **Fairness:** 'That's not fair!' We have all probably heard that phrase during the course of our career at one time or another and it would more than likely have derived from frustration or an inability to see things from an objective point of view. The word 'fair' comes up in many lists of desirable traits for a teacher to hold. The word can be interpreted in many ways, however, it is always held in high regard particularly in relation to building and maintaining relationships with learners. It can be a tricky one to pin down as fairness is a perception, but learners seem to easily decide whether a member of staff is generally fair or not. Fairness towards learners does not in fact refer to all learners being treated the same, however, and this is one of the ways in which approaches to supporting learners can be personalised. It is important for learners to understand that fair does not mean equal and dedicating some time to establish and explore this is crucial as it can avoid learners feeling as though they have received the raw deal if they feel another child has received a different response or consequence than them. Learners want to feel that they are being treated appropriately and fairly as opposed to equally as this means that their starting point/needs are being taken into consideration. There are different ways to practice fairness, for example, through your attitude, through your expectations, through measures put in place within the classroom to support learners and whilst tackling issues and giving consequences. Learners will forgive you of almost anything as long as they feel that you are being fair. Ultimately, it boils down to being consistent in your expectations, being willing to apologise if you need to, setting the standards and be a role model. It also means sticking to your word and following through no matter what. Learners will soon accept you as a fair person as long as they do not perceive favouritism or discrimination.

- **Availability and being ready to connect:** When learners feel that an adult truly cares, the need to challenge, confront or 'battle against' significantly reduces as they feel that they fundamentally belong; as connection increases, negative behaviour decreases. The top down approach to discipline does not consider time for connection and focuses on blame rather than 'connection before correction' (Nelsen, 2006). Learners love to hear about your special interests and to get an insight into you as a person, so why not share this? A child may feel the significance of this as extra belonging. The foundations laid by being available and ready to connect can have a lasting effect. These meaningful connections help learners to replicate this with others and it acts as a model for them to internalise.

- **Trust and responsibility:** Believing in a learner's capabilities and building a culture of trust is a brilliant foundation for any relationship. Our fears can get in the way of trusting a child but by giving them responsibility or trusting them with a job that you would not just give to anyone provides a strong message. Trust them with something significant – start small and build this up. Expect them to be truthful and reliable and nine times out of ten they will rise to the occasion. Some small ways to make a start could be asking them to leave the classroom to pass on a message to someone, watering your favourite plant, feeding the chickens or retrieving something from another room. A learner will feel empowered by having this small amount of responsibility bestowed upon them and the message they will get is 'I am trusted.' This helps them to deepen their connection with you and to feel like they are held in high regard. Visitors were always surprised by the responsibility and freedom that learners were given at the Courtyard AP Academy, for example, being asked to go into the office to retrieve something or being sent to the kitchen to fill up the water jug; however, learners thrived on this. Of course, you would not send a learner who was new to the school to do these things before you knew them properly or had an opportunity to build up this trust but over time, they always rose to the challenge.

- **Letters/cards:** There is nothing quite like receiving a letter from someone you look up to and writing a personal letter to a learner can be a lovely way to make them feel special. A phone call or a positive 'shout out' can be great but a letter feels that much more significant where an adult has taken time out of their day and outside of planned communications to pen a message of appreciation. The words of encouragement or recognition can go a very long way to motivate a learner. Despite what the letter includes, whether it is a 'thanks' for helping out or a 'congratulations' for making so much progress, the underlying message is 'I care about you' and this can only be a good thing in contributing to a strengthened relationship. In addition to a general letter of appreciation, sending a celebratory card can have the same effect – the learners receive the message that they are held in mind. Many may never have received anything in the post for them personally, so this can feel very special.

- **Make learners feel valued:** There are hundreds of ways to make a learner feel valued, some of which have been highlighted already as examples. Learners want to feel cherished so show them how much you value them by displaying some keepsakes in your space whether that is an office, within your working area or on your desk. This could be a photo of them succeeding, a copy of an excellent piece of learning that they have brought to you or it might be the key ring they brought you back from Tenerife. By keeping and displaying these little treasures, learners will feel a connection with you and your efforts will scream 'I care about you.'

- **Quality time:** Spending quality time with learners in the form of a fun activity can be very rewarding for everyone involved. In our setting, a good example of this was face painting on a Friday afternoon. This may seem like a rather simple activity; however, it is the power of the time that is the important aspect and the activity itself can be interchangeable. Make it work for you by choosing something that is easily manageable and does not require any planning, for example, a game of cards, colouring or playdough for example. You can also take into account the learner's interests which might lead to twenty minutes of trawling through a dinosaur book. This special time with an adult is a great chance to catch up in an informal way where learners can feel that they are getting some real quality time and uninterrupted attention.

- **Celebrating success**: Otherwise known in our setting as 'Show me your learning!' This was introduced as part of the 'positive reinforcement' strategy and to move away from the archaic idea of senior leaders only becoming involved when things get difficult. Instead, when learners felt they had gone over and above or were particularly proud of their learning, they were encouraged to present it to the Head of School in exchange for a jolly big 'Well done for engaging so well!' and a tally mark for their class. The display in the office included the names of all the classes and exhibited the tally marks that children from those classes had earned. During the course of the term, this contest encouraged learners to celebrate and share their success with others. It also provided a very special informal opportunity for them to receive some real heartfelt, one-on-one feedback and recognition of their efforts. The days of being sent to the Head's office for a grilling were long gone.

Of course the caveat with many of these strategies is that they can be time-consuming and require you to take time out of your extremely busy day to engage in an activity that may not seem like a priority, but even a small venture a day can make the world of difference to a learner and can mean that the relationship has just received a little boost that will pay off later. The effort you make to build goodwill can be relied on later when the going gets tough and the effort that it takes to build positive relationships pales into insignificance next to the benefits and rewards. Think of it as depositing in your bank account. You will inevitably see something later in the month you would like to buy and having the funds there to do so is a wonderful thing. Similarly, there will be a time that you will need to 'cash in' with a learner, so the more you have in the bank the better. Any strategies, exchanges, activities or interactions that strengthen relationship are worthwhile and will be beneficial to the children that we work with. It can make an individual feel they are valued and belong but can also avoid a tricky situation later when you need to challenge someone without the possibility of the situation escalating. Table 5.1 provides a range of strategies for building relationships with self. Here are some further practical examples of ways in which to build relationships within the three relationships of self, other and curriculum.

Table 5.2 depicts a number of ways in which to develop relationships with others and in Table 5.3 there are some examples of ways to support the development of the relationship with the curriculum.

Table 5.1 Strategies for building relationship with self

Relationship with self:

Key feature	Strategy (to promote each learning behaviour)
Is interested in learning	✓ plan to their interests ✓ a diverse and inclusive range of learning activities ✓ chunked lessons ✓ good pace ✓ visual stimulus ✓ model enthusiasm ✓ give choices ✓ develop an interesting hook for the lesson ✓ change environments ✓ make connections to real life ✓ celebrate achievements ✓ use technology ✓ include interactive elements to the lesson ✓ make the learning meaningful
Has a positive opinion of themselves	✓ highlight what is good about them ✓ plan to their strengths ✓ use positive praise ✓ non-verbal acknowledgements, e.g., thumbs up/nod/smile ✓ show an interest in them ✓ give compliments ✓ use learner as a role model ✓ foster sense of competence ✓ welcome opinions ✓ use affirmations ✓ display learning
Can manage strong emotions such as anger and sadness	✓ teach about emotions and how to self-regulate ✓ model managing emotions ✓ provide regulated responses ✓ validate feelings ✓ relate to feelings ✓ show acceptance ✓ deep breathing ✓ take a break ✓ separate feelings and behaviours ✓ social stories ✓ use of solution-focused approach

(*Continued*)

Table 5.1 (Continued)

	✓ 'draw alongside' ✓ provide safe space outside classroom ✓ listen to understand ✓ use redirection ✓ provide an 'out' ✓ draw up a plan for when things get tricky
Has a belief they can be successful	✓ share learning with others ✓ display learning ✓ publicly praise ✓ use learner as a role model ✓ provide a range of learning opportunities that are not only academic ✓ give reminders of when things went well ✓ build a record of achievement ✓ celebrate risk taking ✓ highlight strengths ✓ non-verbal cues/signals ✓ chunk tasks ✓ scaffolding tasks
Can independently make choices and try to solve problems	✓ provide additional resources ✓ give choices ✓ brainstorm ✓ model effective problem solving by 'thinking aloud' ✓ use open-ended questions ✓ teach self-checking strategies ✓ involve learner in self-monitoring ✓ identify the problem and explore solutions ✓ use prompts ✓ encourage participation in decision making ✓ provide problem-solving opportunities such as puzzles, discussions, design activities
Can accept responsibility for own behaviour	✓ ensure learners are clear about expectations ✓ restorative approaches ✓ reflection time ✓ solution-focused approach ✓ take up time ✓ make it safe for learners to come forward honestly ✓ respond, don't react ✓ use 'repair' rather than punishment
Shows good self-control	✓ role play social scenarios ✓ actively supervise ✓ gentle reminders ✓ play self-control games such as 'freeze' or 'sleeping lions' ✓ step in to redirect ✓ encourage patience, e.g., 'I'll be back to check on you in five minutes' ✓ set clear limits ✓ provide timely reminders ✓ acknowledge the challenge of showing self-control

Table 5.2 Strategies to build relationships with others

Relationship with others:

Key feature	Strategy (to promote each learning behaviour)
Is willing to work independently as appropriate	✓ provide appropriate equipment ✓ use of data to plan effectively ✓ personalised learning ✓ use a timer ✓ scaffolding ✓ set a time limit before going back to check ✓ questions to prompt ✓ use a wait card 'I will be back in . . . minutes' ✓ encourage peer support ✓ take a step back and give space ✓ refer to prior learning ✓ display success criteria ✓ provide check points ✓ plan short tasks and build up
Socially aware of what is going on around them	✓ narrating situations ✓ ask questions ✓ check for alertness ✓ draw attention to and name feelings/events ✓ talk about current events ✓ draw attention to body language ✓ teach non-verbal cues ✓ discuss similarities and differences ✓ role play ✓ explore and discuss real life social interactions
Is willing and able to empathise with others	✓ emotional literacy and social skills taught explicitly ✓ engage in restorative conversations ✓ model a situation into their world ✓ reflection time ✓ social stories ✓ model empathy ✓ discuss ethical dilemmas ✓ expand circle of concern ✓ identify feelings ✓ validate difficult emotions ✓ talk about other people's emotions ✓ read stories about emotions and explore
Is willing to ask for help	✓ red/green cards to indicate when help may be needed without having to verbalise ✓ ensure there is a system in place to gain teacher attention ✓ intermittent checking ✓ learning buddy ✓ provide sentence starters: 'I'm struggling with,' 'I'm not sure what to do next,' 'can you show me . . .' ✓ identify class helpers
Is willing to behave respectfully towards adults in school	✓ model appropriate responses ✓ lead by example ✓ positive correction ✓ positive reinforcement ✓ role play ✓ provide role models ✓ confront head on every time

(Continued)

Table 5.2 (Continued)

	✓ clarify limits/boundaries
	✓ make the most of teaching moments
	✓ meet disrespect with respect
	✓ be consistent
Is willing to behave respectfully towards peers	✓ targeted group work
	✓ consistent approach to challenging inappropriate interactions
	✓ plan for paired collaborative tasks
	✓ paired work
	✓ teach turn taking
	✓ teach appropriate responses
	✓ praise respectful behaviour
	✓ scenario cards
	✓ encourage acts of service
	✓ provide opportunities for learners to make a personal connection
Is able to listen to others and be attentive	✓ regular speaking and listening activities
	✓ debating activities
	✓ listening skills activities
	✓ daily story time
	✓ provide daily opportunities for listening, e.g., sharing personal stories/what you did over the weekend
	✓ encourage learners to give feedback and ask questions after someone has presented
	✓ paired work
	✓ group work
Can cooperate and collaborate when working and playing in a group	✓ structured play
	✓ adult led games
	✓ peer talk activities
	✓ positively gossip during games/group work
	✓ project work
	✓ establish group agreements
	✓ teach how to ask questions
	✓ model negotiation
	✓ match learners who can learn from each other
	✓ consider number in group – start small and build up
	✓ teach language of collaboration
	✓ assign roles within a group

Table 5.3 Strategies to build relationships with the curriculum

Relationship with the curriculum:

Key feature	Strategy (to promote each learning behaviour)
Is willing to engage with the curriculum	✓ use data to plan appropriate activities
	✓ personalised tasks
	✓ display success criteria
	✓ explicit instructions
	✓ scaffolding
	✓ provide high-quality feedback
	✓ give learner an active role
	✓ set targets with learner

	✓ provide interesting resources
	✓ be enthusiastic about the learning
	✓ plan a range of learning opportunities from hands on, more formal and outside the classroom
	✓ provide additional support if needed
Can take responsibility for own learning	✓ offer choices
	✓ self-assessment
	✓ involve learner in next steps
	✓ involve learner in target setting
	✓ ask learner how confident they feel 0–10
	✓ involve learner in decision making
	✓ encourage learners to take notes using a whiteboard/notebook
Is able to access the curriculum	✓ personalised learning relevant to needs and interests
	✓ target setting
	✓ data to plan
	✓ achievable but challenging tasks
	✓ range of resources
	✓ range of learning tasks
	✓ time to reflect on learning
	✓ provide regular feedback
	✓ personalised homework
Is willing to try new things and 'take risks'	✓ start with short and achievable tasks and build this up
	✓ consistent acknowledgement of effort
	✓ additional support of how to overcome mistakes
	✓ modelling
	✓ positive reinforcement
	✓ affirmations
	✓ make the task interesting
	✓ provide opportunities to learn in different contexts
Can make mistakes and move on	✓ meet mistakes with encouragement and support
	✓ make room for deliberate mistakes in the classroom
	✓ create a safe environment
	✓ group correction
	✓ provide immediate feedback
	✓ reward progress throughout the task not just at the end
	✓ model mistakes
	✓ think aloud, 'I made a bit of a mess of that, let me try again'
	✓ praise efforts and show how to move the learning forward
Is self-aware, knows how and when to get help	✓ provide clear instructions
	✓ seat with role models
	✓ make it clear that you want to help
	✓ create a climate of curiosity where it is normal and encouraged to ask questions
	✓ create a 'wonder wall' where learners can write on post its
	✓ ensure learner is clear on process to ask for help within the classroom
	✓ encourage use of 5Bs – BRAIN, BOARD, BOOK, BUDDY, BOSS
Motivated to complete tasks	✓ positive feedback
	✓ positive statements: 'I can't believe how much you have managed to achieve already, wow!'
	✓ use a timer
	✓ offer varied experiences
	✓ praise during and on completion of task

(Continued)

Table 5.3 (Continued)

	✓ stickers/stamps
	✓ use of class reward system (award token)
	✓ non-verbal cues, e.g., thumbs up
	✓ group tasks
	✓ model enthusiasm
Able to work unaided	✓ personalised learning
	✓ personalised level of support/language and expectations
	✓ start with short tasks: 'do you think 10 minutes will be long enough to do this?'
Follows classroom rules and routines	✓ provide crystal clear expectations
	✓ have clear processes
	✓ relentlessly follow through
	✓ visual timetable shared each morning
	✓ be consistent
	✓ revisit and refer to your rules and routines often

Behaviour for Learning language and feedback – a golden thread

During their time at the Courtyard AP Academy, children quickly and expertly adopted a language of Behaviour for Learning. It was the golden thread that was ever present in every aspect of school life and was embedded throughout the curriculum and beyond – it permeated every corner of the school. Adults would often encounter learners having conversations even at more unstructured times about their Behaviour for Learning and using this shared language became natural to them. The journey to achieve this level of embedded culture was not a short one; however, it was achieved through a consistent and persistent focus on learning behaviours and the language that went along with this. It was a day in and day out pursuit of identifying, discussing and reinforcing positive learning behaviours both formally within the classroom and more informally beyond the classroom. The focus on and benefits of learning behaviours themselves cannot be understated and as highlighted in the Improving behaviour in schools report (EEF, 2019) 'Teaching learning behaviours will reduce the need to manage misbehavior.' The language was ever present, relentlessly acknowledged and discussed endlessly. It is fair to say that the learning behaviours were referred to continuously and staff would joke about living, eating and breathing it. Visitors to the school were often astounded by the learners' understanding and use of the language, however, the inescapable nature of it meant that it was quickly internalised and subsequently used routinely by everyone ranging from our youngest learners to the site manager. It would also not be uncommon to see visitors slip into role during their short time at the school. Learners were provided with multiple opportunities throughout the day to not only reflect on their own Behaviour for Learning but to comment on that of their peers. These planned and unplanned opportunities proved to be an effective way to provide greater depth in understanding of the language and to ensure that it remained at the forefront of school life.

The feedback provided to learners, both formally and informally was always firmly rooted in Behaviour for Learning and there was a strong commitment from all staff to utilise this language wherever possible. Every opportunity for its use was seized, contributing to its ever presence – there really was no escaping it. Here are some ways to include Behaviour for Learning in daily practice (Table 5.4).

Table 5.4 Ways of including Behaviour for Learning in daily practice

Some ways to include the language in day-to-day practice:
- Written feedback in books
- Verbal feedback
- Targets
- Compliments
- Discreet Behaviour for Learning lessons
- Throughout planning
- Within the curriculum
- Displays
- Within instructions
- Restorative conversations
- Praise
- General conversation
- Assembly
- Catch up time
- Phone calls and meetings with parents/carers and other agencies
- Written reports

The language and framework impacted and influenced every aspect of the school and one example of this was the way in which staff transformed transition time at the end of playtimes. Tracking data demonstrated that the transition from the end of playtime into the classroom was a flash point during the day where learners would regularly escalate their behaviour and incidents would occur, sometimes from unresolved issues during the break or possibly as the result of an ongoing difficulty with transitioning into the next activity; either way, it was clearly a time that many learners found challenging. The new five minute 'cool down' period in which learners reflected on their Behaviour for Learning gave time and space for individuals to think about their interactions, behaviours, responses to others and the impact of that on their relationships. This short session was led by adult questioning and supported learners to consider the positives that had been displayed alongside the ways in which to improve and move forward.

The examples in Figures 5.1 and 5.2 show how the questions used scaffold and support learners to identify positive learning behaviours and how the reflection provides an opportunity for adults to reinforce and/or re-frame where necessary.

Example 1:

Adult: What did you do well during playtime?

Learner: I didn't get angry when the other team scored a goal.

Adult: That's right, you showed excellent self-control during the match and you managed your strong emotions. That is excellent progress! What else did you notice about yourself?

Learner: I was able to cooperate with others as part of a team by following rules and sharing the ball.

Adult: Fantastic! That meant you were able to really enjoy the game. What do you think you could do next time to make it even better?

Learner: I could show more self-control by waiting patiently while the teams are being chosen.

Figure 5.1 An example of a reflective discussion between an adult and a learner using Behaviour for Learning language

Example 2:

Adult: What did you do well during playtime?

Learner: Not much! I got upset, shouted and stormed off!

Adult: From what I saw, you were able to come back a short time later to re-join the match which showed resilience and an ability to move on after mistakes. What could you do next time to make it even better?

Learner: I could be more willing to ask for help by letting an adult know I was getting frustrated before it got to the point where I was storming off.

Adult: An excellent suggestion!

Figure 5.2 A further example of a reflective discussion between an adult and a learner using Behaviour for Learning language

Following the introduction of the post playtime 'cool down' period, we saw a significantly marked reduction in incidents, leading to a much smoother transition into the classroom for the vast majority of learners. It was not a miracle cure; however, it did prove to be a significant step forward not only as a contribution towards creating a calm and purposeful environment, but also to embedding the perpetual use of the language by drawing learners' attention to their relationships with themselves/others. Thus, the golden thread was woven through all aspects of school life and playtime was no exception.

Alongside the discussions at the end of playtime, staff were adept at using Behaviour for Learning language to support, encourage and de-escalate at all times. The continuous narrative was, in a sense, a Behaviour for Learning commentary of which staff became pundits/storytellers – it was the soundtrack to our school. Over time we observed learners embracing the opportunity to also take on this role and to develop their ability to become mentors to others by supporting them with feedback and sometimes comfort or to encourage their peers by employing the language. It was quite an extraordinary scene to witness learners who are considered to have 'poor social skills' mentoring one another within the Behaviour for Learning framework using the language that became second nature to them.

Breakfast club also became a pivotal period in the day where learners were immersed in the language. How do you like your eggs in the morning? With Behaviour for Learning language! Our resident chickens Nugget, Basil, Drummer and Mavis provided us with a breakfast of champions each day, and conversations across our scrambled eggs included the discussion of our targets, which were also displayed in the dining area, the way in which our relationships with self, others and curriculum were developing and our aims for the week among other conversations about the latest computer game or new craze of the moment and an occasional game of table foosball or trumps.

In addition to learners being awash with the incidental and opportunistic use of Behaviour for Learning language, one of the ways in which this language was developed, disseminated and embedded was through discrete teaching during Behaviour for Learning sessions that were planned and led by the lead learning support professional. This was a weekly 45-minute session that became a highlight for the learners and an opportunity during the week to concentrate solely on Behaviour for Learning by unpicking and unpacking it and modelling it into the world of the learners. These sessions engaged all individuals by providing a space to practice and rehearse the behaviours themselves.

A great deal of time was spent defining the terminology and an essential element was allowing the learners to internalise the language and concepts by exploring, discussing and rehearsing. The lead learning support professional used data provided by class teachers to target specific areas that were emerging as themes within classes, for example, at a time when Pineapple class were struggling with cooperating and collaborating, sessions were aimed at promoting this behaviour where a half term was dedicated to numerous structured and unstructured opportunities to develop the skill. This was achieved through careful and imaginative planning of activities such as designing and creating their own board games with a set of instructions which they then presented to their peers and played as a group. This not only had cross-curricular links to literacy and numeracy in some cases but also allowed the learners the opportunity to rehearse the necessary skills to effectively collaborate, to take turns and to manage strong emotions if things did not go their way.

The support provided during these sessions was always critical, as tackling areas of the assessment that learners found challenging would often give rise to feelings of frustration; however, by giving the space to practice and to make mistakes in a safe environment, learners were able to develop and progress whilst concentrating on that one particular element without distraction. The fact that this was so explicit was crucial as it focused the mind and drew their attention to the aspects of the target that they needed to work on. The feedback from class teachers and data tracking found a strong correlation between the areas covered in the Behaviour for Learning lessons and the learners' progress in general. The impact of the sessions was far reaching, learners showed a very high level of engagement and demonstrated extremely positive attitudes towards their learning both within the discreet sessions and during other learning opportunities. As highlighted by Fox 2013, 'All behaviour can be learned and changed,' and this was certainly evident in our setting where change quickly came about as a result of a focus on the learning behaviours.

The Behaviour for Learning assessments that were used to track progress always showed a substantial improvement of learners' relationships with self, other and the curriculum. Alongside this progress, we saw a significant reduction in serious incidents with an increase in engagement, ultimately leading to strong outcomes academically. Learners made outstanding progress, often over and above what was expected of them nationally.

During the sessions, and throughout the day, staff used praise to best effect to help learners recognise what was expected of a 'successful learner.' These sessions also addressed personal, social and health education as well as citizenship and elements of great British Values.

How we changed learners' attitudes towards learning

A common theme that was evident from new learners on entry to the Courtyard AP Academy was a poor attitude towards school. Many entered well below the national expectations and very few had experienced much success in learning in their educational career up until that point. For many, their negative experiences were entrenched and the predominant barrier for most was their poor attitude towards learning. As a result, staff developed a range of strategies to motivate and engage all learners, some of which have been discussed previously and some which will be explored in the next chapter.

We always strived towards 'inspirational' learning and teaching and a sharp focus was placed on providing opportunities that would stimulate a whole range of learners and that differed from what would be considered to be standard, day-to-day lessons. Time was dedicated to allowing adults to observe one another and to share inspirational practice, which allowed everyone to learn from each other. This included staff who were not teachers but led in other areas of the curriculum such as forest school, Behaviour for Learning sessions and cooking, for example. Adults became adept at quickly getting to know their learners and identifying their interests, which meant that this information could be used to plan lessons that would motivate and inspire. For example, there were lessons where learners were creating magic potions in literacy, visiting a shopping mall in numeracy, travelling to space in science and doing around the world tours in Geography, all within their classrooms. Learners were often intrigued to find out what they would be participating in, especially when they could see that their classroom had been set up in a creative and imaginative way. This approach certainly helped to strengthen and improve their relationship with the curriculum. Some learners who had been disengaged for most of their school life were now mixing cauldrons, driving moon buggies and sailing the seas; however, none of these activities were perceived as 'learning' in the traditional sense – instead, children were having fun and experiencing success.

As a contribution to building and sharing inspirational practice, we moved towards a model of filming lessons in order to gather and preserve some of the creative work that was already happening within the school. These recordings were used as a training tool and to share ideas amongst staff. It proved to be very effective in capturing some of the magic that was being created and that was contributing to the improved relationships that learners were experiencing with themselves, others and the curriculum. Over time, staff became increasingly confident in experimenting with approaches to delivering an engaging and stimulating curriculum and often found themselves operating outside of their comfort zone. It would not be uncommon to see a Little Red Riding Hood, Mary Poppins or Captain Hook strolling down the corridor or to find a room cordoned off with police tape or to discover a giant 'DO NOT ENTER' sign above a classroom door. The awe and wonder that this created for learners made a huge contribution to their progress and learners' relationship with the curriculum was often the area that improved most quickly, which was impressive given their starting points which was usually, 'I'm not doing it' or 'I can't do it.' Over a relatively short space of time, learners' confidence and resilience grew, which depicted a transformation. They began making statements like 'It's difficult, but I'm going to take a risk in my learning' and 'I'm going to move on after my mistakes.' The level of motivation witnessed was also a far cry from the lack of engagement that the vast majority of learners displayed on entry to the Courtyard AP Academy. Children began to value their exercise books for the first time ever, they became proud of their learning and spoke widely of the progress that they were making.

Award assemblies were always a highlight of the week and were used as one of the tools to promote and celebrate the success of the learners, in particular in relation to their Behaviour for Learning. Certificates were personalised for each child and would often be focused on an area that was targeted, for example, a certificate awarded for a trying new things (RC4) or managing strong emotions (RS3). This positive feedback and public recognition of progress was highly valued by the learners and the accompanying compliments that staff and learners would pay each other was a further acknowledgement of progress. The way in which learners were able to recognise and verbalise the positive learning behaviours displayed by others not only strengthened relationships but also demonstrated the depth of their understanding of the Behaviour for Learning framework and how to operate within it.

The compliment system came to be a very important part of changing a learner's attitude towards themselves and started out as an adult's intermittent way of building learner confidence. It was very quickly identified as a tool that had a tremendous impact on learner self-esteem and went a long way to change the narrative and view they held of themselves. As highlighted by Adams (2009), 'It has been found that children who have low self-esteem and a low view of themselves are more likely to be disruptive in the classroom' and for this reason, the investment of time and effort to shift these views was crucial. Learners would often come to the Courtyard AP Academy stating they were 'naughty' or 'angry' and this quickly changed to statements such as 'I show a positive attitude to my learning' and 'I am able to cooperate with my peers in group work.' This was an enormous shift in their attitude towards themselves and for some, it was the first time that they were perceiving themselves to be a positive and successful learner. Figure 5.3 gives some examples of compliments that learners paid each other.

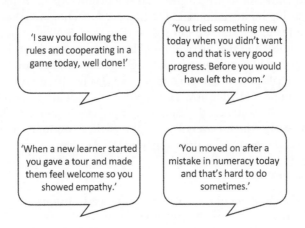

Figure 5.3 Examples of compliments exchanged between learners

As part of the assembly, a 'Star of the Week' was announced and this pivotal moment in the week identified an individual who had made significant progress with their Behaviour for Learning and the accolade celebrated this publicly. A democratic process meant that learners were able to vote for a stand out learner from that week. It was always a joy to see children identifying the progress of others. This award was particularly revered since learners highly valued the recognition from their peers and in addition to that, it meant you had a fast track to the weekly 'Hot Chocolate With the Head.' What an incentive!

Learners' views of themselves were transformed to such an extent that it was often the case that they felt they could tackle anything that came their way. We captured learners' views of themselves in a range of ways such as learner questionnaires, learner voice interviews that were filmed and PASS (Pupil Attitude to School and Self) questionnaires in order to explore their social and emotional well-being, to capture progress and to identify any areas in which learners felt they required support. The information gathered showed that the new narrative that they formed of themselves meant that they increasingly found themselves in a position to take risks and engage with learning rather than respond in a way that was disruptive, which would often have been the case previously.

A love for learning

Another common theme that ran deep throughout the Courtyard AP Academy was the new found love for learning that children would discover a short time after attending. For most, this was the first time that they had experienced a positive relationship with the curriculum and the pride it manifested was astounding. Visitors consistently commented that learners were engaged and confident and consistently showed that they enjoyed the tasks that they were engaged in. There were many ways in which to develop this love for learning, some of which have been mentioned previously but here are some additional examples:

Records of achievement

The 'record of achievement' was born out of learners collecting their most prized pieces and everyone was provided with a folder in which they could store the copies of their best learning along with the certificates that they collected on a weekly basis. Many learners had more than one volume, which was the mark of a seasoned progress maker, and this was always respected by others. They were regularly shared with peers during catch up time and with visitors who came to the Courtyard AP Academy. They were also frequently used during reintegration and multi-agency meetings to demonstrate the progress learners had made and the ways in which they were building positive relationships with themselves, others and the curriculum. They were an excellent source of evidence of a learner's growth and development and highlighted the love for learning that they had developed. In challenging moments, they were also used as a tool to salvage a tricky situation and to remind a learner how far they had come. This powerful document was always taken away with learners at the end of their placement and there have been several instances over the years where leavers have said that they continue to cherish them and enjoy looking back at their time at the Courtyard AP Academy.

Classroom environment

The classroom and school environment were a large part of supporting a love for learning. Each room was decorated with a wide range of learner work and classrooms were purposeful, safe and stimulating. Each class boasted a 'Wall of Fame' for learners who had shown an exceptional effort along with a working 'Wow Wall' for learners who had gone over and above what was expected of them. Learning was proudly mounted and displayed for all to see and in addition, learners took copies home, which proved to be highly impactful in terms of parental engagement.

The classroom environment was ever evolving to suit the needs of the learners. In some cases, learners had the opportunity to design displays and to support an adult in achieving it. One example being: a suggestion was made during pupil parliament that we celebrate the diversity at school by creating a giant display in the lunch room that consisted of a world map, pictures of learners and staff and facts about the countries of their heritage, of which there were 26. Learners were asked to take pictures and to research the countries in order to contribute and take ownership of the display. They felt empowered and proud, not only because of their contributions, but also because they themselves were reflected in the display.

The Behaviour for Learning assessment had a display in its own right in every room in the school. It was one of the ways in which we included learners fully in the target setting process and the monitoring of progress; it also contributed to them being immersed in the language and helped them to gain a familiarity with the terminology. Within each classroom, learners had their own name on an arrow which was used to pinpoint an area of the assessment or learning behaviour that they felt they needed to develop. It was always interesting and rather impressive that they were able to identify just what it was that was causing them difficulties and this was in fact the case for learners as young as Year 1. Learners also completed half-termly assessments alongside the teacher assessment which was an excellent way to gather evidence and to track progress. As we have seen in Chapter 4 the graphical diagrams that were created as an analysis of this progress were extremely powerful in demonstrating and capturing how far each individual had come.

The graphical analysis in Figure 5.4 shows that learner x had made significant progress across the three relationships and in particular in their relationship with the curriculum; the light grey demonstrates the baseline data and the dark grey depicts the progress for this individual. The diagrams are a helpful tool in order to not only celebrate success but to identify next steps; for example, it is clear from the analysis that learner x requires support with RS7 (shows good self-control) and RO3 (is willing and able to empathise with others). This information was subsequently used by staff to plan a personalised package of support to address the areas in question.

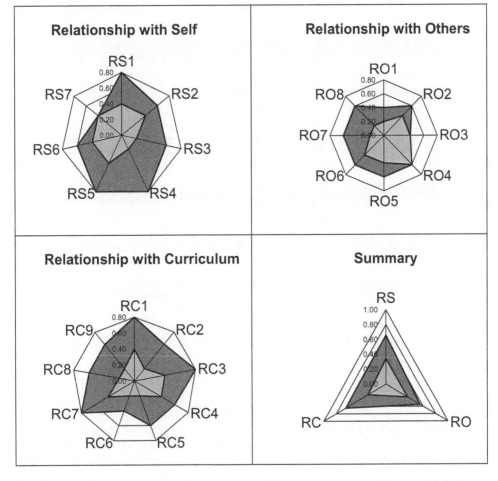

Figure 5.4 An example of the progress made by a Year 3 learner (learner x) who had attended the Court-
     yard AP Academy for two terms

'Catch up'

'Catch up time' was a pivotal time during the day and was developed after a period of time where staff identified a need for learners to talk, socialise and build relationships before formal learning started. For many children, this opportunity to connect with others in a positive way was very rewarding and allowed them to express themselves, to discuss their successes or simply to share personal experiences. In its infancy, 'catch up' was an informal chit chat but quickly developed into a structured part of the day where learners were encouraged to reflect on themselves and their Behaviour for Learning. Each morning during this time, learners would use a solution-focused approach to reviewing their previous day. It was always important to focus on the positives and to discuss how we could make today even better. During this 20-minute session, learners would refer to their Behaviour for Learning target and discuss the ways in which they had addressed this the day before. It was also an excellent opportunity to build relationships as peers were encouraged to comment on the successes of others.

A script was developed which standardised 'Catch Up' across the school as shown in Figure 5.5.

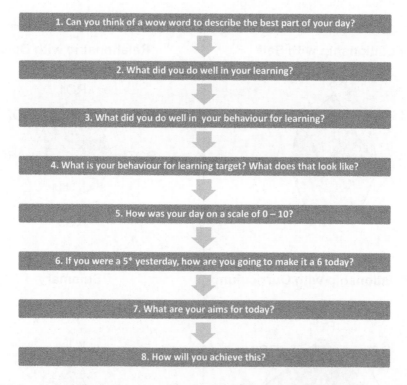

Figure 5.5 Standardised 'Catch Up' script adopted across the Courtyard AP Academy

The constant reminder of what learners needed to work on meant that it was always at the forefront of their minds. As time went on, learners became more and more confident and it was decided by the Pupil Parliament that learners should be given the responsibility of leading the session by asking their peers how successful they felt their day had been on a scale of 0–10 and to choose a wow word to describe the best part of their day. The Key Stage 1 (KS1) learners were supported during this session with visual aids and word banks but were able to access the questions very well and respond appropriately by reflecting on themselves. The feedback that learners provided was extremely discerning and made an important contribution to pupils' understanding and appreciation about how they might improve their own Behaviour for Learning.

A similar model was adopted for staff who engaged in an adult 'Catch Up' session at the end of the day in their class teams which allowed them the space to identify what had gone well, to work together to identify ways of moving forward and to plan for improvements for the following day as shown in Figure 5.6. It also meant that staff were confident

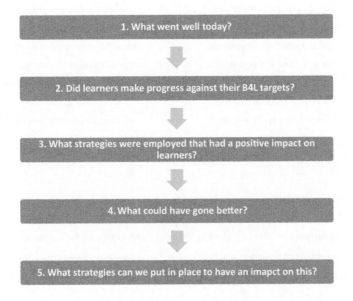

Figure 5.6 The adult 'Catch Up' script that was adopted across the Courtyard AP Academy

in each learner's target and could make a special effort to notice them achieving this particular behaviour across the week.

To be reflective practitioners was a priority in order to continually improve the ways in which we supported learners and the more time that was dedicated to this, the more focused and effective our work became. 'Catch up' time provided valuable and regular reflective experiences and purposeful conversations for both adults and learners and ensured we maintained a sharp focus on Behaviour for Learning and our role in promoting it.

Feedback

Comments made in work books as part of the feedback cycle were pivotal to learners engaging well with tasks and making progress and teachers became adept at high-quality feedback that engaged and inspired the learners. Many looked forward to the opportunity to read the remarks and respond during the course of the day. Coloured pens were used, comments were targeted and next steps were identified for each individual. Staff developed their own style and it was not uncommon to stumble across jokes or doodles which added a special personal touch to the comments and supported the personalised approach we took to learning and teaching. The references made to Behaviour for Learning within the feedback created a wraparound approach and learners were receiving this language for all angles. Figure 5.7 gives some examples.

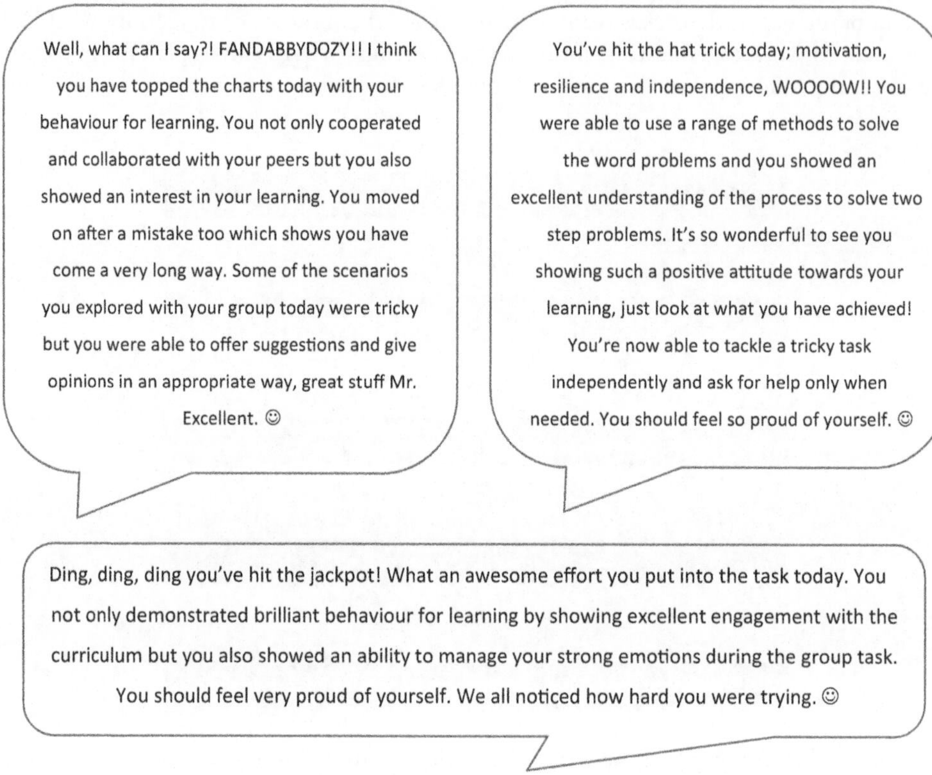

> Well, what can I say?! FANDABBYDOZY!! I think you have topped the charts today with your behaviour for learning. You not only cooperated and collaborated with your peers but you also showed an interest in your learning. You moved on after a mistake too which shows you have come a very long way. Some of the scenarios you explored with your group today were tricky but you were able to offer suggestions and give opinions in an appropriate way, great stuff Mr. Excellent. ☺

> You've hit the hat trick today; motivation, resilience and independence, WOOOOW!! You were able to use a range of methods to solve the word problems and you showed an excellent understanding of the process to solve two step problems. It's so wonderful to see you showing such a positive attitude towards your learning, just look at what you have achieved! You're now able to tackle a tricky task independently and ask for help only when needed. You should feel so proud of yourself. ☺

> Ding, ding, ding you've hit the jackpot! What an awesome effort you put into the task today. You not only demonstrated brilliant behaviour for learning by showing excellent engagement with the curriculum but you also showed an ability to manage your strong emotions during the group task. You should feel very proud of yourself. We all noticed how hard you were trying. ☺

Figure 5.7 Some examples of teacher comments and feedback in learner work books

Additional learning opportunities

There was always a strong commitment to showing the children that learning could happen anywhere and everywhere. School trips and other extra-curricular activities were a crucial part of our curriculum offer and over time, we saw that these opportunities were supporting the learners' progress with themselves, others and the curriculum.

Throughout the year, a variety of 'drop days' were organised and were often used to celebrate national events or special occasions such as 'go green garden day', anti-bullying, road safety, national heroes and many religious events. Pupil parliament were also invited to devise and plan for some drop days to include in the calendar such as Eco day, Christmas around the world and Arts day. During these drop days, all adults, including non-teaching staff, were encouraged to lead a session; this gave everyone the opportunity to contribute to school life and to share a passion of theirs. These events were always a huge success and were a highly anticipated part of the school calendar. During the sessions, learners were encouraged to take risks in their learning and to try new things in a high-challenge, low-threat environment. The fun and engaging tasks were not regarded by the children as 'work,' however huge leaps and bounds were made with learners accessing exciting opportunities that challenged them in many of the Behaviour for Learning areas.

The children were mixed up for the day and joined learners from other classes and year groups which meant that they were able to practice and apply skills and behaviours that they had been developing with individuals that they did not normally interact with. The element of risk taking was a large focus on these days as this was an area that the vast majority of learners struggled with and it often posed as a barrier to their learning. Inevitably children would rise to the challenge and do themselves proud; for example, a learner with a significant stammer attempting a rap about healthy eating in front of the rest of the school during arts day. This was recognised by the whole school as an amazing achievement and ultimately proved to be a transformational moment in his journey, one that supported him to gain the confidence to take more risks in front of others such as reading to his peers or offering answers during class which he previously would have avoided.

In order to explore the benefits and to capture the impact of drop days/additional learning opportunities, children were asked to complete before and after self-assessments. The value of such opportunities was clear and Figures 5.8 and 5.9 demonstrate this following a garden project.

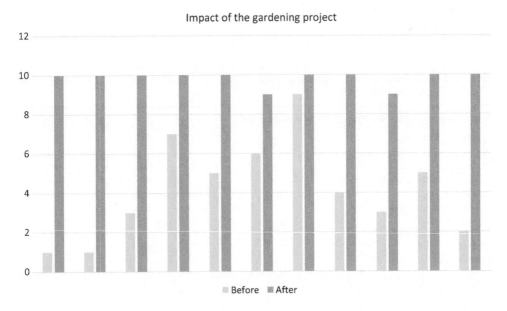

Figure 5.8 A graph to demonstrate the impact of the Gardening Project

Evaluation:

- 100% of learners report improved confidence in gardening.
- Learners make links between the garden project and taking risks in learning.
- Learners also make links between the garden project and showing self-control. This is also reflected in our B4L data.
- Learners who report an improvement in their listening also demonstrate this in their Behaviour for Learning assessments.

Where learners have self-reported an increased ability to show resilience and taking risks, this has been noted in the classroom context by staff and is captured in weekly tracking.

Figure 5.9 A basic evaluation of the impact data gathered following the completion of the Garden Project

Table 5.5 shows how learners responded to a baseline question asked before the garden project began and Table 5.6 demonstrates the ways in which learners responded to a follow up question at the end of the garden project and illustrates the progress that they made.

Table 5.5 Learner responses to the question, 'What do you already know about gardening?' before undertaking the Garden Project

What do you already know?
Some houses have a garden I know how to plant a flower You can grow things x 4

Table 5.6 Learner responses to the question, 'What do you know now/what are you better at?' at the end of the Garden Project

What do you know now/what are you better at?	
How to make healthy snacks	Safety
Following rules outside the class	How much soil you need to grow peas
Different tools x 2	Being socially aware
What insects live in a garden x 3	How to look after plants
Science	How to plant seeds x3
Taking risks in my learning x 4	How to be healthy x2
Good self-control x 3	Listening skills
About the environment	How to look after a garden
Cooperation x 4	Showing a positive attitude
Confident in gardening x11	Showing resilience

Personalised learning

This term is used frequently in education and can mean a variety of things to different people but the personalised approach adopted at the Courtyard AP Academy contributed hugely to the deep learning culture that was developed. Our drive towards precise inclusion was unwavering and took many forms. One of the core values across the trust was 'success by any means' meaning that staff would adapt, change and design a package for learners that ensured they made strong progress; it also meant that success was non-negotiable. Whilst a flexible and creative approach to the curriculum could be a challenge, a commitment to this ensured that learners excelled. This mantra was one of the most important elements used in order to support outstanding progress and was not limited to academic work. Leadership had a sharp focus on ensuring that there was an unrelenting emphasis on learning and a clear vision of learners developing a 'love for learning.'

On entry to the Courtyard AP Academy, staff quickly built a picture of the learner by gathering a range of data from a variety of sources and this was used to drive improvement. Information sharing, partnerships and collaboration were vital and we built strong links with outside agencies and mainstream schools which made this information more accessible. The data gathered from a range of sources included academic information, social and emotional information and likes and dislikes from parents/carers and of course the learners themselves. These records were used to build a personalised profile which was used to inform the design and implementation of a holistic and high-quality intervention support system.

The data received was compiled into a working document which was regularly reviewed and updated to reflect the current circumstances and needs of the learners. In addition to this, when learners started at the Courtyard AP Academy, they completed an assessment in numeracy, reading and writing in order to identify gaps in learning. Having considered a number of different assessments, we decided that the Rising Stars assessments would be an effective tool to use. These diagnostic assessments, alongside the information gathered, meant that we were able to build a clear picture of where the learners were academically which provided us with an excellent basis to build upon. It also gave an indication of where the learner sat nationally which in time, allowed us to track how quickly gaps were closing. Learners were often involved in the process of analysing the assessments and this was used as a talking point to further gain a good understanding of how confident they felt in different areas across the curriculum.

Adults used the learners' Behaviour for Learning assessments and academic data to ensure that the learning and teaching strategies were personalised on every level and this shone through not only in our physical evidence such as in work books but also in the level of engagement shown by learners. Children were always asked to complete a Behaviour for Learning assessment themselves which fed into the suite of interventions provided for them. It was always an insightful exercise and we generally found that learners were easily able to identify the areas in each relationship in which they needed to make progress in order to be successful. Moving forward, this was repeated termly in order to gather progress data and it became an important aspect of the learner self-reflection and the target setting process. Finally, for the part-time learners who continued to attend their mainstream school, information was gathered from class teachers such as long- and medium-term plans in order to ensure that the curriculum was dovetailed.

All learners received a highly bespoke curriculum where gaps in learning were identified quickly and planned for accordingly. We adopted the Chris Quigley curriculum which allowed us to plan for breadth and depth and to plan for progress. It set out essential coverage, threshold concepts and exceeded the standards in the national curriculum. It was a very accessible resource that teachers were able to use which meant that they could spend additional time personalising rather than reinventing the wheel.

Children accessed learning on a daily basis that was matched specifically to their likes where possible, their academic ability and their Behaviour for Learning data. It was challenging to provide this level of personalisation as it could often result in several tasks taking place simultaneously; however, with careful planning and the effective use of adult support, it was not only possible but was extremely purposeful and beneficial, enabling learners to move at their own pace from their own starting points. Teaching reflected not only excellent knowledge of the curriculum, but the diverse needs of learners whilst successfully encouraging and developing appropriate classroom learning behaviours. This combination supported learners to develop a renewed positive view of themselves and to make outstanding progress which often exceeded what was expected of them nationally.

Personalisation was a non-negotiable aspect of our practice and one of the outcomes of this aside from the academic progress discussed previously was the fact that learners were able to concentrate for much longer periods of time and to engage more purposefully with their learning. The vast majority of learners initially had difficulty with accessing the curriculum independently; therefore, skills that enabled them to do so were taught intensively and learners were given ongoing and regular opportunities to practice these skills in different contexts.

What did personalisation look like at the Courtyard AP Academy?

- a wide variety of bespoke learning challenges in a range of environments
- diverse and inclusive resources to support learning
- tasks based on progress against learning outcomes
- interventions to complement classroom-based learning
- opportunities for learners to be involved in the decisions affecting their learning
- a strong cross-curricular element focusing on key skills
- the use of approaches and interventions with a proved track record to have an impact of learning and progress
- curriculum dovetailed to mainstream for part-time learners

As a result of the personalisation techniques, learners also showed increased confidence and took more pride in their learning. They began valuing feedback from adults with one learner stating, 'The comments in my book make me feel happy. I used to rip my books but now I take care of them and do my work neatly.' This was extremely significant for some learners who had previously not been able/willing to access the curriculum.

For each learner, the personalisation was ever evolving and was informed by a number of things such as assessment data, ongoing assessment for learning, feedback from other agencies including therapists, structured conversations with parents/carers and reviews of targets set throughout the year. The highly bespoke approach always reflected the unique qualities of the individuals and allowed for learners to flourish at their own pace.

Tasks were often highly scaffolded where necessary in order to support learners to develop a belief that they were able to take risks and try new things independently. Over time, this targeted support inevitably decreased; however, it was a very important aspect of the plan at the start of the journey for many learners who struggled with their confidence when attempting a task. The methods used to scaffold came in many different forms, for example:

- in-depth modelling
- shared writing
- word banks
- structured work sheets
- writing frames
- peer talk/discussion time

- question and answers before beginning the task
- pre-teaching vocabulary
- key information displayed within the classroom
- verbal prompts
- ample thinking time
- check lists to tick off
- highlighting key vocabulary
- additional visual aids
- peer scaffolding

Scaffolding was also used in order to encourage learners to move away from relying on additional adult support and towards the all-important RO1 'is able to work independently.' The strategies listed proved to be very important stepping stones in this journey for our learners. The '5 Bs' were also introduced in order to further encourage learners to use the range of resources at their disposal as this was something that many struggled with; these were BRAIN, BOARD, BOOK, BUDDY, BOSS. In time, this supported learners to begin to self-scaffold, a hugely important skill to develop in order to be able to sustain their learning within the classroom and in order to master other positive behaviours such as RC6 – 'is self-aware and knows when and how to get help' and RO4 – 'is willing to ask for help.' It was imperative that learners had a host of places to find this help before approaching an adult for support. In addition, developing a range of strategies to help themselves encouraged independence, resilience, increased risk taking and impacted their feelings of having a 'belief that they could be successful' – RS4. Learning and applying these skills and behaviours are part of the 'hidden curriculum,' however they cannot be overstated in their importance in order for learners to access the curriculum and be successful.

Peer scaffolding was also used regularly, for example, encouraging learners to support their classmates by providing clues or pointers if required. This of course was dependent on the individuals, their confidence levels and their ability to work alongside others; however, it was another way to strengthen the children's relationships with others and the curriculum. Underpinning the scaffolding strategies was a level of recognition and praise that reinforced learners when they successfully accessed their learning using one of the strategies.

As with all other elements of the learner's curriculum, the scaffolding was personalised. Different methods and combinations were used with different learners and the amount of time they were employed also varied based on the pace and level of progress over time. Some other ways in which learners experienced personalisation was through ongoing verbal feedback, diagnostic marking, the use of positive language, praise stickers, tokens, certificates and cards. All of these strategies helped to encourage and motivate learners to do well and to engage with the curriculum.

There were also many additional layers of personalisation at play that were not always obvious to the untrained eye; however, the combination of strategies used within the curriculum and beyond had a huge impact on learner progress. We were able to track the unique effects of the personalisation using a range of progress measures including the academic progress and the Behaviour for Learning assessments, both demonstrating a significant progress in the vast majority of cases.

What made our school a success was the foundation of positive relationships upon which everything else was built. Learners experienced an environment that inspired and supported them. Staff took responsibility for removing barriers and were highly committed to creating the best possible opportunities for the children where they could begin to experience success and develop a confidence in their own abilities for the first time.

Without their dedication to the vison and their relentless drive to provide the best, it would not have been possible to implement the Behaviour for Learning framework in such a successful way.

Summary

This chapter explored the importance of building positive relationships with learners and provided some practical ideas and a range of strategies in order to achieve this. It also highlighted the far reaching effects of focusing on relationships with self, others and the curriculum. In addition it offered examples of ways to personalise your approach and to inspire children to develop a love for learning.

Takeaways

- Relationships rule! Do everything in your power to build, nurture and maintain these.
- Tirelessly focus on positive learning behaviours; notice them, talk about them, praise them.
- Embody and clearly communicate your expectations; this will contribute to lasting change.
- Consistently root your feedback in Behaviour for Learning – make it inescapable.
- Catch up! Dedicate time each day to review, reflect and plan ahead.

Reflective questions

1. In what ways do adults build relationships with learners in your setting?
2. Which of the strategies identified in this chapter could you adopt to further enhance your practice?
3. How could you include Behaviour for Learning practices into your daily routine?
4. What indicators of social and emotional progress do you look for and how is this captured?

References

Adams, K. (2009). *Behaviour for Learning in the Primary School* (1st ed.). East Exeter: Learning Matters Ltd.

Dix, P. (2017). *When the Adults Change, Everything Changes: Seismic Shifts in School Behaviour*. Wales: Independent Thinking Press.

Education Endowment Foundation (EEF). (2019). *Improving Behaviour in Schools*. https://d2tic4wvo1iusb. cloudfront.net/eef-guidance-reports/behaviour/EEF_Improving_behaviour_in_schools_Report. pdf?v=1635355216 (accessed 29/07/22).

Fox, E. (2013). *Rainy Brain, Sunny Brain: The New Science of Optimism and Pessimism* (1st ed.). London: Cornerstone.

Nelsen, J. (2006). *Positive Discipline: The Classic Guide to Helping Children Develop Self-Discipline Responsibility, Cooperation, and Problem Solving Skills (revised ed.)*. New York: Ballentine Books Inc.

6 Changemakers

Introduction

In this chapter, we aim to explore the crucial role that adults play as facilitators of Behaviour for Learning progress. More specifically, we will look at some of the characteristics and 'behaviours' of effective adults and discuss the extent to which these behaviours impact learner outcomes.

Through an exploration of topics such as teacher expectations, strategies to de-escalate and the ability to create a positive environment, we invite the reader to reflect on their own practice and to consider the measures in place to meet the needs of all learners in their own setting.

Teaching

Teaching at the Courtyard AP Academy was underpinned by social and emotional aspects of learning. Given the history and needs of the learners, it was crucial that adults were able to manage themselves expertly in the five main domains (motivation, social skills, managing feelings, empathy and self-awareness) in order to provide safe, reliable and consistent role models.

Adult behaviours: the five areas

1. Motivation

   - Show a personal enjoyment and interest in the context of the lesson.
   - Concentrate on how pupils learn as well as outcomes.
   - Attribute failure to the nature of the task, quality of teaching or some changeable aspect of the learner.
   - Develop resilience in learners by promoting mistakes as learning.

2. Social skills

   - Encourage everyone to feel included, cared for and that they belong.
   - Model and promote the skills of listening to, respecting and valuing each other.
   - Develop relationships through fun and humour.

DOI: 10.4324/9781003166672-7

3. Managing feelings

    •   Read and respond to the emotional climate of the classroom.
    •   Create a climate where staff and pupils view mistakes as opportunities for learning.
    •   Use positive affirmation language to promote risk taking.
    •   Validate the worth of everyone's feelings.
    •   Model the language of managing feelings.
    •   Model calming down strategies.

4. Empathy

    •   Demonstrate a genuine interest in your pupils' contributions through active listening.
    •   Model and promote an interest in individual unique experiences.
    •   Model how to challenge discrimination.
    •   Pay attention to nonverbal communication and respond appropriately.

5. Self-awareness

    •   Pay attention to the impact that your self-esteem has on your teaching.
    •   Reflect on your needs and challenges and the impact that this has on your teaching.
    •   Reflect on your strengths and use these to enhance your practice.
    •   Recognise and acknowledge your interests, likes and dislikes and the impact this is having on your teaching.
    •   Pay attention to your communication through body language and the impact this may have on staff and pupils.
    •   Model reflection and learning.
    •   Recognise when you are beginning to feel overwhelmed by feelings and use calming down strategies.

The impact of adult behaviours on the children and their personal progress cannot be overstated; it was one of the most impactful aspects of our work and having the ability to confidently model in these areas was imperative. Developing a culture where adults were expected to take full responsibility for themselves in each area was no mean feat. As individuals, we bring our own style, beliefs and personality to our role; however' presenting consistently positively across the five areas was a non-negotiable. We found that when adults were able to practice and display these behaviours consistently and confidently, learners would imitate and learn from this very quickly.

This principle underpinned our practice and was embedded to the extent that you may not notice it 'just happening' in and around the school. This was evident when visitors would arrive at the Courtyard AP Academy and comment on the excellent learning and behaviour of the children; however, they would not necessarily be able to identify or pin point what was influencing this. Training played a huge role in allowing adults to understand the impact of these behaviours on the progress of the children. A large commitment was made to not only train new staff but also to regularly refresh staff already at the school. Strengths of individuals in certain areas were identified and used as a model and to train others in order to share good practice. This was achieved through 'drop ins,' informal peer observations and filming where staff felt comfortable to do so.

In addition to the social and emotional aspects of learning, lessons were planned with purpose and a great deal of imagination which supported learners to take an active role in their progress and achievement. 'To ensure that children learn effectively we need to engage, motivate and inspire them' (Fisher, 2009). Learning was exciting and motivated learners to engage with the curriculum (RC1) as well as to develop and apply their skills. For example, in Pineapple class, learners opened a Pizzeria where they used toppings for their pizzas as a way of solving fraction problems. In Raspberry class, learners received an apprenticeship and then a full-time contract in a fruit and vegetable shop where they worked as accountants, shop floor managers and stock takers to solve real-life money problems. In Mango class, learners trained as scientists and undertook a paper chromatography experiment to solve clues and to discover who has been leaving funny messages around the school. Staff were passionate about broadening the experiences and aspirations of learners and including exciting new opportunities for them to experience success. PASS (Pupil attitudes to self and school) data consistently showed that learners were happy to be at school and that learning was fun and interesting.

All schools aim to promote an environment and ethos where children's health and well-being is central to everything they do, and many approaches and initiatives can be used to contribute to this, but what did it look like at the Courtyard AP Academy and how did it make a difference?

- **Compliments:** This may seem like an odd thing to have on the timetable, however, as briefly discussed earlier, the impact of providing compliments and positive feedback cannot be underestimated. The powerful element of the compliments was that much of it was peer feedback which helped to build and strengthen relationships. For children who struggled to forge and maintain relationships this was so important and these planned opportunities to give and receive positive feedback was very powerful. Excellent work was shared with peers either during 'catch up' time, assembly or during lessons which gave them the opportunity to praise each other. Learners were encouraged to give feedback using Behaviour for Learning language and this was modelled by adults. Over time, they became more confident and would often to refer to Behaviour for Learning targets for that particular individual (displayed in the classroom) as part of the compliment/feedback. For some learners, this was the first time that they were hearing positive comments about themselves from their peers and it helped to challenge their sometimes negative perceptions of themselves. For the most part, these compliments were pinned onto a compliment tree or other form of display in the classroom and were regularly referred to in order to de-escalate, motivate and inspire. They were even used as reminders during conflicts to help repair relationships.
- **Sensory and occupational therapy programmes:** Many learners were identified as having sensory processing issues which impacted their learning as they could experience emotional, social and behavioural responses to their surroundings which could act as a barrier to their learning and as such required a personalised approach to minimise these barriers. A simple strategy shown in Figure 6.1 was adopted to understand and plan (VOSS, 2011).

- **S** Stop and assess the situation; behaviour happens for a reason.
- **E** Environment change? What can I change, add or omit?
- **N** Note students' response to the change.
- **S** Sensory strategies and tools to be used.
- **E** Embrace the positive and learn from the experience.

Figure 6.1 Steps taken to interpret and understand a learner's behaviour and to plan a support package based on any observations made

The personalised programmes provided included movement breaks, Occupational Therapy programmes, large print, 'move 'n sit' cushions and fidget toys to name but a few. All staff received training from both a Speech and Language Therapist and Occupational Therapist, which was invaluable for staff in gaining a deeper understanding of some of the difficulties facing the learners and to put their behaviour into context. It also meant that staff were able to plan and deliver a range of personalised interventions to support learners in these areas. In addition, those who were identified as having delayed fine motor skills would often be targeted within the classroom with a range of additional activities such as threading beads, cutting, posting and slotting items, weaving and stacking. Delays in gross motor skills were addressed outside the classroom with a similar range of personalised activities such as target practice, balance activities on an exercise ball or hop, skip and jump activities.

- **Personalised timetables:** Some learners with more complex needs required a personalised timetable that sat outside that of the normal school day. This was because their needs and priorities could not be met within the classroom setting at that specific time. Despite this, there were sessions timetabled where learners were included in larger class activities and also opportunities for reverse inclusion. The personalised timetables were time limited and progress was reviewed regularly in order to amend and create targets to work towards that would ensure that the learner could reintegrate into a whole- class setting on a full-time basis as soon as possible. Intense support was provided as part of this bespoke package and often included a high level of support and input around managing strong emotions (RS5) and building relationships (RO5/RO6). The aim of the personalised timetable was always for the learner to re-join their peers in the shortest time frame possible whilst addressing significant barriers to learning.
- **Pupil parliament**: A Pupil Parliament was set up in order to provide learners with leadership opportunities. It was a space for the children to take the lead and to feel empowered about their school. It also gave them the time and space to express their thoughts and to have an influence over some decisions that affected them. Some of the topics discussed included learning and behaviour, resources, charity, enrichment opportunities and learner well-being. The Parliament helped to develop their communication and organisation skills and also encouraged them to practice other behaviours such as compromise and social awareness. These were new experiences for many of the learners and they would often thrive in this environment. We found that the children relished the chance to become a greater part of school life. The links to Behaviour for Learning were also extremely strong, particularly in relationships with others (RO). Learners were increasingly able to apply behaviours such as: 'is

able to cooperate and collaborate when working and playing in a group' (RO8), 'is able to behave respectfully towards peers' (RO6), 'is socially aware of what is going on around them' (RO2) to name but a few. We found the impact of applying these behaviours had a direct impact on the relationship with self, for example 'has a positive opinion of themself' (RS2), 'can independently make choices' (RS2) and 'shows good self-control' (RS7). From tracking data, we saw that learners involved in the Pupil Parliament made strong progress quickly in these areas. In order to make Pupil Parliament extra special, learners who were elected, through a democratic process, were awarded with badges and refreshments were provided during the meetings. One of the outcomes of the Parliament when discussing the school environment was to create a 'You said, we did' display. This was an inspirational display and exhibited the achievements of the Parliament, for example, providing additional games and resources for the playground and providing a more varied breakfast club menu. Learners were also involved in a range of other activities: writing to the prime minister, visiting the Houses of Parliament, creating posters to display around the school to promote positive Behaviour for Learning, raising funds for local charities, collecting food for the local food bank, networking with Pupil Parliaments from other schools and creating a manifesto of ideas for change within the school. Learners developed an understanding of how citizens can influence decision making through a democratic process and as a result, they showed a deep understanding of the process and were able to devise different ways in which learners could contribute to change. This came in many forms such as naming the school chickens, budgeting for additional school resources, improving the range of reading books and influencing the enrichment calendar. Learners also developed improved ownership of the school and felt influential which impacted positively on their relationship with self (RS2). Behaviour for Learning data showed that learners were also more able to take responsibility for their learning (RC2). One learner stated, 'Being on Pupil Parliament was a fun experience and made me feel helpful. We did loads of things to help the school community' (Child Z).

- **Thoughts box:** This box was introduced as part of an initiative to create a smoother transition from unstructured time into learning time. Many learners, as discussed in the previous chapter, would end playtime with anxieties and issues that would spill over into the classroom and so the high-tech tissue box, which had usually been lovingly decorated with gems, glitter and stickers, was designed to be a vehicle to help learners to manage their feelings and strong emotions (RS3). It gave them the chance to record how they were feeling in the knowledge that it would be addressed at a more appropriate time and was an outlet for worries, questions or comments they felt they wanted to share but hadn't had the opportunity to do so yet. Over time, the box supported learners with self-regulation, in particular managing strong emotions (RS3) and showing self-control (RS7) as they felt that they were able to 'park' their thoughts rather than carry them into the next session. This of course took time and practice and did not happen overnight; however, focusing on supporting learners to access it as an outlet was certainly worthwhile. The thoughts box, however, took a rather surprising turn and quickly and unexpectedly evolved. Staff discovered that in amongst the usual worries and questions, positive comments began filtering though including Behaviour for Learning feedback for other children, suggestions about the school and compliments for others. This astonishing shift was welcome and celebrated as a sign of progress. We found that the more learners were able to manage their emotions and self-regulate, the less they relied on recording their concerns. An example of a comment from a learner: 'I've made so much progress since mainstream I'm proud of myself.' 'I followed the rules and routines all morning and I finished my learning!,' 'learner A took risks in his learning today and tried something new.'

- **Buddy system**: The buddy system at the Courtyard AP Academy was introduced in breakfast club in order to contribute to a positive start to the day. Unlike other buddy initiatives, it did not involve learners specifically supporting younger children. It in fact began cross-phase during this unstructured time and was then extended into peer support within the classroom. The role of the buddy was flexible and generally consisted of inviting others to sit and chat or including them in a game or activity. The system helped learners to feel valued and supported and contributed to a safe and caring school environment where learners felt that they could rely on one another. Buddies were given important opportunities to practice care, respect and patience, resulting in improved empathy, resilience and compassion. Impact data and learner feedback demonstrated that they developed an increased sense of responsibility, improved relationships with peers, increased confidence and an increased ability to make choices independently.

- **Restorative approaches**: These provided a consistent framework within which to tackle incidents of poor behaviour without descending into punishment mode as this has very little, if any impact at all. The approach improved overall relationships, enabled learners to understand the impact of their actions and gave them some responsibility in relation to influencing next steps following an incident. Ultimately, restorative approaches allowed all parties to be heard and resulted in a deeper understanding of others, increased empathy and improved communication. It also encouraged learners to appreciate the perspective of others and resulted in a more respectful climate overall. Some feedback following the use of restorative approaches: 'It's helped me to make friends again when I thought I'd lost them and it felt nice to be listened to even though I made the wrong choice' (Child yr6). 'I liked it because it helped me to move on after a mistake' (Child yr5). 'The restorative conversation had a really positive impact on our relationship and impacted on the support I was able to give him going forward. So helpful.' (Learning Support Professional). 'It has helped me to see it from someone else's side and to be kinder' (Child yr 5). According to our impact data and analysis, 100% of the individuals involved found the process successful, 100% of victims felt they were listened to and 100% of wrongdoers felt that their perspective was taken into consideration.

- **Relaxation time:** Play time into learning time can be chaotic in schools if it is not managed effectively. Alongside the 'cool down period' and thoughts box, relaxation time was introduced to further support learners to manage this transition and to prepare them for the next learning activity. Within our setting, the learners benefitted hugely from this period of 'relaxation' which included cushions, deep breathing, relaxing music, a story, a snack and a drink and an opportunity to unwind independently before preparing for focused learning activities. The link between good mental health and successful learning is crucial and a calm and relaxed learner is more able to engage well with the curriculum (RC1). Tension and anxiety deeply affect a learner's relationship with themselves, others and the curriculum and so relaxation time became invaluable. Inner reflection was an additional byproduct and children became more aware of their emotions and how to manage them independently. The self-management and self-regulation skills practiced during this time linked directly with a number of areas on the Behaviour for Learning assessment, for example, 'is able to manage strong emotions' (RS3) and 'is willing to engage with the curriculum' (RC1). The readiness for learning that relaxation contributed to was a crucial aspect of learners engaging positively following unstructured time.

- **Garden project:** The garden project was introduced as a cross-academy initiative and was a huge success at the Courtyard AP Academy. It provided a stimulating and motivating environment where learners could become more actively involved in their outdoor environment. Some of the activities that took place were habitat hunts, planting seeds and bulbs, creating bird feeders to hang in the garden, creating a compost heap and a 'grow your own' project for a range of vegetables that when harvested, were used during cooking lessons or sent home with the learners. The project contributed significantly to learner well-being and had strong links with health and nutrition and cooperating and collaborating (RO8). The links to Behaviour for Learning were strong and this was part of the continuum of provision that learners were immersed in. The project also contributed to Behaviour for Learning progress and this was clear following analysis of the impact documents. Learners completed an impact self-assessment at the end of the project and they all reported an improvement in confidence. They also made links between the project and taking risks in their learning (RC4) and reported an increased ability to show good self-control (RS7).

- **Votes for schools:** This was a trust-wide initiative that had a significant impact on the learners. The weekly lessons enabled children to voice their opinions on issues that affect them, tackle and understand current affairs and to make sense of the world around them. It also enabled us to consistently embed SMSC and British values across the school. The voting platform provided age-appropriate information and the opportunity for the children to express themselves on challenging national issues while developing skills in oracy and participation. The sessions, which included a large amount of debate and discussion, very much supported a range of the Behaviour for Learning areas. Learners reported that they felt an increased sense of being part of the wider community and enjoyed being informed and curious.

- **Enrichment**: A big dedication and investment was made into enrichment at the Courtyard AP Academy with a firm belief that the impact was far reaching, including providing culturally rich experiences that would enhance day-to-day learning. The challenge came in the form of staffing and budget constraints; however, we discovered that a lot could be achieved with a little creativity and playing to the strengths of staff, for example, an ad hoc lunchtime session playing chess or knitting, street dance in breakfast club or app building in golden time. Enrichment opportunities complemented the academic curriculum and extended children's learning through new and exciting experiences. Many activities and trips outside school to the theatre, for a meal, on a residential stay and to the seaside for example, were planned to help broaden the horizons of our learners and to raise aspirations. In addition, a Friday afternoon was devoted to enrichment activities which were planned and delivered by our Learning Support Professionals. An example of this was media studies which took place during this time and which proved to be very popular. It culminated in a red-carpet event where parents and carers were invited in for the screening of the movies that had been produced, which we all enjoyed together. Enrichment was also interwoven throughout the curriculum and not always a stand-alone activity, particularly for learners who had been identified as requiring additional opportunities. Given the bespoke nature of the offer for each child, enrichment took many forms and a very flexible approach was taken. One of the most revered prizes at school was the enrichment activity that was undertaken with the champions of the 'Show Me Great Learning' contest. We experienced learners growing in confidence, showing increased resilience and independence and impact data showed that progress was most significant in 'relationship with self.' Enrichment questionnaires captured the impact of these experiences where learners told us that they felt more confident as a result of engaging with a range of extracurricular opportunities. Weekly BMX-ing lessons were a huge hit for example and feedback showed that learners had an increased ability to follow instructions in the context of school as a result. Learners independently made links between BMXing and an increased ability to take risks in their learning (RC4) and in line with this, Behaviour for Learning data reflected the learners' increased ability to listen attentively (RO7) within the classroom environment. The annual talent show was another high point during the school calendar and this chance to meet up with the other academies to share hidden talents provided an incredible opportunity to step outside comfort zones and to perform in front of an audience with one Year 6 learner reporting 'Now I've done that, I can do anything!' Weekly circus skills sessions were enjoyed very much and supported the children to not only develop their gross motor skills but to try new things (RC4) and to cooperate and collaborate (RO8). A Year 5 learner reflected that, 'Circus skills helps us to learn new skills and it helps us manage our strong emotions. Then our learning is better in class.' Other examples of enrichment activities included: *Face painting *cooking *garden projects *caring for the school chickens *enterprise projects *bi-annual family and friends' tea party *yoga *sewing *drop days *small group activities *girl group *debating *Keep fit sessions *meditation *sports day *book day *charity fundraising *visiting speakers *photography *putting on a performance *voting in a school election. We found that the DFE's activity passport was a great place to start for under 11s as it provided a wide variety of ideas and a good platform upon which to build and develop our ideas. Enrichment, building character and life skills can often be left behind amid a culture of focusing solely on academic performance; however, the benefits of dedicating time to these cannot be overestimated.

- **Structured play**: This played a crucial part in supporting learners to develop positive relationships with others. Whilst it could be time-consuming and required a significant level of adult input, the effort more than paid off. Some learners had very little experience of playing effectively with others and the modelling in the context of structured play helped them to understand and internalise the expectations. It is often taken for granted that learners understand how to play appropriately with others; however, for learners with SEMH in particular, this can be somewhat of a challenge and unstructured times can often be a trigger as they may not yet have developed the skills to manage themselves independently. This is usually because they missed out on early experiences of this. All playtimes at the Courtyard AP Academy contained an element of structured play with a high level of adult support. This ensured that learners were being modelled to at all times but also supported to manage their emotions when things became overwhelming. The de-escalation techniques used by staff during these periods were extremely effective, not only in preventing incidents and maintaining positive interactions between learners, but also in teaching the children how to manage these scenarios independently. The Behaviour for Learning language used supported individuals to understand what they needed to do in order to be successful in playing alongside others appropriately. Staff were adept at personalising these interventions with learners in order to ensure that they did not become overreliant on support. Over time, the instances in which learners relied on these interventions from staff decreased and their ability to manage strong emotions and cooperate and collaborate increased. Following the introduction of structured play, we saw a dramatic reduction in incidents and an increased ability from learners to manage interactions and conflict independently.

- **Pivotal's hot chocolate with the Head (#hotchocfri)** (Dix, 2017): This was a highly revered opportunity in the week that was awarded to learners who had gone over and above what was expected of them and had shown excellent Behaviour for Learning progress throughout the week. It caused quite the stir when first introduced and the competition was fierce to say the least. After all, who would turn down a cup of hot chocolate and a good old chat about how wonderful they are? To recognise and commend those putting in that extra special effort was powerful, and it was established as a real celebration of success. It also provided an additional opportunity to reinforce the links between the positive choices that had been made and the progress that had occurred as a result.
- **1:1 time with a special adult**: Many learners at the Courtyard AP Academy were disconnected from others and had disproportionate experiences of fractious or broken-down relationships. As a result of this, maintaining positive and productive connections with others could prove challenging. These relationships crucially affected all aspects of their learning; therefore, providing time to establish and nurture them was a valuable investment of time. This 10–20-minute period provided a safe space which normally involved a game together, participating in a focused play activity or just a good old chat. Following the learner's lead was an important aspect of this role in order for them to feel that they were able to express themselves and discuss any issues that were troubling them. The time was invaluable in helping them to feel understood and provided a space in the day to tackle any difficulties that had been identified that needed to be discussed away from peers in a non-threatening way. Turn up and connect!
- **Forest school**: Forest school played a large part in our drive towards inspirational teaching. Incorporating play, exploration and risk-taking helped learners to develop socially and emotionally as well as physically and spiritually. They were able to solve real-life problems and to apply knowledge across the curriculum by engaging in activities such as building dens, learning to cook in the outdoors and whittling sticks. Learners exercised creativity and independence and we saw them bringing these skills into the classroom. The core beliefs that forest school are based upon are as follows and were aligned with the philosophy adopted across the curriculum: Everyone is *equal, unique and valuable *competent to explore and discover *entitled to experience appropriate risk and challenge *entitled to choose, and to initiate and drive their own learning and development *entitled to experience regular success *entitled to develop positive relationships with themselves and other people *entitled to develop

a strong, positive relationship with their natural world (forestschoolassociation.org). Feedback from learners who engaged in forest school showed that they benefitted significantly from the sessions, for example, 'I like it that we all feel free and it is enjoyable and entertaining' (Child Year 6 learner). 'We have a chance to learn about cool things that we would never learn about normally' (Child Year 4). Interactions with nature brought unique joy to the learners; it also allowed them to develop their Behaviour for Learning skills in an exciting and stimulating environment.

- **Art therapy**: In house therapeutic support was offered to learners whose progress was affected by SEMH difficulties. Art therapy was used as a vehicle to tap into their creative side in order to express themselves in safe and healthy ways. It also supported them to better manage unwanted and overwhelming feelings, which often affected their relationships with themselves, others and the curriculum. This emotional expression had a big impact on the learners involved and there was a strong correlation between access to art therapy and engagement with the curriculum. The process of art making and creative engagement helped to aid self-expression and to communicate emotions that may be difficult to verbalise.

- **Lego therapy**: This social development programme was aimed at our learners with additional social communication difficulties. The programme was highly structured, systematic and predictable and the sessions were facilitated by a trained LEGO therapist who would guide and support the learners to address and resolve any issue that arose. Staff received training to deliver the sessions and were able to support the children to develop skills such as communication, problem solving and collaboration which also reflected many of the learning behaviours that the children were familiar with. The sessions also helped them to develop a positive relationship with the world around them. The multi-sensory and versatile experience was personalised and tailored to suit the needs of individuals and to address any specific issues that were a barrier to their learning. Emotions can run high during these sessions and things can escalate quickly as frustrations play out; therefore, the role of the adult was crucial in redirecting, de-escalating, verbally supporting and using Behaviour for Learning language to reinforce positive interactions. There was a significant improvement in learners' receptive language and there was a positive impact on verbal expressions by defining terms, describing, comparing and contrasting items and events. This was reflected in increased access to the curriculum and an improvement in speaking and listening skills.

- **Monitors**: This is very common role found in many primary schools that promotes the formation of good habits, allows children to feel valued and helps them to understand the importance of being responsible. Our monitors ranged from reading monitor, snack monitor and eco monitor to name but a few. We were passionate about developing young leaders and this was one of the ways in which this was addressed. Learners developed a sense of pride in the classroom and their school and felt valued for the role that they played.

- **Ambassadors**: All visits to the Courtyard AP Academy were led by school ambassadors. This revered role was developed over time and established itself as an initiative that learners worked hard to be a part of and felt proud to be associated with. Learners as ambassadors had a significant impact on their sense of self from being selected as a result of their positive attitude, to the special badge and clipboard afforded to them; they were always proud to show off their school. Visitors were often surprised by the astute comments made by the ambassadors and their honest and unscripted viewpoints were always well received and were a real insight into the school and its culture. Learners were very proud of their school and felt it was their duty to show it off to the best of their ability with one Year 3 learner stating, 'This school is impeccable because they help with your learning but also because it is challenging.' These representatives taking an active role added an authentic insight into the school while developing their communication and leaderships skills.

- **Routine:** The highly structured and routine driven day was a crucial aspect of the school. As with all routines, the limits and boundaries and predictability of the day removed a source of anxiety for the learners which was particularly important for those with additional needs. The routine was an ideal way of communicating that they were in a safe place and that they could predict what was going to happen next. Sharing the timetable first thing was a very important way of setting the tone for the day and by involving the learners in this, provided an opportunity for them to develop shared responsibility and reduced stress, particularly for hypervigilant learners. Every moment of the day was accounted for and activities and sessions were broken down into a maximum of 45-minute slots as this was found to be the most effective in maximising learner concentration and engagement. Visual timetables were present and visible in every room and were included in the morning routine in order to ensure that everyone was clear about what to expect during the day. The stability that this created for learners was so important and helped them to engage positively in the school day. The welcome that learners received was also planned and incorporated into the routine. Each and every learner would be greeted as they entered the building with a smile and a, 'It's so great to see you!' This not only set the tone for the day but enabled adults to identify and address any issues that may have occurred before school, allowing for a smooth transition into breakfast club. At every transition point during the day, for example between breakfast club and learning time or between playtime and learning time, class teachers would also collect their learners and escort them to the next session. This helped to reduce incidents and was an opportunity for praise and reinforcement. At the end of each day, the Head of School would dismiss the learners with a hand shake and comment on something positive they had seen the learner doing during the day in relation to their Behaviour for Learning. Routines were in place for all aspects of school which created a safe and stable environment for the learners to thrive in.

Over time, and as part of a suite of interventions including some of those just discussed, motivation and engagement with the curriculum increased which naturally impacted positively on learner progress. It was a combination of these interventions, amongst others, that were put together as part of a personalised package for individuals at the Courtyard AP Academy that impacted their relationships with self, others and the curriculum in conjunction with quality first teaching. It goes without saying that where possible, high-quality class delivery rather than interventions outside the classroom is the most impactful approach and investing in what happens inside the classroom has the highest payoff; however, that high-quality delivery, supported by a wide range of other interventions, can have a profound effect on the outcomes for children.

Table 6.1 provides some factors to consider within your own setting. Use the points included to reflect on your classroom and practice rate on a scale of 0–5.

Table 6.1 Some examples of factors to consider in your own classroom

Environment	✓ well-spaced furniture and appropriate lighting
	✓ well ventilated space
	✓ easily accessible materials
	✓ labelled resources
	✓ stimulating display that reflects ethnic and cultural diversity
	✓ arrangement of tables (horse shoe, clusters, rows)
	✓ good examples of learning displayed
	✓ classroom expectations displayed
Communication	✓ regular verbal reminders of routines and expectations
	✓ positive reinforcement
	✓ clear, concise instructions
	✓ targeted questioning
	✓ verbal instructions supported by visual prompts
	✓ specific praise in relation to learning and effort
	✓ checking for understanding
Systems and structures	✓ entry and exit routine
	✓ visible reward system
	✓ visual timetable
	✓ predictable routine
	✓ consistency to embed routine
	✓ 'do now' settling exercise
	✓ monitors, e.g., hand out books and resources
Learning	✓ Clear learning outcomes
	✓ success criteria
	✓ personalised tasks
	✓ wide range of resources
	✓ multi-sensory approach
	✓ high order/open-ended questions
	✓ opportunities for collaboration and independence
	✓ key information displayed

Teacher expectations

The Courtyard AP Academy was characterised by high expectations and high achievement. This permeated the school and was largely attributed to staff behaviours and attitudes and this golden thread was what we were all about. In order to achieve a whole-school culture of high expectations it was crucial to develop skilled and reflective practitioners, which was a main priority. The key role that adults play in whether or not a learner is successful is not something that can be left to chance. Children thrive when they are immersed in a culture of high expectations and excellence which in time has a positive impact on their behaviour and achievement. Hook and Vass (2011) talk about providing clear guidelines to support children to make positive choices and this was very important to us. Inconsistent and unclear expectations lead to confusion and grey areas and certainly do not have the power to create a reality where learners achieve extremely well. The psychological phenomenon that is the Pygmalion effect wherein high expectations lead to an improvement in performance apply to the classroom and the age-old adage: 'they will never amount to anything' can be a powerful force. Learners are highly astute and can recognise with some ease the kind of expectations at play through tone, responses, verbal and non-verbal communication and what adults are willing to accept; what you allow will continue. The goal is to create an environment where there is a culture of hard work and self-belief. Demand the best and expect the learners to meet you there.

Here are some examples of how to make your expectations clear:

- Say exactly what you mean.
- Demonstrate/teach what you mean.
- Have good examples around the room/school.
- Provide detailed feedback.
- Set challenging goals.
- Only praise behaviours and learning that is praiseworthy.
- Praise effort.
- Make examples of learners going above and beyond.
- Model characteristics that you would like to see.
- Relentlessly positively reinforce.
- Continuously refer to the expectations.
- Take every opportunity to pick up on learners doing the right thing and who are displaying positive learning behaviours.
- And most importantly of all, be consistent; it is the most important way to communicate what we want from our learners.

Initially, it can be hard work to set these high expectations; however, the hard yards are worthwhile. It will take time, dedication and a whole load of consistency to achieve but by employing the previously listed strategies, what you are communicating to the learners is that you believe that they are capable of living up to your standards in the classroom and beyond. You will also develop a reputation of high expectations which will bring out the best in the children; it will also contribute towards the development of intrinsic motivation and a love for learning. It is vital that adults set the tone for their classrooms and leave absolutely nothing to chance. There are so many things to think about:

- Where will learners sit?
- How you would like learners to respond to questions/instructions?
- How you will get the attention of the class?
- What they should do if they are unsure?
- What will the daily routine look like?
- What shape will the line-up procedure take?
- What presentation is acceptable in work books?
- How will they interact with others?
- How will they get your attention?

The list goes on! The vision you have for your classroom can only be brought to life by sharing, teaching and relentlessly reinforcing your expectations – nothing happens by accident. Standards need to be crystal clear and you must be extremely vigilant in order to maintain them. By creating an environment where your expectations are explicit, opportunities for conflict and grey areas are minimised. There will inevitably be times when they are challenged; however, if the time has been spent to embed them into everyday practice and they continue to be clear, it will be simple to tackle these instances through reinforcement. In addition to the expectations within the classroom, it is vital that all adults show a steadfast commitment to sustain the culture and expectations of the school in the wider context.

There will always be learners who will exhibit 'challenging behaviour'; however, there are a plethora of proactive strategies that can be employed in order to de-escalate and that can be put in place as preventative measures. Table 6.2 provides some examples.

Table 6.2 Examples of preventative measures that can be taken to de-escalate

Positive greetings	Move in for closer proximity	Positive reinforcement
Actively supervise	Non-verbal cues	Providing choices
Use of a reward system	Hand on shoulder or similar	Take up time
Reminder of expectations	Redirection	Reminder of previous positive learning

Recognition and reward

Reward systems come in many shapes and sizes and have caused a great deal of debate over the years: Do they work? How should they work? Should the reward be tangible or not? A report from the Department for Education (2017) found that in a study on 'Behaviour management systems in schools rated Outstanding' 100% of those schools utilised a system to promote positive behaviour. What comes out of the many studies that have been conducted around rewards is that learners respond positively to being treated positively, which will not come as a surprise to anyone. 'Schools should have in place a range of options and rewards to reinforce and praise good behaviour, and clear sanctions for those who do not comply with the school's behaviour policy' (Behaviour and discipline in schools, advice for headteachers and school staff, DFE, 2016). But what should this look like in practice? The foundation of positive relationships and positive reinforcement is what the reward system at the Courtyard AP Academy was built upon as we were fully aware that the best form of reward was relational. We decided that a physical representation of the positive learning behaviours would help children to sustain their good choices and this manifested itself in our simply named 'Token system.'

Many discussions took place around reward systems and how this should work within our setting and we concluded that what we really wanted was a 'recognition system.' This system would be used to provide worthy praise for positive learning behaviours displayed by the children. A token economy is a very contentious topic and whilst our recognition system was called the 'token system' its main aim was to draw attention and be a physical representation of a positive learning behaviour. The physical act of placing a token on a chart whilst receiving positive reinforcement was powerful and learners responded very well to this, and by rewarding these specific behaviours with tokens, habits were formed over time.

The token system could be used in a broad sense in relation to a wide range of learning behaviours or could be adapted to be used in a more targeted way in direct relation to a learner's Behaviour for Learning targets. The approach with each learner was personalised and tokens were normally awarded in direct relation to individual targets or other additional areas for improvement which were easily identifiable. The token system helped learners to find value and fulfilment in actively participating in positive learning behaviours and fundamentally the reward system that we developed was driven by learning behaviours.

Tokens in action:

1. Actively supervise.
2. Notice positive learning behavior.

3. Recognise this verbally by providing praise: 'Fantastic, you showed motivation by starting your task straight away!'
4. Award token.
5. When 10 tokens are collected, learner to place sticker on personalised sticker chart (1 space for each day).
6. When 5 stickers are collected, certificate awarded and presented publicly.

This extremely simple yet effective approach to recognising and reinforcing positive learning behaviours was low-effort and high-impact. Learners felt acknowledged and proud of themselves and did not view the reward system as transactional where they expected something at the end of it. Instead, the recognition and feedback provided highlighted their abilities and progress and offered a high level of satisfaction and fulfilment.

Responses and consequences

There are few topics that cause more debate in schools than consequences for poor behavior – it can be an extremely divisive topic. One of the challenges associated with this topic is that consequences can mean very different things to different people and staff can witness or experience the same behaviour or incident and have a wide-ranging response or idea about an appropriate consequence as a result of what had happened. If there is no clear process in place, this can have an adverse effect on staff and learners. Tackling challenging behaviour on a case- by-case basis is draining and unpredictable and can leave staff feeling disillusioned and children with a limited understanding of how their actions have affected others. One thing is for sure and that is that staff and learners need clarity and certainty.

'Consequences,' depending on the direction that they are coming from, can also be a way of attempting to control behaviour rather than to teach. There are many practices that simply add fuel to the fire, for example, placing names on the board when learners make poor choices and racking up tally marks every time they misbehave. This is a practice in shame and a vain attempt to encourage learners to accept responsibility or some accountability for their behaviour but ultimately often leads to anger and frustration. It is also highly unlikely that this approach would have any lasting effect on their behaviour. It will, however, serve to have a negative impact on a child's learning and progress. In addition, staff may also perceive the role of consequences to be very different. Punishment under the guise of a consequence will offer the illusion that a learner has 'got what's coming to them' and has taken responsibility for their actions but in fact it simply serves to reinforce anger and to breed resentment. This can also negatively impact a learner's sense of self and certainly does not support individuals to learn, grow or develop. Consequences as the result of poor behaviour are designed to teach and must be built on a foundation of respect whereas punishment is designed to chastise.

Consequences at the Courtyard AP Academy were transformed into 'responses to poor behaviour' and we quickly moved away from the inherited process of learners sitting in silence during their break time following an instance of poor behaviour. The original system had no long-term impact whatsoever and didn't contribute towards learners taking responsibility for their actions or making any progress. The same learners appeared day after day to pay their dues; it was clear that something had to change. Staff worked tirelessly in order to protect learning time within the classroom through quality first teaching, relationship building and using the wide range of techniques discussed previously as well as the underlying message to learners that it was a privilege to be in class and so any disruption of this learning time was taken very seriously. We did not adopt a punitive approach but we developed a very clear system that meant that any learning time that was missed due to poor behaviour or disengagement was made up for at a time when learners were able to engage productively. A script was developed that supported learners to re-engage quickly; however, if this was not the case, a process was in place to manage the situation (see Figure 6.2).

Ready for learning script:

1. When an adult becomes aware of a pupil not engaging with learning, offer to help using a variety of strategies dependent on learner (refer to resources, model, ask question to prompt etc.).
2. If the learner continues to * provide a verbal prompt: 'It's learning time now, please continue with your task.'
3. If learner continues to * ask 'Are you ready for learning?' YES: learner continues with task. NO: remind learner that this is learning time and that this will have to be made up for in their own time.

(*distract others, not follow instructions, disrupt the flow of learning)

Figure 6.2 The ready for learning script used at the Courtyard AP Academy

The predictability of adult responses made learners feel safe and kept the focus on the importance of learning. The challenge came with pressures on staff and their time when following up on any issues, however, over time we saw the impact of the approach with learners spending less and less time 'making up' for any learning that was missed. Learning was 'made up' during alternative times during the day that were considered to be the learner's own time, predominantly break time, however some learners chose to get it done and dusted before the school day started or took it home to complete.

Behaviour perceived as 'disruptive' is often a communication and a symptom of a problem, not the problem itself. It can stem from a lack of skills to manage or respond appropriately to difficult situations and all learners will experience this at one time or another during their time at school. It is noteworthy to talk about de-escalation and responses to poor behaviour as the focus should always primarily be on prevention. That is not to say that it is possible to control the behaviour or choices of learners by any stretch of the imagination but the role of an adult can certainly have an impact if the intervention is timely and appropriate and grounded in respect. Attempting to help a learner regain their footing in a difficult situation can also strengthen your relationship with that individual.

Adult responses must always be based on our knowledge of the child and should aim to calm and de-escalate early signs of distress. Whatever concerning behaviour a child is displaying the 3Rs (Dr Bruce Perry) should always be practiced in the first instance. For learners who struggle with emotional regulation, who are highly sensitive to correction or are unable to manage their intense emotions appropriately, this is so important. For the dysregulated child, their ability to listen, to process and to respond appropriately to information is significantly impacted and depleted.

In order to support a learner to re-regulate, adults should follow the 3Rs (Figure 6.3).

★Regulate – calm and soothe the learner. Children are not able to reason when they are in a state of anxiety or distress
= moving from alarm to calm
> Do this by using soothing but limited language, give time and space

★Relate – validate feelings and label them. Help children to label their emotions to manage their behaviours. It is important that we 'name it to tame it'
= focusing on the relationship
> Do this by validating their feelings and acknowledging how they feel

★Reason – set limits on their behaviour and problem solve with the child
= provide new brain memory
> Do this by teaching the language of emotions and sharing strategies

---

Figure 6.3 The 3 Rs (regulate, relate, reason)

This method can feel difficult as we all possess our own triggers. The natural response can be to attempt to regain control through attempts to ask questions, demand and direct; however, this can simply escalate a situation and when we are confronted with further challenges, can lead us as the adult to dysregulate also causing the child's behaviour to intensify, escalate and ultimately compound the situation. Table 6.3 gives examples of learner communication and behaviors with suggested responses to support and de-escalate.

Responses that are not attachment and trauma aware:

- Dismissing a child's feelings by telling them they are overreacting, being silly or wrong.
- Using shaming language or sanctions.
- Using tokenistic praise.
- Telling children how they are feeling.
- Being confrontational with verbally or body language.
- Ignoring the child.
- Using too many words, which can overwhelm them.
- Isolating or leaving children on their own when they are distressed.
- Expecting children to self-regulate independently.

Some examples of de-escalation strategies

Verbal:

1. Validate the learner's emotions.
2. Maintain a low and even tone of voice.
3. Use distraction and diversion techniques.
4. Provide choices.
5. Use limited soothing language: 'I wonder if . . .' 'would you like to . . .'
6. Ensure there is take up time.
7. Attempt redirection.
8. Provide reassurance.

Table 6.3 Examples of learner communication/behaviours and suggested responses to support and de-escalate

Underlying communication:	Behaviours:	Possible responses:
*I don't feel safe *I don't trust you *I don't know how I feel *I feel rubbish or stupid *I feel anxious or scared *I feel sad *I feel angry *I can't cope with my difficult feelings *I feel overwhelmed *I need to escape *I need to protect myself *I don't know whether I still exist *I need you to attend to me to feel safe and loved *This is the only way I know to make you like me	LOW LEVEL: *Fast breathing *Restlessness *Stiff body posture *clenched fists or jaw *Rapid or high-pitched speech *continually talking, asking questions making noises *not sitting still	• Respond to attachment-seeking by moving closer to child, using their name and acknowledging their need, e.g., "I haven't forgotten you Sam. I will just finish marking this work and then I'll come to you." • If appropriate use a soothing touch • Offer a movement break • Offer a sensory support such as a stress toy • Move things on without making demands, e.g., "It can be hard to stay calm when we're not sure what to do. Maybe we can try the next question together and come back to this one later."
*I need to be in control to feel safe *I don't have the skills you're expecting *I don't believe you won't leave		• Use "I wonder . . ." to help child identify feelings, e.g., "I'm wondering if you are shouting "it's boring" because you feel scared about getting the answer wrong?" (Use this technique 1:1 so as not to embarrass) • Validate their feelings, e.g., "I know what that feels like. It can be scary to have a go in case you fail at something." "I know it's hard to think right now." "I'm sorry that it's made you so cross."

MEDIUM LEVEL:

*refusal to do work *refusal to follow instructions

*non-compliant behaviour

*Disrespectful language

*minor damage to school property

*argumentative *non-directed swearing

SEE PREVIOUS RESPONSES:

Quiet correction 1:1 with child to avoid public shame

- Acknowledge their feelings of unfairness
- Re-phrase requests so they don't imply a demand, e.g., instead of "Tidy away your books" try "we can't go to break with everything out on the desks."
- Try to problem solve with the child, e.g.,
"You want to go to break. I want you to complete your work so you can do well in Maths. How are we going to solve this?"
- Link the consequence to the action', e.g., if they have broken a calculator, they don't get to use one the next session.
- Use a light tone of voice to suggest a child has another go using different words.
- Give choices about what will happen next calmly, repeating as often as necessary.
- Repeat your request or expectation and don't become drawn into an argument.

HARMFUL BEHAVIOURS:

*Aggressive/threatening/racist/ homophobic/sexist language

*Damage to school property

*Threats

*throwing objects *kicking objects

*kicking, hitting, spitting

SEE PREVIOUS RESPONSES.

- Use self-regulation techniques to keep yourself calm.
- Make sure your hands are visible, palms towards the child so they know you will not hurt them.
- Keep your body posture, facial expression and tone calm.
- Keep a distance so the child does not feel trapped.
- Use a low, slow, strong voice.
- Speak rhythmically like you would to an infant.
- Narrate what you see in a calm voice, e.g., "I can see you are feeling very frustrated right now."
- If a child needs to be removed, ensure they are with an adult who can support them to self-regulate.
- Do not chase a child unless they are in danger as it can seem like an attack. Reassure them, "I'm still here when you're ready."

9. Identify what you can see, hear, feel, smell.
10. Give reminders of success.

Non- verbal:

1. Remain calm and regulated.
2. Maintain neutral body language/face.
3. Give personal space.
4. Provide an alternative safe and comfortable space.
5. Planned ignoring.

A restorative response to an incident of conflict involves asking the questions in Figure 6.4 as a script.

To the person responsible for the harm

- Tell us what happened before the incident.
- What happened next?
- Who has been affected by what you did?
- How were they affected?
- What were you thinking at the time? What were you feeling?
- Is there anything else you would like to say?

Person harmed

- How did you feel at the time?
- How have you felt about this since?

Person responsible for harm

- What can we do to put things right?
- How can we make sure this does not happen again?

Person harmed

- What would make things better for you?
- What can we do to stop this happening?

Figure 6.4 A script that can be used in response to an incident of conflict

Adapted from Structured Intervention script, Restorative Solutions, 2007

Restorative approaches in educational settings are increasing in popularity and when used effectively, are interwoven into the culture of the school. The intentional, clear and systematic approach to dealing with incidents minimises any discussion or debate around an appropriate consequence for learners. It also contributes towards facilitating social and emotional progress whilst preserving a child's relationship with themselves but improving relationships with others. The approach contributed to lasting change at the Courtyard AP Academy and gave individuals confidence that their views were going to be taken into consideration in a non-judgemental and safe space. The key features of respect, responsibility, repair and re-integration lent themselves to creating a harmonious learning environment where strong relationships were maintained.

Our desire to belong is part of who we are and our relationships define us. From the earliest moments we search for those who will nurture, protect and teach us. As adults in schools, we have the ability to impact the lives of our learners in these positive ways by focusing on precise inclusion and aiming for success by any means. We must pour our efforts into creating an environment that allows our children to flourish and develop into confident and independent individuals. We must also focus on building trust and respect and become role models to those who need us. Finally, we must recognise what our learners need most from us and provide opportunities for them to develop into successful young people.

Summary

This chapter focused on the impact of adult behaviours on learners' personal progress with a particular emphasis on the role of the adult in promoting positive learning behaviours in the classroom and beyond. We discussed a range of approaches that contribute to personalisation and learner well-being and highlighted a number of interventions that support motivation and engagement with the curriculum.

Takeaways

- Be relentless in your pursuit of excellence and set your standards high – learners will meet you there.
- Symbolise your vision, be who you want them to be.
- Personalise your approach on every level, always taking into account a learner's starting point.
- Take an intentional and systematic approach to including Behaviour for Learning in all aspects of what you do.

Reflective questions

1. What measures are in place in your setting to ensure that the individual needs of learners are being met across all the three relationships?
2. What impact are your current rewards and sanctions/consequences having on the Behaviour for Learning of children, especially those with SEMH?
3. What steps are taken to ensure that high expectations are clear and consistent?
4. What preventative measures are utilised in your setting to de-escalate and how effective are they?

References

Department for Education (DFE). (2016). *Behaviour and Discipline in Schools. Advice for Headteachers and School Staff.* London: DFE.
Department for Education (DFE). (2017). *Case Studies of Behaviour Management Practices in Schools Rated Outstanding' Research Report.* London: DFE.

Dix, P. (2017). *When the adults change Everything changes: seismic shifts in school behaviour.* Carmarthen, Wales: Independent Thinking Press.

Department for Education and Science (DFES). (2005). *Learning Behaviour: The Report of the Practitioners on School Behaviour and Discipline (The Steer Report).* London: HMSO.

Restorative Solutions. (2007). *Restorative Practice Pack.* Preston: Restorative Solutions CIC.

Fisher, J. (2009). *Puppets, Language and Learning.* Featherstone, London, UK: Featherstone.

Hook, P. and Vass, A. (2011). *Behaviour Management Pocketbook.* (2nd edition) Hampshire: Teachers' Pocketbooks.

Voss, A. (2011). *Understanding Your Child's Sensory Signals. A Practical Daily Use Handbook for Parents and Teachers.* (3rd edition) Scotts Valley, California: Create Space Independent Publishing Platform.

7 Promoting Behaviour for Learning across schools

Introduction

This chapter focuses on the Primary Inclusion Development Service (PIDS) and how we assessed and evaluated the requests for interventions and the work of the service as a whole. It was important to have a systematic approach to recording our interventions and to decide the specific areas that we were going to monitor (Hallam, 2007). To develop the service, we used the 'Quality Standards for Special Education Needs Support and Outreach Services' (DCSF, 2008) The standards enabled the team to evaluate the previous outreach provision and identify areas for the development of PIDS. We share the quantitative and qualitative data that we used to monitor and evaluate the service. We then take the reader through each stage of the request for intervention process so that you gain insight into the information that was collected at each stage and how it was used. The chapter ends with a focus on our work in partnership with schools.

Was the Behaviour for Learning approach going to improve behaviour?

We decided to inform schools of the new service and sent out the following brief:

> A new service will be developed targeted at supporting primary schools to enhance their own capacity to respond even more effectively to the needs of primary school-aged children with SEBD and to secure each child's entitlement to learning within their own mainstream school.

These were the key questions for us as a service:

> Was the focus on Behaviour for Learning improving outcomes for children?
> Was there an understanding of the interrelationship between learning and behaviour?
> Did the behaviour of children with SEMH needs improve following the intervention?

These were the questions that needed answering and we had to have answers. We were taking a risk adopting a new approach to improve behaviour by focusing on learning and using the Behaviour for Learning framework. We were shifting to a focus on the learning behaviours and the three relationships: 'relationship with self,' 'relationship with others' and 'relationship with the curriculum' (Ellis and Tod, 2009, 2018, 2022). Behaviour for Learning was the only approach that met the aims of the service and what we were trying

DOI: 10.4324/9781003166672-8

to achieve. It was important for us to be able to track, monitor and measure the impact that we were having by implementing Behaviour for Learning.

Self-evaluation had a key role to play in the development of the service. It was a priority and the responsibility of the leadership team to ensure that the Primary Inclusion Development Service [PIDS] incorporated ways in which we could review, monitor and evaluate the interventions that were going to take place across schools (Halsey et al., 2005). The headteachers and staff in schools had to see evidence that this approach was going to make a difference – for them, the requests for intervention sent to school were primarily focused on the behaviour of children improving. Our agenda was much broader than that. We wanted to improve outcomes for all children, and work with staff in a way that further equipped them to meet the needs of children with SEMH difficulties who were at risk of exclusion. In any service provided by a local authority there is always a level of accountability to the stakeholders, staff in schools and of course parents. We wanted parents to have confidence in the approaches that we were implementing and to have them fully involved in the whole process.

Changes to the outreach service

In Chapter 2 we describe how we reviewed and evaluated the Behaviour Support team using the Quality Standards for Special Education Needs (SEN) Support and Outreach Service (DCSF, 2008), standards 1–6.

As a team we used the six standards as a framework to evaluate each standard to identify the strengths of the previous outreach service and areas that we would have to develop and ensure that they were incorporated into the PIDS. Working on this collaboratively with staff in the Primary Inclusion Development Service provided an opportunity for all staff to contribute and be involved in the evaluation process. The involvement of a local authority Inspector and Senior Education Psychologist supported the evaluation process and clarified how the service would relate to and interact with the local authority and other professionals.

The Quality Standards for Special Education Needs support and outreach (DCSF, 2008) were an effective tool for raising expectations and developing a high-quality service to meet the needs of children, including those with SEMH. The areas identified for development were incorporated into the PIDS Improvement Plan. Alongside this, we developed strategies that would support the monitoring and evaluation process of the Primary Inclusion Development Service and the evidence that would be collected. It was important throughout to ensure that we were explicit about equal opportunities so that we could measure the impact of our interventions in a systematic way.

The PIDS plan

As well as the priorities and targets being identified on the service plan we identified how we would monitor and evaluate the success criteria.

The areas identified which were a priority for us to focus on were:

Standard 1: Progress towards outcomes is systematically recorded and monitored, and
    Standard 3: Parents should always be consulted and where appropriate; they should
    be involved in supporting the learning and development of their child as part of any
    intervention. Standard 6: The service regularly collects feedback about its interventions and uses it to improve the quality of service (DCSF, 2008).

Table 7.1 Quantitative and qualitative data used for monitoring, evaluating and measuring impact in PIDS: the outreach team

Quantitative	Qualitative
Intervention form	BFL assessments
Reasons for request for intervention	Record of Support
Attainment data	6/8-week review
Attendance data	Feedback from Pupil
Exclusion data	Feedback from Parent
Parental feedback	Feedback from Staff
Data on year group	Feedback from PIDS team
Data on gender, ethnicity	Feedback and reports from other professionals and agencies
	Case Study
	Transition plan
	Action plan
	Annual report
	Evaluation form
	Headteacher feedback on service

We had to look in more depth at how we were going to systematically monitor the interventions and collect data that could be used to evaluate the impact on different groups of children. Parents needed to be much more involved in the intervention process than they had been previously, so we made sure that they took on more of a key role throughout the process. The approach that we developed gave us the opportunity to ensure that the Behaviour for Learning assessment (Appendix 1) was incorporated into the process. All requests for individual children included a Behaviour for Learning assessment and it formed the basis for looking at approaches and strategies that would be used to improve behaviour.

We collected a range of quantitative and qualitative data to monitor and evaluate the impact of our interventions which can be seen in Table 7.1.

PIDS Process

We will discuss each stage of the PIDS process (Appendix 2) and show what data was collected, how it was monitored and evaluated.

Stage A Request for Intervention

A REQUEST FOR INTERVENTION

The request for intervention (Appendix 3) was an important stage in the process. We were giving a message to schools that it was an intervention. It was at this stage that we had to ensure that the data that was collected was accurate, especially the data on attainment

so that we could monitor the intervention and regularly review progress and impact for each child. The data collected for all children was also used to monitor the impact and effectiveness of the service across the year. The data collected included the following:

- Reason for a request
- Who the request was for? – Individual/group/class/teacher/school
- The strategies that had been used

A request for an individual child would also include the following initial data about the child, school and family:

- Baseline data on attainment,
- DOB
- Year group
- Ethnicity
- Language spoken at home, EAL
- Looked After child(ren)
- Behaviour incidents
- Exclusions
- Involvement of other agencies
- The Behaviour for Learning assessment

Tables 7.2 and 7.3 are examples of the Behaviour for Learning assessment completed for individual children at the initial stage of the intervention.

At the initial consultation meeting, further information was gathered. This was an opportunity to confirm and clarify the reasons for the request for intervention, the attainment data and look at the Behaviour for Learning assessment. Parents were involved at this stage and the intervention would only take place if the parent/carer had agreed to it. The parent attended the initial consultation meeting so that we could gain their perspective on the request and for them to share any concerns and add information. The use of the Behaviour for Learning assessments became a much more positive focus for conversation with parents. We did not talk about children being 'disruptive.' Instead, the language in the assessment was very clear and engaged parents more effectively. It was also a good opportunity to discuss all the learning behaviours, especially the children's relationship with the curriculum and the strengths that had been identified by the member of staff. A classroom observation of the child, group or class, based on the three relationships of the Behaviour for Learning framework was carried out to identify and help clarify the areas that were going to become the focus for the intervention. The focus would include the areas that the member of staff had concerns about. Behaviours observed in the classroom are often a result of the interaction between emotional, social and cognitive factors. Joint observations with school staff proved to be helpful; it was an effective way of becoming familiar with the Behaviour for Learning framework as well as looking at which adult behaviours were having a positive impact on the child's learning behaviour. Classroom observations gave a great insight into when, where and how learners were engaging in such positive behaviours. It was also an opportunity to provide feedback to staff on what was working well. The involvement of other professionals, for example the Educational Psychologist or Early Years Specialist, always helped to clarify the judgements that had been made about the child's Behaviour for Learning and to identify a starting point and a focus for action.

Table 7.2 Completed Behaviour for Learning assessment for a child, Noah

Primary Inclusion Development Service
Behaviour for Learning Assessment for School Staff

Date: _____**9.9.15**_____   School: _____**HP**_____

Name of pupil: _____**Noah**_____   D.O.B: _____

Completed by: ____**JP**_____   Relationship to Pupil: _____**Teacher**_____

The numbers represent the percentage over time for each category	5	25	50	75	95
RELATIONSHIP WITH SELF (Predominantly Emotional) To want to, and be able to, include him/herself in the learning opportunities and relationships on offer in the classroom and school context. This includes how the learner feels about themselves, their self-esteem, self-efficacy and their perceptions of the relevance of school learning.	Rarely	Sometime	Fairly Often	Often	Always
Key Features	1	2	3	4	5
RS1. Is interested in learning	x				
RS2. Has a positive opinion of him/herself		x			
RS3. Can manage strong emotions such as anger and/or sadness		x			
RS4. Has a belief that he/she is capable of being successful		x			
RS5. Can independently make choices and try to solve problems	x				
RS6. Can accept responsibility for own behaviour	x				
RS7. Shows good self-control			x		

RELATIONSHIP WITH OTHERS (Predominantly Social) Being able to take part in learning that involves others, and join in aspects of school life as a member of the school community. This involves being willing and able to interact socially and academically with others, including the teacher and other adults.	Rarely	Sometimes	Fairly Often	Often	Always
Key Features	1	2	3	4	5
RO1. Is willing to work independently as appropriate	x				
RO2. Is socially aware of what is going on around him/her			x		
RO3. Is willing and able to empathise with others	x				
RO4. Is willing to ask for help	x				
RO5. Is willing to behave respectfully towards adults in school		x			
RO6. Is willing to behave respectfully towards peers		x			
RO7. Is able to listen to others and be attentive		x			
RO8. Can cooperate and collaborate when working and playing in a group		x			

(Continued)

Table 7.2 (Continued)

RELATIONSHIP WITH CURRICULUM (Predominantly Cognitive) The dynamic interactions that make up the reciprocal activity between the learner and the curriculum. This involves being able and willing to access, process and respond to information available through the curriculum.	Rarely	Sometimes	Fairly Often	Often	Always
Key Features	1	2	3	4	5
RC1. Is willing to engage with the curriculum		x			
RC2. Can take responsibility for own learning		x			
RC3. Is able to access the curriculum			x		
RC4. Is willing to try new things and 'take risks'	x				
RC5. Can make mistakes and 'move on'	x				
RC6. Is self-aware, knows how and when to get help		x			
RC7. Motivated to complete tasks	x				
RC8. Able to work unaided		x			
RC9. Follows classroom rules and routines			X		

This table can be used to collate information from the first three sections

List the pupil's strengths from the assessment		
Relationship with Self (RS)	**Relationship with Others (RO)**	**Relationship with Curriculum (RC)**
RS7 Shows good self- control	**RO2 Is socially aware of what is going on around him/her**	**RC3 Is able to access the curriculum**

List areas of concerns from the assessment		
Relationship with Self (RS)	**Relationship with Others (RO)**	**Relationship with Curriculum (RC)**
RS1 Is interested in learning	**RO1 Is willing to work independently as appropriate**	**RC7 Motivated to complete tasks**

Key focus areas identified based on assessment (RS, RO, RC)

Table 7.3 Initial assessment for pupil, Judah, completed by school staff

Primary Inclusion Development Service

Behaviour for Learning Assessment

Date: _____2012_____   School: X_____

Name of pupil: _____Judah_____   D.O.B: _____

Completed by: _____Class teacher _____   Relationship to Pupil: _____

RELATIONSHIP WITH SELF (Predominantly Emotional) To want to, and be able to, include *him/herself in the learning opportunities and relationships on offer in the classroom and school context. This includes how the learner feels about themselves, their self-esteem, self-efficacy and their perceptions of the relevance of school learning.*	Rarely	Sometimes	Fairly Often	Often	Always
Key Features	1	2	3	4	5
RS1. Is interested in learning	x				
RS2. Has a positive opinion of him/herself	x				
RS3. Can manage strong emotions such as anger and/or sadness	x				
RS4. Has a belief that he/she is capable of being successful	x				
RS5. Can independently make choices and try to solve problems	x				
RS6. Can accept responsibility for own behaviour	x				
RS7. Shows good self-control	x				

RELATIONSHIP WITH OTHERS (Predominantly Social) Being able to take part in learning that involves others, and join in aspects of school life as a member of the school community. This involves being willing and able to interact socially and academically with others, including the teacher and other adults.	Rarely	Sometimes	Fairly Often	Often	Always
Key Features	1	2	3	4	5
RO1. Is willing to work independently as appropriate		x			
RO2. Is socially aware of what is going on around him/her		x			
RO3. Is willing and able to empathise with others	x				

(Continued)

Table 7.3 (Continued)

RELATIONSHIP WITH OTHERS (Predominantly Social) Being able to take part in learning that involves others, and join in aspects of school life as a member of the school community. This involves being willing and able to interact socially and academically with others, including the teacher and other adults.	Rarely	Sometimes	Fairly Often	Often	Always
RO4. Is willing to ask for help	x				
RO5. Is willing to behave respectfully towards adults in school	x				
RO6. Is willing to behave respectfully towards peers	x				
RO7. Is able to listen to others and be attentive	x				
RO8. Can cooperate and collaborate when working and playing in a group	x				

RELATIONSHIP WITH CURRICULUM (Predominantly Cognitive) The dynamic interactions that make up the reciprocal activity between the learner and the curriculum. This involves being able and willing to access, process and respond to information available through the curriculum.	Rarely	Sometimes	Fairly Often	Often	Always
Key Features	1	2	3	4	5
RC1. Is willing to engage with the curriculum		x			
RC2. Can take responsibility for own learning		x			
RC3. Is able to access the curriculum			x		
RC4. Is willing to try new things and 'take risks'	x				
RC5. Can make mistakes and 'move on'	x				
RC6. Is self-aware, knows how and when to get help	x				
RC7. Motivated to complete tasks	x				
RC8. Able to work unaided			x		
RC9. Follows classroom rules and routines	x				

This table can be used to collate information from the first three sections

List the pupil's strengths from the assessment		
Relationship with Self (RS)	Relationship with Others (RO)	Relationship with Curriculum (RC)
Tries to solve problems, works independently, gives up if something is 'too challenging'	Mostly disinterested in the same things as his peers (football/video games). Sometimes works well with selected pupils depending on mood.	Enjoys history, maths, Art and DT and has strengths in these areas. *Prefers* to work unaided.

List areas of concern from the assessment		
Relationship with Self (RS)	**Relationship with Others (RO)**	**Relationship with Curriculum (RC)**
Very low self-esteem, unable to control strong emotions.	Lacks empathy, very often disrespectful towards adults and children, doesn't like talking about things or listening to what people have to say.	Lack motivation to learn therefore often doesn't like taking advice, moving on from mistakes.

B IDENTIFICATION OF NEEDS

Examples of a range of learner observations made of each focus behaviour in context, are as follows:

Relationship with Self

RS1. Is interested in learning:

- Learner asked two questions relevant to the topic, during the 10-minute class discussion.

RS2. Has a positive opinion of him/herself

- Learner stated that he was a good friend because he liked to help others whilst writing describing themselves to someone they had just met.

RS3. Can manage strong emotions such as anger and/or sadness

- Learner was observed going straight to the 'calm corner' in the classroom following playtime, as he was 'furious that his team hadn't won.' Showing good self-awareness of his needs.

RS4. Has a belief that he/she is capable of being successful

- 'I have done this before so I know that I can do it this time.'

RS5. Can independently make choices and try to solve problems

- Moved to the other side of the table when children were squeezing into a small space to look at artefacts being shared.

RS6. Can accept responsibility for own behaviour

- Was able to identify that something she had said to another child may have made her feel very upset.

RS7. Shows good self-control

- Was able to wait for his turn to share his ideas with hand up and not calling out.

Relationship with Others

RO1. Is willing to work independently as appropriate

- Participated in quiet reading time, remaining focused on his own book for a period of 10 minutes.

RO2. Socially aware of what is going on around him/her

- Followed the lead of some other children putting away classroom equipment during tidy up time.

RO3. Is willing and able to empathise with others

- Invited a new boy to join his game in the playground commenting that he himself 'used to be the new boy.'

RO4. Is willing to ask for help

- Sought help from the support adult in the class when he wasn't sure of where he needed to store his new reading books.

RO5. Is willing to behave respectfully towards adults in school

- Ready to stop playing with the bricks as soon as he was asked to do so by his teacher.

RO6. Is willing to behave respectfully towards peers

- Thanked his friend when he was prepared to share to pencils with a peer.

RO7. Is able to listen to others and be attentive

- Listening carefully to a peer sharing news about a new pet and ask a relevant question about its size and colour.

RO8. Can cooperate and collaborate when working and playing in a group

- Helped to devise and adhered to a new ball game during a PE lesson.

Relationship with the Curriculum

RC1. Is willing to engage with the curriculum

- Contributed to a class discussion about choice of topics they wanted to explore over the year.

RC2. Can take responsibility for own learning

- Without being prompted to do so, he was reading through comments recorded in his book by his teacher, with next steps for learning.

RC3. Is able to access the curriculum

- Was able to complete the first set of questions with ease and then attempted the 'extra for experts' quiz, with some success.

RC4. Is willing to try new things and 'take risks'

- Sounding out and writing spellings in her 'have a go' book.

RC5. Can make mistakes and 'move on'

- Responded positively when the teacher addressed a misconception during a maths lesson. He was able to accept this feedback and apply it to the next set of equations.

RC6. Is self-aware, knows how and when to get help

- Observed using each step of the 5Bs approach to find suitable adjectives for his sentences.

RC7. Motivated to complete tasks

- Using a timer, he was able to complete the required task in the allocated time.

RC8. Able to work unaided

- Was able to answer 4 out of 5 of the comprehension questions with minimal distraction.

RC9. Follows classroom rules and routines

- Observed following the classroom routines for completion of jobs, collecting reading books and lining up for lunch.

The next stage was the planning stage, which included all those who were going to be involved in the intervention.

C   PLANNING AND IMPLEMENTATION

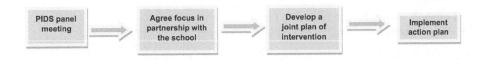

The purpose of the PIDS panel meeting was to agree on the focus for the intervention and clarify the roles of the staff who were going to be involved. The meeting was attended by the parents/carers, the class teacher, any learning support professionals who supported the child, the headteacher and a member of the PIDS team leading on the intervention and the head of service. It was an opportunity to share and go through the request, listen to parental views and decide on the next steps. The joint action plan (Appendix 4) was a crucial part of the process; it was at this stage that we identified the target and actions that were going to take place and how they would be monitored over the next 6–8 weeks. In the action plan, we would include all the staff who were going to be involved in the intervention and include the role of the learning support professional if there was a teaching assistant in the class. The success criteria were used to identify the changes that we were looking for, track progress and measure the impact. The action planning form shows the questions that were asked and discussed which were very much in line with a solution focused approach.

D   MONITORING

> Regular
> review of
> progress

It was at this stage that monitoring took place every 6–8 weeks. This time frame gave a good indication as to whether the targets were the correct ones and whether the member of staff believed that their perspective was valued and that the weekly support they were receiving was empowering them. It was a good opportunity to build trust and confidence amongst school staff. The review of the intervention form was completed (Appendix 5), and a Behaviour for Learning assessment (Appendix 1) was updated for discussion at the meeting. All reviews were attended by the parent, class teacher, headteacher, PIDS intervention lead and head of service. The meeting was an opportunity for everyone to be reflective and honest about the effectiveness of the actions that were taking place. On some occasions, the focus and actions were changed as they were not having the intended positive impact on improving the learning behaviours identified on the action plan. The regular reviews supported staff expertise and confidence, thus enabling us to work with schools in a way which increased their own capacity to meet the needs of children with SEMH. Table 7.4 is an example of a child's completed review.

Review of Intervention

Name of Pupil: Rosemarie   **School: School**   **X Yr: 5**

Intervention: PT-PPRU Placement
Placement Commenced: 27th June 2012   **Date of Review:** 27th September, 3.40pm
School X Attendees:– SENCO, Class Teacher:1– Mother, Rosemarie – Pupil
PPRU Attendees: Head of PIDS, PPRU teacher, Development worker.

This review, Table 7.4 is for a child who attended the PPRU part time and was also supported by a member of staff from PIDS, a development worker. It is a good example of how the staff from PIDS and the PPRU worked together to support the reintegration of a child back to school. The reviews usually lasted for one hour and the focus is on what has been done, the key strategies used to promote behaviour, progress in the three relationships and a response to the intended outcomes at the PPRU which can be seen in Table 7.4 Everyone who had been involved in the intervention contributed to the

Table 7.4 Completed review form of child, Rosemarie, who was supported by the PIDS and attended the PPRU

Work completed	Progress against outcomes
• 7-week part-time placement at the PPRU. • Personalised learning for literacy, numeracy and reading based on levels provided by the school, PPRU's initial baseline assessments and mainstream planning. • Range of learning activities, linked to mainstream curriculum where possible. • Development worker supporting at school X. • 1:1 reading and guided reading sessions on a daily basis. • Targeted support at the beginning of tasks. • Highly structured literacy tasks planned that Rosemarie can access independently. **Key Strategies to support and promote Behaviour for Learning:** • Reinforcing expectations. • Weekly food technology sessions to develop healthy lifestyles knowledge and cooperative work skills. • Discussions with Parent to give feedback regarding progress and attitude to learning. • Support from an adult during written tasks. • Choice language and take up time have been identified as key strategies to use with Rosemarie to help her make the right choices with her learning and behaviour. • Positive evidential praise based on learning and learning behaviours. • Use of humour to de-escalate. • Take up time.	**B4L Progress:** Assessment data shows that Rosemarie has made progress in all assessed areas. • <u>Relationship with Self</u> –Assessments show that Rosemarie is more interested in learning, is more able to accept responsibility for her own behaviour and is showing more self-control. • <u>Relationship with Others</u> –Assessments show that Rosemarie is more willing and able to empathise with others, is more willing to behave respectfully towards adults and is more capable of cooperating and collaborating when working or playing in a group. • <u>Relationship with Curriculum</u> – Assessments show that Rosemarie is more willing to engage with the curriculum, that she is able to follow classroom rules and routines and is willing to try new things and take risks. **Intended Outcomes (from Request for PPRU Placement)** For Rosemarie to: • Undertake and complete learning tasks. • Be able to follow instructions. • Be able to speak to adults and peers appropriately. • Be able to manage strong emotions such as anger. • Be able to interact appropriately with her peers. • Rosemarie has shown a positive attitude to learning whilst attending the PPRU. • Rosemarie has developed positive relationships with the adults who support her from the PPRU. • With support, Rosemarie completes work tasks. • Rosemarie has developed and maintained positive relationships with her peers at the PPRU. She is able to play appropriately and can work collaboratively, unsupported. • Rosemarie shows a positive attitude to learning and follows classroom rules and routines. **Rosemarie's Views:** • 'My behaviour is better' • 'I do more work' • 'I listen to adults' • 'I want to get back to Mainstream' **Mum's views:** • Her relationships with others have improved. • She is more able to be rational. • She is better with new people. • Wants as much help as possible for Rosemarie's learning.

(Continued)

Table 7.4 (Continued)

Work completed	Progress against outcomes
	Class teacher's views: • Rosemarie is more relaxed and happy. • She is more able to reflect. • Her reactions to situations are not as extreme and she is able to calm down much quicker. **Intervention teacher views:** • Rosemarie is more cooperative and a difference has been noted. • She will benefit from the Speech and language intervention which will continue as often as possible.
Barriers	**Next Steps** • PPRU teacher to send Class teacher examples of writing frames used at the PPRU. • Development worker to continue to support at school. • PPRU teacher to photocopy work for Rosemarie to bring back to school for her to celebrate her success. • Rosemarie to return to mainstream full time by half term. Week 1: Monday, Tuesday and Friday at School Week 2: Monday, Tuesday and Friday at School. Week 3: Monday, Tuesday, Thursday and Friday at School. Week 4: Monday, Tuesday, Thursday and Friday at School.

feedback, including the child and parent. This process was positive for the child as they were having feedback on the progress they were making from all those involved in the process. After everyone has shared, next steps are discussed; in this case it was Rosemarie being reintegrated back to school.

There were no surprises in this process as the reviews were regular and records of support were shared with the school staff after each visit. A solution-focused approach always helped staff to focus on the improvements that had been made. Some children benefitted from having a part time place at the PPRU for a short period of time, before being integrated back into their mainstream school.

E   EVALUATION

Evaluation
meeting and
form

Evaluation was an important part of the process (Appendix 6). These were the key questions that were asked:

- **What have been the outcomes of the intervention?**
- **How has the input from the Primary Inclusion Development Service contributed to this?**
- **What strategies/systems/actions have made an impact?**
- **What are the sustainable Next Steps?**
- **What is the agreed Date of Follow Up Meeting?**

The process was completed with all staff who had been involved, including the parent and headteacher. An important part of this process was not only identifying what had an impact on the intervention, but also reflecting on the following: Were the strategies and/ or actions implemented sustainable? Did the teacher and school believe they had been empowered? Was the child confident in the improvements they had made?

Evaluation of service across the schools in the local authority

An annual service report was produced yearly for the local authority and distributed to headteachers. The report included a reminder of the vision, aims and an analysis of the data from the following interventions:

- Requests by type
- Individual
- Class
- Group
- Teacher
- Whole school

The majority of the requests for intervention were for individual children that had been identified by the school as having SEBD. They were children who were either at risk of being excluded or had had a fixed-term exclusion. The children referred to PIDS did not have a statement or education health care plan. Groups of children were also referred for specific reasons, for example, 'there were concerns about how they managed their anger.' Whole classes were also referred where there were concerns about the behaviour of the whole class. Teachers who needed further support and training were also included in the intervention requests. We received a few requests for whole-school support which was usually for specific training for all staff. Projects, for example, a playground project and on one occasion this was because behaviour was a concern throughout the whole school and had been identified as an area that needed improving.

Evaluation of the Primary Inclusion Development Service (PIDS)

The report gave an evaluation of the service and included an analysis of the interventions by gender, year group, ethnicity, school and intervention type. The data was analysed termly and led to training and further support for staff and children, for example, leading a playground project. Headteachers were asked for specific feedback about PIDS which included whether the service had met their needs, the strengths, and areas for development. The annual report also included written review of the achievements of the service in relation to the service plan and targets.

In Chapter 2 we share the data from our first year. This is a sample of data taken from our report dated 2009 to 2013 which was sent to headteachers and local authority officers so that they had an overview of the Requests for Intervention that were being carried out across the Local Authority by PIDS. We also had exclusion data for each school which we did not publish as part of this document.

See Figure 7.1 and Table 7.5 for data on Request by Type September 2009 to June 2013.

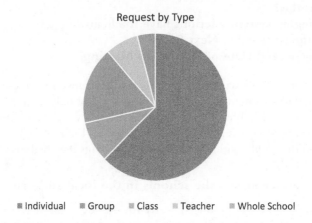

Figure 7.1 Pie chart showing the type of requests received by the PIDS from September 2009 to July 2013

Table 7.5 Type of requests for interventions received from September 2009 to June 2013

Type	Number of Interventions
Individual	125
Group	18
Class	34
Teacher	15
Whole School	8
	200

See Figure 7.2 and Table 7.6 for data on Request by year group September 2009 to June 2013.

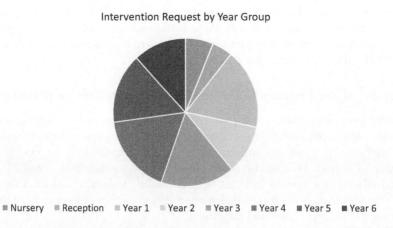

Figure 7.2 Pie chart showing the requests for intervention for each year group received by PIDS

Table 7.6 Requests for nursery, reception and each year group received by PIDS

Requests by Year group (Individuals, groups, class)

Year group	Number of Interventions
Year 1	31
Year 2	19
Year 3	29
Year 4	31
Year 5	27
Year 6	21
Reception	8
Nursery	11
	177

Table 7.7 Headteacher feedback from those who used the service 2012–2013

Headteacher feedback on service

	Consultation Advice	Interventions	PIDS process	Reviews	Work with	INSET training	Capacity Building	Support	Phone, email
Very good	10	11	12	10	9	6	9	5	10
Good	6	6	5	7	6	4	6	1	6
Satisfactory	0	0	0	0	0	0	1	2	0
Poor	0	0	0	0	0	0	0	0	0
N/A	1	0	0	0	1	7	1	9	1

Impact on children

There was a significant impact on children across schools. The analysis of the Behaviour for Learning assessment which was completed by the staff in the school was evidence of this. The children's relationship with the curriculum was always the first area to show improvement and then the others would follow. The improvement in the child's relationship with the curriculum also made a difference to their academic progress as their learning was improving and they were more motivated and engaged. The timing of the intervention varied from 8 weeks to a term for some children and up to a year for others. Over time staff became more confident in the process and in a few schools there were senior staff who led on the intervention and we would support their leadership team. Children also gained an understanding of the learning behaviours and contributed to the reviews. In Chapter 4 we see how children used the Behaviour for Learning framework to provide feedback to each other. Across the schools that we worked with, there was a reduction in the number of children being excluded as the strategies and approaches being used by staff were having an impact on improving the behaviour of the children. If at the review process it became apparent that a child was making slow and inconsistent progress, they would then be referred to the Primary Pupil Referral Unit either for a part-time or full-time placement.

Parents

The involvement of the PIDS helped parents to reengage so that they were empowered to be able to work in partnership with the school and support their child. All parents were actively involved in the intervention process; they had a shared understanding of the progress their child was making in their Behaviour for Learning and they had opportunities to contribute to their child's next steps. Parents felt involved in the whole process and as a result, gained a better understanding of the needs of their child, this included special educational needs where relevant (DFE, 2014). In most instances, there was a reduction in parental worries and fears surrounding their child being 'labelled' or they themselves being blamed for their child's behaviour. As PIDS worked effectively in partnership with other agencies, parents gained an understanding of the role of different agencies and how they could support their child. A parenting programme was also provided for some of the parents: 'Strengthening Families, Strengthening Communities' (Steele and Marigna, 1994).

Staff in schools

The training provided by the PIDS team meant that staff in schools received a range of specialist training which deepened their understanding of the needs of the children they were working with in schools, especially meeting the needs of the children in early years as well as those with SEMH. The team also provided training for schools on Behaviour for Learning. The impact on the processes used by PIDS was that staff were focusing on approaches and strategies that would improve Behaviour for Learning, the specific areas identified in the child's assessment. This was evident in the records of support and pupil reviews. The staff moved away from focusing on what to do to get the child to behave better. The headteacher feedback showed that the majority of them identified 'capacity building' as good or better – this meant that they could see that staff were developing a wider range of skills and approaches to meeting the needs of children, those with SEMH needs and those exhibiting poor behaviour in class and around the school. Table 7.7 reflects the feedback from headteachers who used the service.

The feedback from headteachers as part of the annual evaluation was that they valued the training that they received on team teach, especially the de-escalation strategies.

The most effective interventions were those where the school adopted a whole-school approach to the interventions which included training for all staff. Peaston (2011) stresses the importance of adopting whole school approaches. This was recognised by schools following the reviews and the impact on children's learning behaviours. In some schools a senior member of staff or the SENCO would partner with a member of staff and work together on the intervention request from the school.

Summary

In this chapter we shared how we used the Quality Standards to develop the PIDS. We identified the quantitative and qualitative data that we used in the service to evaluate the impact of the PIDS interventions on individual children, groups and classes.

We described the process that we used in PIDS and shared how BFL was incorporated into the processes and how children, parents/carers and staff were involved.

We showed how the 6–8 week review was an effective strategy for tracking the impact of approaches and strategies to improve specific areas of the child's Behaviour for Learning.

We identified strategies that helped us to build capacity and empower staff so that they were even more effective at meeting the needs of children with SEMH in mainstream schools.

Takeaways

- 🖑 Be clear about the nature of the partnership you are setting up with schools and the roles within it.
- 🖑 When the focus is on building capacity, you are working with staff in schools so that they are empowered and not creating a dependency culture.
- 🖑 Always consult parents and consider all the ways that they can be involved in supporting the learning and development of their child.
- 🖑 A regular and consistent review process which includes all stakeholders is an effective way of working in partnership to improve a child's Behaviour for Learning.
- 🖑 Incorporating the three relationships of Behaviour for Learning into your existing systems and structures will ensure that they are addressed throughout the school/provision.

Reflective questions

1. In what ways would the use of the BFL tool help to address any inequalities identified?
2. What additional strategies could you use at your school/provision to empower teachers and support staff to meet the needs of vulnerable children?
3. As a support service how do you assess whether the work that you have done in school is sustainable?
4. An analysis of our data showed that a disproportionate number of black children were referred to PIDS. In your school, how do use your analysis of data to change any trends identified from your behaviour analysis?

References

Department for Children, Schools and Families (DCSF). (2008). *Quality Standards for Special Educational Needs (SEN) Support and Outreach Services*. Nottingham: DCSF Publications.

Department for Children, Schools and Families (DCSF). (2009). *Special Educational Needs (SEN): A Guide for Parents and Carers*. Nottingham: DCSF.

Department for Education (DFE). (2014). *Special Educational Needs and Disability. A Guide for Parents and Carers*. London: DfE Publications.

Ellis, S. and Tod, J. (2009). *Behaviour for Learning: Proactive Approaches to Behaviour Management*. Abingdon: Routledge.

Ellis, S. and Tod, J. (2018). *Behaviour for Learning: Proactive Approaches to Behaviour Management* (2nd ed.). Abingdon: Routledge.

Ellis, S. and Tod, J. (2022). Behaviour for learning. In H. Cooper and S. Elton (eds.), *Professional Studies in Primary Education* (4th ed.). London: SAGE.

Hallam, S. (2007). Evaluation of behavioural management in schools: A review of the behaviour improvement programme and the role of behaviour and education support teams. *Child and Adolescent Mental Health*, 12(3), 106–112.

Halsey, K., Gulliver, C., Johnson, A., Martin, K., and Kinder, K. (2005). *Evaluation of Behaviour and Education Support Teams*. London: DfES.

Peaston, H. (2011). *Mainstream Inclusion, Special Challenges: Strategies for Children with BESD*. Nottingham: National College for School Leadership.

Steele, M. and Marigna, M. (1994). *Strengthening Families, Strengthening Communities: An Inclusive Parent Programme*. London: Race Equality Foundation.

8 Transforming learning

Introduction

In Chapter 1 we talk about the impact of Behaviour for Learning on the children, parents/carers and the staff. We share how the Behaviour for Learning approach permeated the whole school and had an impact on the children's outcomes, attitudes to learning, self-esteem, attendance, self-control and their understanding of what successful learning looked like. Children made outstanding progress and some exceptional. In this chapter we look at the evidence that we collected to evaluate the provision at the Courtyard AP Academy. The whole culture of the Courtyard AP Academy was transformed, and we identify what we have called a tapestry of strategies which had an impact on everyone in the school community. We were very rich in data and share the quantitative and qualitative data that we collected and include the approaches that we used. The reader may not be familiar with all of the strategies, for example, the door handle test; we also adapted the way that we carried out learning walks. Even though we carried out classroom observations as part of the monitoring cycle, we describe how we also used leverage leadership observations and feedback (Bambrick-Santoyo, 2012) as the approach to improve the quality of teaching and learning and implement Behaviour for Learning for all staff. All staff wrote case studies, one a term, and we include two examples as they were important for sharing and building capacity across the team. Children's voices played an important part in our work at the Courtyard AP Academy, and we include the voices of more children. Finally, we reflect on our work across the Primary Inclusion Development Service and Courtyard AP Academy and how the implementation of Behaviour for Learning transformed children's behaviours and how children, staff and parents were empowered.

Self-evaluation at the primary pupil referral unit

Our self-evaluation process in the PPRU and the Courtyard AP Academy was informed by the OFSTED framework. In the same way that schools were expected to have a self-evaluation process in place and complete a self-evaluation form (SEF) as part of the OFSTED school inspection framework, the expectation was the same for Primary Pupil Referral Units. The school evaluation form was a document which summarised the evaluation and incorporated judgements on the quality of the provision and the outcomes for children. The purpose of self-evaluation can be defined as a process of reflection, made systematic and transparent with the aim of improving pupil, professional and organisational learning. It was a requirement as a part of the new relationship with schools and

DOI: 10.4324/9781003166672-9

was a crucial piece of evidence available to the inspection team (DFES, 2004a, 2004b p. 24, DFES/OFSTED, 2005). Alongside this there was a conversation with our school improvement partner to discuss and advise on targets, priorities and support. The PPRU improvement plan identified the targets and success criteria that we would be using to track progress and the evidence that would be collected. The progress of the targets informed our self-evaluation.

Self-evaluation at the Courtyard AP Academy

We continued to have an effective self-evaluation process in place at the Courtyard AP Academy when we became part of an alternative provision. It was imperative to have a rigorous and robust monitoring process in place so that we could evaluate the impact of our approach to Behaviour for Learning at the Courtyard AP Academy; that is on the children, parents/carers and staff.

Our aim was to have an outstanding provision where all learners regardless of their background, heritage, ethnicity, gender and social class were successful.

The questions we asked ourselves were:

- What do we know about our children?
  This included academic ability, language, English as an additional language, special education needs, gender, ethnicity and pupil premium.
- What do we know about the school where they have come from?
  This was important because some of the children were attending the Courtyard on a part-time basis and would be slowly reintegrated back into their school full time.
- Where are we now? What are our strengths and what areas needed developing?
- How do we know? What evidence are our judgements based on?
- What do we need to do to improve the quality of the provision?
- How can we ensure that Behaviour for Learning is an integral part of our whole school development and improvement?

The answers to the questions informed our school improvement plan, the success criteria being used to track the progress of our priorities and the evidence on our plan identified the data that we would collect.

School evaluation was embedded into the way we did things. It was an ongoing process, and we found many different ways of collecting evidence, of how we were implementing Behaviour for Learning as well as the impact it was having on the school community. We incorporated Behaviour for Learning into our school development plan and used evidence from the children's assessment of their relationship with self, relationship with others and relationship with the curriculum to assess the progress and impact of Behaviour for Learning on individual children.

The introduction of 'Bluewave Swift,' a school improvement product online system adopted by the Tri-Borough Alternative Provision (TBAP), was instrumental in helping us to manage our school improvement processes, that is collecting and analysing data, producing our school improvement plan and tracking targets.

All staff were involved in the self-evaluation process which helped us to get a broader and more detailed perspective of the areas that needed developing and strengthening. The process also helped us to 'drill down' systematically and identify how Behaviour for

Learning was impacting outcomes for children. This is what Chris Banks says about drilling down:

> Drilling down will help to highlight areas and aspects of the schools' performance where improvements are most needed and pinpoint exactly what needs to change. It will also illuminate how parts of what the school does are successfully managing to support pupils to achieve rapid rates of progress.
>
> Banks (2012)

This broad range of evaluation tools that we used and partnership with the school improvement partner and the education psychologist was invaluable and enabled us to sharpen and deepen the focus of our evaluation and collect evidence showing the impact. We used a variety of quantitative and qualitative tools to evaluate the quality of the provision at the Courtyard AP Academy, based on the OFSTED framework which included: Teaching, Learning and Assessment, Effectiveness of Leadership and management, Personal development behaviour and welfare. Table 8.1 shows the tools that were used in the self-evaluation process.

Most of these tools are probably very familiar to anyone involved in monitoring and evaluation in schools; however there are a few, for example, the 'door handle test' and 'pen portraits,' that we used to give us additional information that may not be as well known – we describe these in more detail later in this chapter. Data was tracked rigorously and routinely analysed. In this way we were able to track the academic and Behaviour for Learning progress of children individually and across the school. We were also able to

Table 8.1 Quantitative and qualitative data collected at the Courtyard AP Academy

Quantitative	Qualitative
Attainment data, individual and group	BFL review
Attendance, individual and group	Learner feedback, children's voices
Reading	Parental feedback
Behaviour for learning	Staff feedback
Lesson observation	Feedback from members of local advisory board & trust board
Ready for learning exits	PASS
Continuing professional development events	Leverage leadership observations
Learning walks	Learning walks
Work scrutiny	Door handle test
	Questionnaires
	Children's reports
	Transition plan
	Case studies
	Pen Portrait
	Curriculum analysis and review
	School Evaluation Form – SEF
	Reports for local advisory board, trust board, management committee
	Challenge partners review
	Lollipop Challenge

Table 8.2 The context, purpose and frequency of the self-evaluation tools that we used at the Courtyard AP Academy

Tools of evaluation	Context and purpose	Frequency
Analysis of quantitative data	Attainment data formative and summative, individual, group, ethnicity, gender Reading, literacy, numeracy, SPAG BFL Assessment individual, group Behaviour ready for learning exits Attendance, individual, whole group	Every 8 weeks Every 8 weeks Ongoing Daily, Weekly
Reports	SEF Report to Management committee Report to local advisory Board Report on Achievement analysis Report on the Quality of teaching, Learning and assessment Report on Behaviour and safety Safeguarding review	Termly update
Learners' work	Classroom environment Feedback to children on work Classroom routines, expectations Scrutiny of work written, visual, verbal, art Looking for evidence on quality of teaching and learning, achievement and attainment, consistency, marking	Weekly (informally) Half termly
Observations, formal, informal	Formal observations to assess the quality of teaching and learning	Termly As part of individual assessment for a child
Leverage leadership	Joint observations with other professionals: EP, local authority inspectors, speech therapist, early years practitioner Leverage leadership identifying areas of development	Every 2 weeks
Case study, Pen portrait		Termly Updated termly
Learning walk	Opportunity to get quick feedback on what is happening and identifying strengths to be shared	Half termly
Door handle test	Identify and share good practice	Every Friday
Video	Used to identify good practice Identify the BFL approaches that impact children's behaviour and attainment	1/term
Interviews	Learners, parents, used as part of review process with children, parents and staff Part of challenge partners and inspection process parents, children and staff interviewed about the provision	
Diaries and logs	Running record kept of conversations with parents	
Questionnaires	PASS for children NFER staff Feedback on activities Visitor feedback Children's feedback	1/year 1/year
Photos	Evidence of work, learning, activities children had taken part in. Evidence for Spiritual, Moral, Cultural, Social curriculum	Ongoing, especially from trips or drop days when visitors led sessions Weekly – Star of the week
Scrapbooks	Photos and individual feedback on the social, emotional cultural development	Ongoing

evaluate the progress of specific groups including gender, those with special education needs, looked after children, children of different ethnic groups, English as an Additional need and those with Pupil premium.

Table 8.2 gives more insight into the use of the tools and how frequently we used them to gather information.

Demonstrating the impact of working within the Behaviour for Learning framework was a brilliant way to not only acknowledge the work of staff but to keep everyone motivated and on track. The data was clear and was a powerful depiction of the progress that learners were making. The range of Behaviour for Learning data collected was shared with staff on a regular basis including the reduction in 'ready for learning exits' which depicted the amount of learning time missed. Along with this, excellent assessment data and a significant reduction in serious incidents further supported the effectiveness of working within the framework. This intentional approach to sharing positive data often helped to boost morale and to reinforce the indisputable effect of working within the Behaviour for Learning framework and with minimal intervention, the information was there for the taking so sharing it was simple. Regular and scheduled times were set aside to share this information, for example during team, whole staff meetings and line management meetings. They were used to analyse and celebrate the data for individual classes. Celebrating this and amplifying the work being done helped to energise the team and created a reality rather than a discussion around effective practice and avoided conversations based on perceptions.

The SEF

Table 8.3 is an extract from the SEF, the section on Personal Development, Behaviour and Welfare. It shows how Behaviour for Learning was included as evidence in this section.

Table 8.3 The section on Personal development, behaviour and welfare taken from the SEF 2015–2016

Key Blue for Outstanding
Personal Development, Behaviour and Welfare

Summary

Summary: Blue

We judge the personal development, Behaviour and Welfare of our learners to be outstanding because:

- In the extremely safe, friendly environment, learners make excellent improvements in managing their behaviour.
- Learners show a very high level of engagement, extremely positive attitudes to learning and enjoy their time at the Courtyard AP Academy (CAPA).
- Parents, carers, staff and learners all confirm the substantial improvements that the school makes to the lives of learners both at school and home by developing positive attitudes to learning.
- The Behaviour for Learning assessments demonstrate that learners make progress in relation to themselves, others and the curriculum. (See BFL data.)
- The number of serious incidents reduces for each learner as they spend more time at the CAPA.
- All parents' and carers' feedback shows that they believe that their child's behaviour has improved since attending the CAPA.
- The discerning feedback that learners give to each other, for example during reflection time, assembly or when they write compliment slips to their peers, make an important contribution to pupils' appreciation about how they might improve their own behaviour and learning.

(Continued)

Table 8.3 (Continued)

- The overall attendance has improved with individual learners making significant improvements.
- Staff are adept at enabling learners to address any difficulties they have in managing their own behaviour.
- Staff ensure that learners settle in quickly and adapt to the very high expectations that are set not only with regard to behaviour but also to safety.
- Team Teach safe touch philosophy is promoted across the CAPA, with all staff trained.
- Some staff are also trained in solution-focused approaches, restorative approaches and cognitive behavioural approaches and this supports learners in managing their Behaviour for Learning.
- All staff have received extensive training in how to establish Behaviour for Learning and they use praise to best effect to help learners recognise what is expected of a 'good learner.'
- With the exception of 1child, all CAPA reports that have been submitted for child in need meetings or case conferences report that there has been a significant improvement in behaviour of the learners.
- The very strong liaison between the school staff, a range of agencies and mainstream schools is a crucial factor in the school's high level of success in promoting learners' progress and achievement.

Even betters . . .

Summary: *Blue*

To provide Lego therapy for our learners
To look at how we can implement an OT programme for more of our learners
To continue to monitor the impact of OT on our learners

Main strengths

Summary: *Blue*

Implementation of the Behaviour for Learning framework by focusing on the teacher behaviours and structures in place to promote learning and learner progress
The ready for learning script which is used consistently by all staff
Use of de-escalation strategies by staff

Door handle test

The door handle test was used to capture a range of positive experiences that had taken place during the week. This ranged from individual achievements to whole class. The member of staff had to focus on something positive that they remembered as they opened the door – this referred to positive learning that had taken place throughout the week. The idea was that staff would write this down on a 'Post It' as they left on a Friday afternoon (See Figure 8.1). These were displayed for all staff to read. The door handle test provided a wealth of evidence of the success of implementing Behaviour for Learning that took place throughout the school as well as positive feedback to staff and children. It is possible to go through each of the door handle tests, feedback and link it to one or more of the areas of the three relationships of Behaviour for Learning. It was always good to leave on a Friday with a positive focus on the learning and achievements that had taken place.

The learners in Pineapple class did a great job of recalling adverts during the starter. They were engaged and taking risks through the use of role play.

C has made an awesome start at CAPA. He engaged so well across the curriculum.

The learning that took place in the 'magnificent veg shop' and pizzeria – amazing learning and engagement, superb – all working to their potential. Lots of smiles and awesome progress.

K, M. J, & A worked collaboratively during their Media lesson. All learners showed a positive attitude towards their learning.

W has been so focused on his learning and achieved star of the week – he was so proud and so was his family.

Class supporting each other with their learning. They worked well as a team.

L's ability to use a solution-focused approach to lead the catch up session was great. (L is a child, catch up was usually led by an adult)

Figure 8.1 Examples of the Door handle tests, 'Post Its' written by different members of staff

Classroom observation

Lessons were observed as part of the monitoring cycle on a termly basis using the OFSTED framework (OFSTED, 2015). Evaluation of teaching and learning overall which included work scrutiny, curriculum planning and assessment showed that over time from 2012 the quality of teaching improved from good to consistently outstanding in 2 years and Behaviour for Learning was being consistently implemented across the school. The key to the improvement in such a short time was the result of the introduction of Leverage leadership observations and feedback which were more frequent and based on a coaching model (Bambrick-Santoyo, 2012).

Leverage leadership

As we worked in partnership with schools, we were introduced to Leverage Leadership by a senior leader following a discussion of building capacity in the classroom and empowering teachers. Leverage leadership is advocated by Paul Bambrick-Santoyo (2012)

in his book *Leverage leadership: A practical guide to building exceptional schools.* According to Bambrick-Santoyo (2012) effective observation and feedback is not about evaluation; it is about coaching. We focused on this approach to observation and feedback as we were keen to build capacity not only at the Courtyard AP Academy but across schools as well.

Following observations of this model of leverage leadership observations and feedback in practice in a school where it was well established, we decided to adopt this approach in our school. We were trained and then started using the observation framework with the leadership team. We then introduced it to the whole school. The impact was amazing and very significant. The pace at which staff were developing new skills, especially in Behaviour for Learning, was fast. This was true not only for the teaching staff but also for the Learning support professionals.

Observations were held more regularly once a fortnight for a shorter period of time – 15 minutes – and feedback given which included strengths and what was called 'high leverage action steps.,' the action that was going to have the biggest impact most quickly. The change that was going to take place had to be measurable with the expectation that it could be made in a week; otherwise the action was not small enough. This helped us to use small incremental steps which improved the quality of teaching and learning and impacted the progress of all children.

We decided to use these observations at the Courtyard AP Academy alongside our termly observations based on the OFSTED framework. We continued with our termly observations for teaching staff which was part of the monitoring framework and timetable across TBAP. All teacher observations were recorded and tracked including the leverage leadership observations. The leverage leadership observations were so successful and effective in improving outcomes for children that we continued to implement it across the school. 'The primary purpose of observation should not be used to judge the quality of teachers but to find the most effective ways to coach them to improve students learning' (Bambrick-Santoyo, 2012). Staff are given an action step with the opportunity to role play or simulate how to implement the action to improve their practise using a coaching model.

This was the process that we used following our training:

The Six steps to effective feedback

1   Praise: praising what is already going well, e.g., positive ongoing feedback
2   Probe: asking a targeted question in relation to something you have observed, e.g., was learner A engaged in the main task?
3   Action step: come up with bite sized action step to implement during the week, e.g., learner A could not access all the information in the board which affected his engagement in the task
4   Practice: role play/simulate how to improve current class or lessons
5   Plan ahead: design or redesign upcoming lessons to implement actions, e.g., ensure PowerPoint is accessible to all by keeping slides simple
6   Set timeline for follow up: set the date and time

(Based on effective feedback Leverage leadership, Paul Bambrick-Santoyo (2012, p. 352).

These 15-minute fortnightly sessions were used in order to help adults to focus on their use of language, structures, systems and strategies that supported Behaviour for Learning progress. This approach supported strong and sustained improvement of staff practice and required very precise feedback and lots of practice as well as specific action steps identified as part of the feedback process. The coaching model had a deep impact in classrooms and beyond and was a great way to build layers of expertise and essentially create a treasure box of tools to support the children and their Behaviour for Learning. It kept a sharp focus on continuing to improve practice and to support staff to include as many successful strategies as possible in their practice and there was a strong cumulative effect on practice across the school. All teaching and learning support professionals were involved in these observations and therefore the impact was greater.

The pace of staff development and learning increased much more that the observations that we were doing once a term with broader areas to improve. This was evident from our tracking records for each teacher and learning support professional across the school. More frequent observations and actions provided the opportunities to include and focus in on Behaviour for Learning strategies across the school. Our tracking data for individual staff meant that we had a good record of the aspects of teaching and learning that were being followed up. All adults, teachers and learning support professionals improved in their practice, lessons were outstanding, but what was more important was the impact that this had on the children who were making accelerated progress. Teachers became highly effective in personalising the curriculum and Behaviour for Learning for each child. The learning support staff used their skills to support children so that they could be successful learners, able to engage and work independently. The data from the tracking system also gave us an overview of the effectiveness of the teaching and learning strategies that were being used and the impact of Behaviour for Learning.

These observations were seen in a very positive way, especially by the Learning Support Professionals who valued the specific feedback they gained about the support they were providing in the classroom or when they led groups or an area of the curriculum. According to Bambrick-Santoyo (2012) regular weekly observations and feedback can impact a teacher's development, developing as much in one year as most teachers do in 20.

Filming/videoing

Filming was a strategy used by some of our schools to develop classroom practice. Our involvement in the 'securing good to better' project had shown us how filming was used to enable staff to reflect on their practice, their behaviours and the impact on the child's learning. At the Courtyard AP Academy we used filming to successfully capture good practice and even though staff were not comfortable with the process initially it was highly effective in contributing to self-reflection and also to gathering an insight into your own teaching. It can also be the most powerful experience you have in terms of gaining a deeper understanding of your own approaches, your behaviours, mannerisms, tone of voice; in fact, how your behaviours were impacting the learning of children. If you were to ask a teacher what they do to make the children listen to them, for example, they may respond with a generic and humble answer such as 'we have a relationship and they know what I expect' but they would rarely list the behaviours, strategies or structures they have put in place and developed in order to achieve this. The filming not only helped staff to recognise their strengths and to witness effective strategies and behaviours in action but the footage was also an extremely useful training tool. Another byproduct was that staff could also identify their own areas for development and subsequently seek out support with this. The approach that adults took with individual learners was also a focus as our approach was so personalised that often each and every learner in the room was managed in a different way and required different approaches to support them within the classroom. Capturing some of the behaviours and strategies used with individuals was useful not only in being able to recognise the impact of these in the moment but also to share with others. The footage provided a great insight into other teachers' classrooms without the time constraints and cover implications and to witness the impact of their practice on learners and their engagement and progress. Learning support professionals were also filmed/videoed as their role was crucial in becoming more self-aware and knowledgeable so that they could reflect on the strategies that they used. Filming lessons occurred once a term and staff had the autonomy to decide when it would take place and how long it would last – they were in control. Following the recording, staff would watch the clip back by themselves at first if that was what they wanted and then with a member of senior staff following this. During the 'watch back' both parties were tasked with identifying the systems, structures and strategies employed that had a positive impact on Behaviour for Learning, for example, and these were discussed and recorded and later shared with staff. As a result, adults became far more conscious of their practice and became more able to describe in detail the behaviours and strategies that they used that were successful. This increased level of consciousness was important in order to maximise the expertise and to tap into the pool of talent already in place and to capitalise on it.

Filming was used effectively to support the implementation of Behaviour for Learning and to be able to specifically identify the teacher behaviours and structures that were working well and having an impact on the children's relationship with self, others and the curriculum. We took videos of staff taking star of the week assemblies, breakfast club, going to and into class as well as different sessions in class, for example, catch up as well as a subject lesson. Staff learning about Behaviour for Learning was enhanced by the use of videos. The focus was either on one area of the relationships, for example, what does the teacher do to promote the children's relationship with self and staff observe and identify the strategies, the teacher behaviours being used.

Learning walks

Learning walks are one of the monitoring processes that was built into the self-evaluation cycle. The purpose was to collect evidence about teaching and learning and Behaviour for Learning across the school. The process involved a visit by a senior member of staff to classrooms – they were structured and had a specific focus, identifying good practice and areas for development. Feedback would be given formally and used to inform the progress or improvement identified in the school improvement plan. Learning walks were also a good opportunity to visit classrooms informally, share good practice and give positive and evidential feedback to children about their learning.

We decided to highlight excellent practice which had a significant impact on the children's learning and share this with staff. Examples included strategies to engage learners. All staff were then encouraged to try out the strategy with the group or a learner. It was a good opportunity to give personal and professional positive feedback for the good practice that had been observed in a staff meeting.

Over time our learning walks became more focused on the Behaviour for Learning framework which gave us a specific focus and were used to capture the systems, structures and strategies and the impact of these on the learners or the classroom environment as a whole. Each learning walk had a specific focus taken from the Behaviour for Learning assessment such as: 'RS1–is interested in learning' and therefore all of the information and evidence gathered would be in direct relation to how this learning behaviour was supported by adults and/or the environment.

Table 8.4 Strategies that had an impact on the children at the Courtyard AP Academy

Strategies that had an impact on children across the school or individually

Personalised learning	Redirection	Occupational therapy
Use of 'ready for learning' script	Choice language	Art therapy
B4L targets	Restorative approaches	Peer Massage
Written feedback in books	Take up time	Lego therapy
Motivational feedback	Non-verbal cues	Speech therapy
Blanks questioning	Positive reinforcement	EP intervention
Relaxation time after break	Blue chairs	Blanks level questioning
Parental/carer contact	Token system	Adult present at transition times
PiXL	Consistent routines	Sensory circuit
SEAL & BFL programme	Lexnoic	
BFL Self-assessment	Emotional currency	Staff modelling

A tapestry of strategies

Table 8.4 lists all the strategies that had an impact on the outcomes of the children who attended the Courtyard AP Academy.

Data rich

It was the combination of all the quantitative and qualitative data that we collected that gave us feedback on the implementation of Behaviour for Learning across the school. A multi-method approach which included data, pupil voice, adult voice, observations, questionnaires and formal reports captured many insights into Behaviour for Learning and the impact on the school community. The focus on learning helped us to revisit the structures that were in place and the strategies that we used to engage learners. Monitoring and evaluation is and was important as it provided us with a strong evidence base and confirmed that the permeation of Behaviour for Learning across the school had resulted in securing improved outcomes for all children.

Behaviour for learning assessment for a group

As outlined in Chapter 2, assessment data was collected every 6–8 weeks and a graphical analysis would be produced for each child, their relationship with self, relationship with others and relationship with the curriculum. The graphical analysis would be an indication of the progress the child had made in their Behaviour for Learning. The case studies included in this chapter are an indication of the progress children made across the three relationships, 'relationship with self,' 'relationship with others,' 'relationship with the curriculum.'

Figures 8.2, 8.3, and 8.4 show the progress of the same 10 children at the Courtyard AP Academy across the three relationships. Children's relationship with the curriculum developed first and we could see that from their engagement in the classroom and classroom observations both informal and formal. Children's relationship with self then followed as children became more confident and saw themselves as learners and felt more positive.

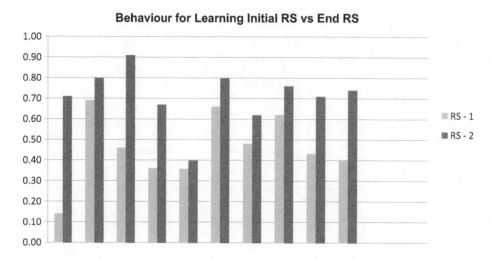

Figure 8.2 Behaviour for Learning assessments for the children showing progress of relationship with self, academic year 2013–2014

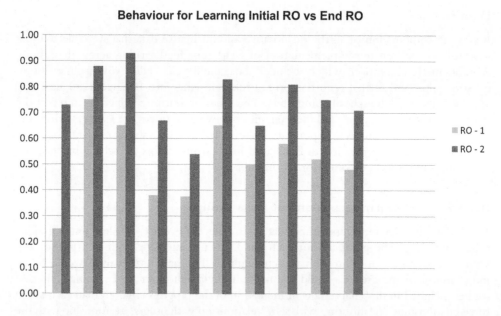

Figure 8.3 Behaviour for Learning assessments for the children showing progress of relationship with others, academic year 2013–2014

The analysis from the Behaviour for Learning assessments helped us to focus in on support that would be needed not only for specific children but across classes and the school as well as identifying strengths.

RS 1 line is base line assessment

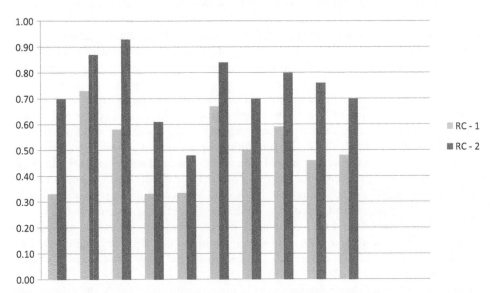

Figure 8.4 Behaviour for Learning assessments for the children showing progress of relationship with curriculum, academic year 2013–2014

RS 2 line is progress

We had good narratives for the many children who attended the Courtyard AP Academy that we then shared with our local advisory board. Here is one example:

> Learner H has made amazing progress and he is a good example of a learner who has made accelerated progress over and beyond what would be expected nationally. He has made 10 sublevels of progress the equivalent of 5 years progress in 2 years. He is also one of our pupil premium learners and started at the academy on P levels.

This was the trend at the Courtyard AP Academy – children would engage quickly, have a belief in themselves, make rapid, accelerated and sometimes even exceptional progress.

Parents/Carers of children at the Courtyard AP Academy

Parents quickly engaged with staff at the Courtyard AP Academy, including those who had previously not engaged in mainstream school. The learning environment had a significant impact on parents. This was evident from their initial visit to the school as they went around classrooms, looked at children's work and met staff. One parent said that she wished she had known what the Courtyard AP Academy was like because she would have agreed for her son to come earlier and it may have stopped him being permanently excluded.

As the approach to Behaviour for Learning became more embedded into the school, the relationships with parents/carers strengthened. The strong links with parents was a result of fostering and maintaining a dialogue in a number of ways, the formal induction process, questionnaires, open invitations to one off events, informal meetings, annual reviews, child led parent meetings, home visits and of course the regular 6–8 week reviews and weekly feedback. The use of the three relationships meant that the language used was more accessible to parents and they engaged well. The approach to review the child's progress was one which was much more solution-focused. Working towards what we wanted to achieve helped parents to feel engaged and that their contribution was valued. Parents were empowered. Table 8.5 is an example of a review which includes parent/carer contributions.

In the review there is a summary of the work completed and a list of the strategies that have contributed to the child's progress. Everyone was able to take part and their contributions were equally valued. There was an emphasis on the positive, that is, what was working and even though children might have an incident, for example an emotional outburst, the focus would still be on the progress that the child had made. It was important for all staff to say what their next steps were going to be and any plan for returning to school would be specific. This stage was important as the next review would start with actions agreed to by each member of staff. The next steps were always gradual which can be seen by the 4-week timetable for returning back to the school. It was important not to set the child up to fail but to ensure that they would be successful; the review was a good indication. The strategies and approaches implemented had to be sustainable.

The ability to understand the concerns of parents from different ethnic and cultural backgrounds had a positive impact and reduced any suspicions that they might have had. The children made so much progress that the parents were pleased and ready to support the next step for their child.

Parents talked about their relationships at home changing. The use of the relationships was very accessible to parents; the different language helped parents to get engaged much more. Parents had been told their child was disruptive, physically aggressive, verbally abusive and the list goes on. Making a judgement on whether they are able to manage their emotions and looking at what we need to do next so that their child is able to manage it better, proved to be a much more positive conversation. Parents were very honest about their child's behaviour and also open about their own experiences.

We became advocates for parents as we realised that some of them had difficulty accessing services or completing forms. The Behaviour for Learning assessments helped to highlight areas where children may need support from another service/agency so we were able to work in partnership with parents to access services. On occasions this meant having a joint visit with a parent to meet a member of the Child and Adolescent Mental Health Services (CAMHS) team or Educational Psychologist.

Table 8.5 is an example of a review which was held for a child.

Name of Pupil: Howard   **School:** Primary school   **Yr.: 2**
Intervention: PT-PPRU Placement
Placement Commenced: 13th June 2013   **Date of Review:** 7th October 2013–1pm
Staff Attendees: Deputy headteacher, SENCO, Class teacher,– Mother, – Father,–
    Parent partnership
PPRU Attendees: Head of PIDS – lead teacher – development worker

Table 8.5 Example of a child's review

Work completed	Progress against outcomes
<ul><li>12-week part-time PPRU placement.</li><li>Mainstream support from LSP.</li><li>Personalised learning for literacy, numeracy and reading.</li><li>Range of learning activities, linked to mainstream curriculum where possible.</li><li>Weekly reflection sessions where Howard is encouraged to consider what he has done well and what he needs to do to make his learning and behaviour even better.</li></ul>	**B4L Progress:** Assessment data shows that Howard has made progress in all assessed areas.<ul><li>**Relationship with Self** – Howard is now able to show good self-control, he is more able to make choices independently and is able to accept responsibility for his behaviour.</li><li>**Relationship with Others** – Howard demonstrates that he is able to ask for help, he is able to listen and be attentive to others and is able to work well alongside others.</li><li>**Relationship with Curriculum** – He is more able to make mistakes and move on, he is more able to ask for help and Howard is now able to cooperate and collaborate when working and playing in a group unsupported.</li></ul>

Key Strategies to support and promote Behaviour for Learning:
- Modelling of expected behaviour and use of language.
- Choice language.
- Use of positive praise particularly based on learning.
- Implementation of token system as recognition of expected learning and behaviour.
- Sharing positive learning with other pupils and adults.
- Sense of humour.
- Consistently high expectations and rigid boundaries.
- Use of visual timetable.

Intended Outcomes (from Request for PPRU Placement)
For Howard to:
- Be able to manage in the mainstream environment safely.
- Be able to engage with his learning.
- Howard consistently shows a positive attitude to learning.
- He is more confident in his abilities.
- He is always included safely at the Courtyard.
- He is able to interact well with all other pupils unsupported.

Parents' views
- Howard has been much more settled and is positive about his work.
- He seems to be enjoying school more staying in class.
- He likes going to the PPRU and says he can do his literacy and likes numeracy.
- I haven't had to deal with a lot of incidents, less phone calls home.
- He is much better behaved.
- Playtimes are going well.

Development worker's views:
- Howard is thriving.
- He is keen to complete his learning.
- He is contributing during class discussions.
- He has become more confident in his learning.

Child's Views:
- I want to go back to mainstream more.
- I like numeracy, I'm better at it now.
- I got used to school so I know how to behave.
- I am good at learning and listening now.
- I like my teacher.

(Continued)

Table 8.5 (Continued)

Work completed	Progress against outcomes
	Actions from previous review: • Mother to arrange a visit to the PPRU. • As of September, will attend the PPRU on Thursday and Friday. • Therapy to continue. • Support from Development worker to continue (building capacity with members of staff at school). • Arrange a visit for new class teacher to the PPRU. • Head of service and headteacher to arrange some dates for training around Behaviour for Learning. • Headteacher to begin statementing process. • Howard picked up at 3 and wait in reception for 15 minutes, reading. **Class teacher views** • Howard has settled into working. • In the afternoons he becomes tired but remains on task. • No incidents. • His behaviour is impeccable. • He is keen to engage in discussion. **Deputy head/SENCO views:** • He is making progress. • He is responding well to a consistent approach.
Barriers	**Next Steps** • Development worker to support at School on a Wednesday morning – continue to build capacity with staff including teacher and • Howard to attend Mainstream 4 days a week (Monday – Thursday) in the week beginning 14.10. • In the week beginning 18.11, Howard to attend Mainstream on a full-time basis. • Review @ mainstream – 1pm 25.11.13. • Mother to speak to therapists to see if the time for therapy can be changed. Parent partnership to support with this. • Professionals meeting – 11th November 2pm.

Pen portrait

Pen portraits were recommended by the Education psychologist who supported our team to enable us to plan effectively for children's individual needs. Our primary purpose was to document the journey they had had from the start of their involvement with the service to the current. It was a document that would make it clear to everyone what we knew about the needs of the child, recommendations and what we were doing in response. We used pen portraits to collate qualitative and quantitative data for our children, that is data we had about children's strengths and concerns, serious incidents, attendance, Behaviour for Learning and attainment during their time at the Courtyard AP Academy and Behaviour for Learning graphical analysis. The pen portrait was a way of bringing all the data we had about a child together including the school they had attended, their date of entry to the Courtyard AP Academy and background information. It is an effective way of being clear about the strategies that are being put in place to meet the needs of a child and to see the impact both academically and in Behaviour for Learning across the relationships. As well as identifying strategies which worked across the class and school there are those which are specific for individual children which was important in our provision. General strategies and individualised information sharing were important for an effective transition either to another class or school. Staff would be able to use the individualised 'portraits' and incorporate strategies into their classroom practice.

Reports

Reports were written for the local advisory board and trust board who we were accountable to. The report was written by the Head of School and included contributions from the staff team. They provided an analysis of all of the work of the school and we wrote four reports for the local advisory board (LAB) for the year, which were:

1. A general report of the school.
2. Report on the Academic year – Achievement Analysis, September This report included an analysis of standards for the academic year. Analysis of Key stage 2, analysis of Key stage 1, analysis of data for all learners and comparing with expected progress. Performance of different groups and our judgement on attainment. Individual good news stories.
3. Report on the Quality of Teaching, Learning and Assessment, March.
4. Report on Behaviour and safety.

Each report included an evaluation on the work at the Courtyard AP Academy, the school evaluation form with an analysis of data to show the impact. The school evaluation form was also submitted to the trust board who were actively involved in monitoring and reporting on the performance of the academy, that is the outcomes, quality of teaching and learning and personal development, behaviour and welfare. Safeguarding was monitored and included a monitoring visit by the member of the trust board with responsibility for safeguarding.

Each report includes the progress and development of the school improvement plan. The school evaluation form provided information for these reports. In each report there is evidence and judgements made about the quality of the provision in that area. In all areas our judgement was outstanding and, in the reports, there is evidence cited to validate the judgements that we have made. By the end of the academic year the reports have covered all aspects of the school. The reports also formed the basis of a discussion – an opportunity for the members of the board to scrutinise the data, ask questions and contribute. As they had responsibility for monitoring and reporting to the trust board, people had a more realistic understanding of the reports when the members of the board visited the school and gave feedback and also when we use case studies as evidence of a child's progress and achievements.

Challenge partners

Challenge Partners is a professionally led peer review that is led by practitioners focused on school improvement. The review identifies areas for development, bringing key challenges to schools for the coming year and it also provides continuing professional development for the visiting team. The Challenge Partners review took place on a yearly basis. As part of the process, we were asked to identify one or two areas of excellent practice. The questions that were asked were:

- What is your area of excellent practice?
- What actions have you taken to establish the expertise in this area?
- Which key staff have led on this, which phase/year, group/department/subject area?
- How have you capitalised on the area of excellent practice in your school?
- What evidence is there of the impact on pupil outcomes?
- How have you shared your practice beyond your own school? What has been the extent of the impact of this?
- How will you continue to build your expertise in this area?
- What are your next steps?

Our relationship with Challenge Partners was significant as it helped us to confirm that Behaviour for Learning was excellent practice in our school, providing specific evidence which related to teaching and learning, pupil progress and behaviour. The three members of the team scrutinised the data and evidence of our evaluation and provided additional evidence which validated the judgements that we had made. The review, which included conversations with staff, parents, pupils, and headteachers, confirmed the impact that we were having not only on the outcomes for children but also the staff, parents and schools we were in partnership with. It reinforced the fact that all staff were committed to the approach and had bought into the ethos and culture of the school.

Table 8.6 is the form we completed for Challenge Partners showing the identification of excellent practice at the Courtyard.

> The impact of the strategy was evident in so many ways – pupils' outcomes, attitudes to learning, engagement with learning, high self-esteem of learners, high attendance, good self-control and an understanding of what successful learning looks and feels like'
>
> Challenge Partners review, 2013

> The implementation of BFL has had a significant impact on improving outcomes for pupils with SEMH difficulties. The links between learning and behaviour have encouraged all staff to focus on strategies and structures that promote active learning. The school's analysis of behavior for learning assessments shows that for all learners there are improvements in relationships with self, others and the curriculum over time.
>
> Challenge Partners review, 2017

Table 8.6 Identification of excellent practice for Challenge Partners review

CHALLENGE PARTNERS: Identification of Area of Excellent Practice

Name of School:	The Courtyard AP Academy
Date:	22nd – 23rd October 2013

Please give details of the area of excellent practice that you have identified to support school
improvement across the Challenge Partners. Identify no more than 2 areas. Please complete a
proforma for each of the areas you have identified and continue on additional sheets if you need.
Thank you.

What is your area of excellent practice?

Behaviour for Learning

Why have you identified this area as a strength?

Implementation of the Behaviour for Learning framework has had a significant impact on improving
outcomes for learners with SEBD. It has helped us to address behavioural concerns in the
Courtyard AP Academy and schools.

What actions have you taken to establish the expertise in this area?

We developed how we could measure the impact of interventions for individual learners in schools.
Staff in the Primary Inclusion Development Service developed the framework based on the research
by Tod & Ellis.
Two education psychologists, a consultant and OFSTED inspector have supported the development
of the framework.
A presentation of the Behaviour for Learning framework was shared with primary schools in
Hammersmith & Fulham in Westminster LA.
Training on Behaviour for Learning was provided as part of the Behaviour management training for
NQT & Kensington & Chelsea.
Training has been provided for primary schools. The Behaviour for Learning assessment is completed
at the start of interventions and then 8 weeks.
In the CAPA staffs complete the Behaviour for Learning assessment at the start of the placement and
then every 8 weeks.
We have analysed the Behaviour for Learning assessments for individual learners in the Courtyard and
mainstream school.
We met Tod & Ellis to review the Behaviour for Learning assessment and identify next steps.

Which key staff (please state their roles) have led on this?

Head of School,
Teacher Consultant-Assessment-Primary Intervention Development Service,
Lead teacher
Senior Education Psychologist

**Which phase, year group, department or subject area demonstrate the strongest elements
of the area of excellent practice?**

There is a good understanding of the framework amongst staff in the CAPA. Staffs have a good
understanding of the teacher behaviours which impact the learning behaviours of learners.
Analysis of our Behaviour for Learning assessments shows how learners' relationships with staff,
others and the curriculum improve during their time at the CAPA. The improvement in learners'
attainment and progress is underpinned by implementation of the Behaviour for Learning strategies.
There is also a reduction of incidents of poor behaviour.
Teachers are able to identify and develop the learning behaviours that are relevant to the learners.

(Continued)

Table 8.6 (Continued)

How have you capitalised on the area of excellent practice in your own school?
In mainstream schools implementation of the framework has resulted in a reduction of exclusion, reduction of incidents.

What evidence is there of the impact on pupils' outcomes?
Attainment of all learners' analysis of Behaviour for Learning data shows that learners make progress during their time at the CAPA. Behaviour and safety at the PPRU were identified as outstanding and all learners make accelerated progress in English and maths. The progress is also evident in the 6/8-week reviews where all learners make significant progress in their relationships with self, others and the curriculum.

How have you shared your practice beyond your own school? What has been the extent of the impact of this?
Our practice has been shared within 1, All primary schools in Hammersmith & Fulham HT & key staff 2, HTs in Westminster 3, EPS in Hammersmith & Fulham 4, Locality Teams 5, Target secondary schools 6, NQTS

How will you continue to build your expertise in this area?
Project-based work in primary schools. Focus on identifying the teacher's behaviours which impact learning using following to ensure that learners complete the assessment.

What are your next steps?
To provide a training package that identifies the learning behaviours which impact behaviour and progress. To pilot the framework in a secondary school.

Signed:	Head of School	Date:	Oct 2013

Case studies

All staff completed case studies each term. Figure 8.5 shows what was included in each case study.

Case Study
• Background information about the child and school • Reason for the Request to PIDS or the Courtyard • Strategies implemented • Impact of the intervention • Behaviour for Learning progress data, graphical analysis, pictorial analysis • Mainstream feedback or feedback from school staff involved • Feedback from the child • Feedback from the Parent/Carer

Figure 8.5 Key elements of a case study

Case studies were incorporated into staff meetings with each member of staff sharing how they had built capacity in the school and the impact of Behaviour for Learning on the child's learning and behaviour. This was also an opportunity for professional learning, development and a chance for staff to further develop their skills knowledge and understanding of Behaviour for Learning. Specific strategies were shared, and we were also able to see the complexity of some of the interventions as well as similarities. In addition to case studies for individual children and groups, there were also whole-school case studies, for example, for a playground project.

See Case study 1 of Anthony (Table 8.7) and case study 2 of Stefan (Table 8.8).

Case study 1 is an example of a child who was one of the first involved in an intervention following a request from the school. Following his 8-week review where he was at risk of being excluded, the decision was made that he would benefit from attending the PPRU. His mother was very supportive as he was very vulnerable.

These case studies are good examples of how much progress a child can make both academically and in their Behaviour for Learning.

Table 8.7 Case study of Anthony, Year 6 pupil

Case Study of Anthony year 6

Background information:
Home:
Anthony was born 5 weeks premature weighing 4lbs and spent a period of time in hospital following his birth. He now lives with his mother and younger brother. He does not have any contact with his father. He has witnessed ongoing domestic violence in the family home and has been diagnosed with ODD and conduct disorder. A clinical psychologist described Anthony as 'unable to adhere to social norms.' He was subject to a child protection plan under the category of neglect.

School:
Anthony attended a local primary school until Year 3 when a request for intervention was made to the Primary Inclusion Development Service following concerns that 'his behaviour had escalated to such an extent that he was at risk of harming himself.' He received several fixed-term exclusions following a series of serious incidents which included absconding, physical and verbal aggression and his inability to follow school rules. Anthony has a statement of special educational needs in relation to his SEBD.

Reason for request (taken from referral):
➢ Behaviour that has escalated to such an extent that Anthony was likely to harm himself.
➢ Physical aggression towards peers
➢ Biting/spitting
➢ Running away/scaling walls
➢ Verbally abusive towards adults and peers
➢ Lack of empathy
➢ Inability to manage his behaviour

Intervention strategies implemented:
• Full-time placement at the PPRU/Courtyard.
• Personalised learning for literacy, numeracy and reading.
• 1:1 PixL sessions for writing, reading, SPAG and numeracy.
• A range of learning activities based on Anthony's learning styles.
• Weekly reflection sessions.
• Regular contact between the Courtyard and parent.
• Modelling of expected behaviour and use of language.
• Choice language.
• Use of positive praise.
• Implementation of token system as recognition of expected learning and behaviour.
• Sharing positive learning with other pupils and adults.

(Continued)

Table 8.7 (Continued)

- Weekly SEAL sessions.
- Visual timetable.
- Reinforcement of positive choices through verbal written praise.
- 'Ready for learning script.'

Impact of Intervention:
- Exceptional progress in relation to his engagement and learning.
- Anthony developed a love for learning.
- Anthony showed the ability to accept consequences for his inappropriate choices.
- A significant reduction in serious incidents and ready for learning exits from the classroom.
- Anthony's ability to self-regulate improved significantly.
- He demonstrated an ability to adhere to school rules and routines.
- He was nominated as star of the week on 5 occasions.
- Anthony developed the ability to adopt a solution-focused approach to problem solve.
- Mother reported a significant change in Anthony's behaviour, including whilst in the family home.
- An improved relationship between Anthony and his mother.

Area	KS1 data	Baseline on entry	SATS results	Progress
Reading	P7	1b	4	+ 8 sub levels
Writing	P7	1c	4	+ 9 sub levels
Maths	1c	1a	4	+ 7 sub levels

Behaviour for Learning progress in diagram form

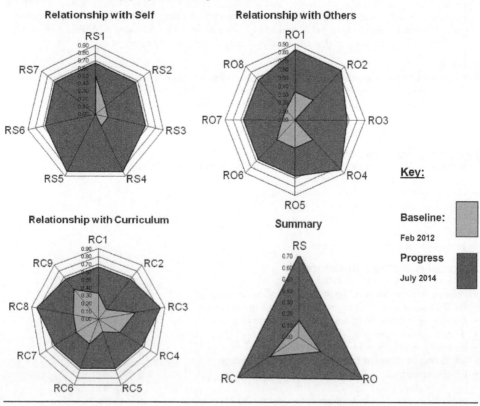

RS1. is interested in learning	RO1. is willing to work independently as appropriate	RC1. is willing to engage with the curriculum
RS2. has a positive opinion of her/himself	RO2. socially aware of what is going on around him/her	RC2. can take responsibility for own learning
RS3. can manage strong emotions such as anger and/or sadness	RO3. is willing and able to empathise with others	RC3. is able to access the curriculum
RS4. has a belief that she/he is capable of being successful	RO4. is willing to ask for help	RC4. is willing to try new things and take risks
RS5. can independently make choices and try to solve problems	RO5. is willing to behave respectfully towards adults in school	RC5. can make mistakes and move on
RS6. can accept responsibility for own behaviour	RO6. is willing to behave respectfully towards peers	RC6. is self-aware, knows how and when to get help
RS7. shows good self-control	RO7. is able to listen to others and be attentive	RC7. motivated to complete tasks
		RC8. able to work unaided
		RC9. follows classroom rules and routines

Table 8.8 Case study of Stefan, Year 6 pupil

Case Study of Stefan Year 6

Focus: BFL progression
Year 6
Attendance: 98%

Background information:
Home:
Stefan lives with his mother and is the only child. Stefan presents with a complex combination of health issues which affect his ability to access his learning effectively on a daily basis. Stefan has co-morbid conditions including ASD, ADHD and Hyperkinetic Conduct Disorder. In addition to this, a lack of boundaries and routines within the home impact Stefan's ability to learn in a structured environment. There has been intermittent involvement from Children's Services due to safeguarding issues. The relationship between Mum and Stefan is highly enmeshed and this has impacted his development and social communication skills. Stefan's living arrangements have been a cause of some difficulty as he was moved out of the borough. This required him to travel for up to 3 hours a day, causing him great distress on public transport where he regularly became involved in altercations with members of the public. Stefan lacks a sense of danger and the travel became a great source of anxiety for both Mum and Stefan and escalated to the point where she was not able to manage him in public. They were moved back to Hammersmith and Fulham in February. He now travels to school by foot.

School:
In 2013, the Courtyard AP Academy received a referral from a local primary school for support in their setting as Stefan was finding it increasingly difficult to operate within the systems and boundaries of school. He received a fixed-term exclusion for physical assaults on adults, other children, absconding, displaying unsafe behaviours (with little regard for his own safety or that of others) and inappropriate/concerning outbursts. Despite such challenging behaviours, Stefan was able to make good academic progress across all areas of the curriculum. In 2013, a referral was made to CAHMS following concerns around mental health and self-harming. Attempts were made to work with Stefan; however, this was unsuccessful due to his extreme and challenging behaviours inhibiting his ability to access the sessions. Stefan was then permanently excluded following a part-time placement at the Courtyard. Stefan is now currently awaiting an EHCP in relation to SeMH, communication and interaction difficulties and sensory needs.

(Continued)

Table 8.8 (Continued)

Reason for request (taken from referral):

➢ Physical assaults on adults and peers.
➢ Persistent disruptive and attention-seeking behaviours.
➢ Significant learning and emotional needs.
➢ Refusal to follow instructions.
➢ Stealing.
➢ Concerning and inappropriate behaviours, e.g., kissing and licking adults and children.

Intervention strategies implemented:

• Full-time placement at the Courtyard.
• Art therapy.
• Consistently high expectations – same approach from all adults.
• Rigid boundaries.
• Restorative approaches with peers following incidents.
• Redirection and take up time.
• Personalised learning and targets.
• Daily reflection sessions – catch up.
• Modelling of expected behaviour and use of language.
• Choice language.
• Explanation of choices and consequences.
• Individual working station.
• Use of specific positive praise.
• Implementation of token system as recognition of expected learning and behaviour.
• Sharing positive learning with other pupils and adults.
• Structured games once a day.
• Visual timetable.
• Reinforcement of positive choices through verbalwritten praise.
• 'Ready for learning' script.
• Regular contact with mum.

Impact of Intervention:

• Stefan's mother reported that she feels that Stefan has made accelerated progress and his needs are being met.
• Stefan has made accelerated progress in writing, maths and reading.
• Increased confidence and self-esteem.
• Increased engagement across the curriculum.
• High level of motivation and resilience in his learning.
• Stefan has improved his ability to interact with others appropriately and is becoming more socially aware of how his actions may affect others.
• Stefan stated 'Miss Mariela is proud of me when I work diligently and exceed her expectations. Others like when I work and play collaboratively with my peers. The adults at the Courtyard help me to achieve my full potential and the smaller learning environment helps me with my concentration as a result, I excel in my learning!'

Area	KS1 data	Current working at:
Reading	2A	Milestone 3 Deep1
Writing	2C	Milestone 3 Deep1
Maths	2A	Milestone 3 Deep1

Behaviour for Learning progress in diagram form

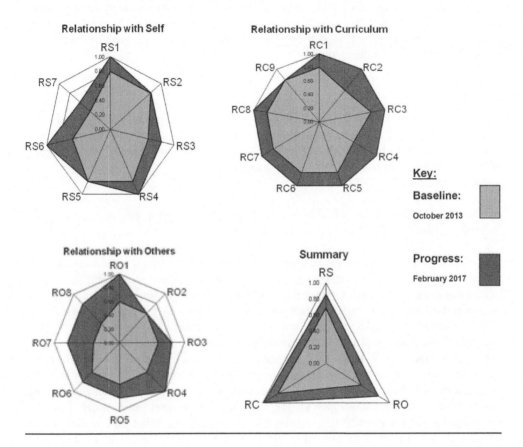

The staff

Staff had to have the knowledge, understanding and skills to be able to work in partnership in schools using the Behaviour for Learning framework. Implementing an extensive training programme involving all staff on a regular basis paid off as within 2 years we were seeing evidence of a shift from a sole focus on improving behaviour, behaviour management to one which was building on Behaviour for Learning. We developed a learning culture across the school where staff were involved in developments and contributed ideas and were willing to take risks. The focus on staff learning, personalised learning and being reflective practitioners meant that staff bought into the ethos and culture of the school – there were no exceptions. Leverage leadership observations and feedback helped staff to identify the teaching behaviours and put them into practice. Teaching staff and Learning Support Professionals had access to the same training and opportunities at the Courtyard AP Academy. The consistent approach was not about whether every staff followed the same rules per se but about a shared understanding of Behaviour for Learning, an inter-pretation of the framework which we had worked on together. All staff became passionate about Behaviour for Learning and worked collectively and collaboratively to implement and model the strategies that were developing throughout the school. As children made progress in the three relationships, they were making accelerated progress in their learn-ing, and attendance was improving.

Children's voice

One of the most powerful forms of feedback is what children have to say about their school. Children had a lot to say, it was their school, and they were not shy in coming forward and saying what they thought. They had a good knowledge and understanding of how the school operated and the expectations of staff.

As Suzanne SooHoo (1993) says:

> Student perceptions are valuable to our practice because they are authentic sources; they personally experience our classrooms first-hand.

The children were immersed in the culture of the school and talked with confidence to visitors ranging from parents and teachers to TV celebrities about school and the impact of Behaviour for Learning. If a visitor did not know anything about Behaviour for Learn-ing, then they sure did by the time they had experienced a tour from one of the children at the Courtyard AP Academy. They not only talked about Behaviour for Learning, but they also showed they had a good understanding of what it looked like.

Children's narrative of themselves changed over time, and their relationship with them-selves became the strongest feature, when compared with relationship with others and relationship with the curriculum. As children had opportunities to reflect on and evaluate their learning, their relationship with the curriculum improved, they gained a greater understanding of their academic progress, the targets set, and what they needed to do to make more progress. Children were and became experts in Behaviour for Learning, the learning behaviours in the three relationships. They had a good understanding of the Behaviour for Learning approach because not only had they been taught about the learn-ing behaviours in their weekly lesson, but it was also modelled and incorporated into their learning. It was part of their experience on a daily basis.

Children talking about their experiences

In Figures 8.6 and 8.7, we hear the voices of two children sharing their experiences while attending the Courtyard AP Academy full time and the impact of BFL on their learning.

Reflecting on the work that we did across the Primary Inclusion Development Service and at the Courtyard AP Academy

Using an assessment tool based on Behaviour for Learning across schools – what did we learn?

Using an assessment tool which incorporated the three relationships meant that any school involved in an intervention would be focused on improving the learning behav-iours identified in the child's Behaviour for Learning assessment. Staff would be working

> *My behaviour for learning is exquisite. Things that I am really good at are taking risks in my learning by trying something new, cooperating and collaborating and showing empathy. When I first came to the Courtyard I found everything hard but now everything is easy peasy lemon squeezy. Also I have impeccable manners and I always remember to thank people when they have helped me. My homework helps me to make progress and I always get it done on time. Things that help me at school are Miss N because she gives children an education. Also when teachers tell me I am doing good work it makes me feel proud. When I am older I want to be a headteacher and a singer. My favourite subject is Spanish because it is fun and I learn new things and when I go to Spain I will know everything. I have made progress in numeracy because now I am better at my times tables and written methods. K Year 6*

Figure 8.6 Child talking about her experience at the Courtyard AP Academy

> *Hi, I am ZBand I am 6 years old.*
>
> *I go to school at the Courtyard AP Academy.*
>
> *When I first came to the Courtyard it was because I found it hard at mainstream school because I didn't get enough help.*
>
> *This year I have got better at my learning. The things that have helped me are the ways that teachers teach us is interesting. Also the adults are always there to help when we need it. Now I am more interested in my learning and my favourite subject is Spanish. I always get excited when I do my work and I have to show Miss F to get a tally for Raspberry class.*

Figure 8.7 Child talking about his experience at the Courtyard AP Academy

collaboratively with a member of staff from PIDS focusing on the approaches and strategies that need to be implemented to improve the learning behaviour of the child. Sometimes you have to change the structures for change to take place. Our reviews show that children did improve in their learning behaviours and staff could see the changes. We were intentional about Behaviour for Learning being an integral part of the work at the Courtyard AP Academy and looked for many ways for this to happen, involving staff in the process.

The impact of teaching children their learning behaviours

These Behaviour for Learning sessions were fundamental to the success of implementing the Behaviour for Learning framework and reinforced the emphasis that was placed on learning rather than behaviour. How did the sessions contribute to the bigger picture?

- Promoted the development of positive learning behaviours.
- Reinforced children's personal and cultural identities.
- Supported the move away from a blame culture and damaging relationships.
- Promoted and enhanced relationships with self, others and the curriculum.
- Provided a way to break down 'good behaviour' into small measurable chunks.
- Provided a specific focus for intervention.
- Supported a language of learning.
- Provided opportunities to use specific positive praise and reinforcement.
- Established a shared understanding of what the behaviours looked like on a practical level for the adults and children.
- Gave learners the opportunity to put these behaviours into practice and to apply them in a range of contexts.

It is important that children are taught learning behaviours so that they can make progress socially, emotionally and academically (EEF, 2019). We would also stress that it is equally important that staff model the learning behaviours, and it is part of their practice. Children's knowledge and understanding of their learning behaviours was reinforced by what they could see, what they heard and experienced.

Transition – changing class

We became very aware that any transition could have an impact on a child's learning behaviours. Even though children had gained a good understanding of their learning behaviours and what they looked like, it was essential that they were modelled by staff. Changing classes for some children affected their relationship with self. It was important for staff to not only look at the Behaviour for Learning assessments but also to get an understanding of the strategies that had had an impact on their learning behaviours. Staff who shared the data for those children who had been involved in an intervention with the next class teacher enabled the child to continue to make progress and build on what they had learnt and achieved.

Transformation

We saw the transformation of children's behaviour as we used the Behaviour for Learning framework to inform all aspects of our work. Children developed socially, emotionally and academically, their narrative changed, they believed in themselves, they believed they could be successful and they had plenty of evidence to support their achievements.

We reframed Behaviour management, focusing on the learning behaviours that children needed to learn so that they made progress regardless of their backgrounds and needs. Children who were academically underachieving as a result of their previous behaviour made accelerated progress and some exceptional given their starting points. This was true for all children regardless of gender, heritage, ethnic and cultural background.

We believe it was the staff's passion, shared vision and the understanding of Behaviour for Learning embedded in their practice that enabled this to happen successfully. Of course, the children had a good understanding of their learning behaviours; it was part of their weekly Behaviour for Learning programme and daily diet – they could not escape from it. However, it was not enough for children to only be taught about their learning behaviours or learn about them; they had to see it and experience it throughout the school. It is important that Behaviour for Learning is an integral part of the school ethos and permeates the curriculum. We know from our practice that having a staff committed to modelling and teaching learning behaviours had a great impact on children's relationships with self, others and the curriculum.

> When the adults change, the children change.
>
> Dix (2017)

We were certainly testament to this. The adults certainly changed their understanding of how to improve the behaviour of children. It was the staff modelling the behaviours they wanted to see, their actions, strategies and approaches which embodied Behaviour for Learning that was the most influential on children. Staff were good at balancing all the three relationships. There was an element of the cognitive, social and emotional elements in their interaction with the children. We know that relationships are paramount in the school environment and everyone who worked at the Courtyard AP Academy made a significant difference in the children's lives.

The children:

- developed a love for learning.
- believed that they could be a successful learner.
- had higher expectations of what they could achieve.
- had a strong sense of their personal and cultural identity.
- made accelerated progress.
- had an understanding of their Behaviour for Learning which increased their readiness to learn.
- Improved their Behaviour for Learning.

Empowerment

Empowering the school community was key to the successful implementation of the Behaviour for Learning approach across the schools we supported and at the Courtyard AP Academy. Building a learning culture where people felt safe and secure to be open and could learn from mistakes resulted in staff growing in confidence. The emphasis on continual professional learning and our approach to specifically tailored staff training to meet the needs of our provision meant that all staff were equipped with the knowledge and confidence to adopt a personalised approach to meet the needs of individual children. The learning support professionals developed leadership skills and had opportunities to take on responsibilities which traditionally would not have happened in a mainstream setting. Staff gave professional feedback to each other which was specifically focused and also created a positive atmosphere and culture which reinforced their strengths. It was paramount that children and parents were also empowered. Throughout the whole process, their views were valued, and we took the time to ensure that they too had a good understanding of our approach.

At the Courtyard AP Academy, our vision was to foster a love for learning for all children:

> Instead, we should try to turn out people who love learning so much and so well that they will be able to learn whatever must be learned.
>
> Holt (1964)

Staff were committed to the vision, inclusion and equal opportunities and it underpinned everything we did – the training, our curriculum offer and our work with the whole school community. We constantly reflected on our approaches and strategies to ensure that we were having a positive impact. Managing change effectively is a journey. It requires you to create an environment and ethos where the whole school community are involved in the process and feel empowered to not only be a part of change by reflecting on practice, but to be instrumental in working to drive change forward collaboratively.

Summary

In this chapter we talked about the importance of self-evaluation and shared the quantitative and qualitative data used which showed the impact of Behaviour for Learning on children's attainment, progress, relationship with self, others and the curriculum and attendance.

The graphical analysis of the children's Behaviour for Learning assessments shows the progress that individual children make across each of the three relationships.

The Door handle tests and learning walks were used to capture good practice and give positive feedback to staff.

The review by Challenge Partners was an excellent opportunity to get feedback on Behaviour for Learning which we had identified as excellent practice.

Strategies which were effective in implementing Behaviour for Learning and improving the quality of learning were observations of adult behaviours (teachers ad learning support professionals), filming and videoing.

Leverage leadership observation–feedback coaching model had a greater impact in relation to the development of staff classroom practice especially implementing Behaviour for Learning and improving the quality of teaching and learning.

Leverage leadership observations, learning walks, the door handle test contributed to the positive ethos of the school.

Strong relationships with parents/carers are important and their role in the 6–8-week review process allowed them to be fully involved in the learning and development of their child.

Finally, we talked about how the implementation of Behaviour for Learning transformed the whole school community and how through the process children, staff and parents were empowered in different ways.

Takeaways

📋 Finding opportunities so that staff can identify and share positive feedback will promote a positive ethos.

📋 Celebrate what you have identified as excellent practice and find ways of evaluating it so that it is shared.

📋 Providing opportunities for staff to self-reflect on their teacher behaviours and structures in place in the classroom can support staff to further develop their practice.

📋 Provide parents with materials that are accessible and easy to understand and involve them in regular reviews where they have a key role in supporting their child.

📋 Children's views are important when we are evaluating all aspects of our school.

Reflective questions

1. What are the teacher behaviours and structures that you have identified from observations that promote Behaviour for Learning?
2. How could you use the Behaviour for Learning assessment to engage parents so that they are actively involved?
3. What strategies do you use which enable all staff to be actively involved in promoting good practice and giving feedback?
4. Are there any ways that you could adapt the monitoring processes that you have in place to continue to promote a positive ethos?
5. How effective are the strategies that you are using to empower staff across your school/provision? Are there any further developments that could take place?

References

Bambrick-Santoyo, P. (2012). *Leverage Leadership: A Practical Guide to Building Exceptional Schools.* San Francisco, CA: Jossey-Bass.

Banks, C. (2012). *Handbook for School Leaders & Leadership Development: Achieving Sustained Improvement.* London: Chris Banks.

Department for Education and Skills (DFES). (2004a). *A New Relationship with Schools: School Improvement Partners' Brief.* London: DfES.

Department for Education and Skills (DFES). (2004b). *A New Relationship with Schools.* London: DfES.

DFES/OFSTED. (2005). *A New Relationship with Schools: Next Steps.* London: DfES.

Dix, P. (2017). *When the Adults Change, Everything Changes: Seismic Shifts in School Behaviour.* Carmarthen: Crown House Publishing.

Education Endowment Foundation (EEF). (2019). *Improving Behaviour in Schools.* https://d2tic4wvo1iusb. cloudfront.net/eef-guidance-reports/behaviour/EEF_Improving_behaviour_in_schools_Report. pdf?v=1635355216 (accessed 29/07/22).

Holt, J. (1964). *How Children Fail.* London: Penguin.

OFSTED (2015). *School Inspection Handbook.* London: OFSTED.

SooHoo, S. (1993). Students as Partners in Research and Restructuring Schools. *The Education Forum,* 57(4), 386–393.

Appendix 1

Primary Inclusion Development Service Behaviour for Learning Assessment for Staff

Date: _____   School: _____

Name of pupil: _____   D.O.B: _____

Completed by: _____   Relationship to Pupil: _____

The numbers represent the percentage over time for each category	5	25	50	75	95
RELATIONSHIP WITH SELF (Predominantly Emotional) *To want to, and be able to, include him/herself in the learning opportunities and relationships on offer in the classroom and school context. This includes how the learner feels about themselves, their self-esteem, self-efficacy and their perceptions of the relevance of school learning.*	Rarely	Sometimes	Fairly Often	Often	Always
Key Features	1	2	3	4	5
RS1. Is interested in learning					
RS2. Has a positive opinion of him/herself					
RS3. Can manage strong emotions such as anger and/or sadness appropriately					
RS4. Has a belief that he/she is capable of being successful					
RS5. Can independently make choices and try to solve problems					
RS6. Can accept responsibility for own behaviour					
RS7. Shows good self-control					

RELATIONSHIP WITH OTHERS (Predominantly Social) *Being able to take part in learning that involves others, and join in aspects of school life as a member of the school community. This involves being willing and able to interact socially and academically with others, including the teacher and other adults.*	Rarely	Sometimes	Fairly Often	Often	Always
Key Features	1	2	3	4	5
RO1. Is willing to work independently as appropriate					
RO2. Is socially aware of what is going on around him/her and is able to sustain and form friendships					
RO3. Is willing and able to empathise with others					
RO4. Is willing to ask for help					

RELATIONSHIP WITH OTHERS (Predominantly Social) *Being able to take part in learning that involves others, and join in aspects of school life as a member of the school community. This involves being willing and able to interact socially and academically with others, including the teacher and other adults.*	Rarely	Sometimes	Fairly Often	Often	Always
RO5. Is willing to behave respectfully towards adults in school					
RO6. Is willing to behave respectfully towards peers and is able to manage disagreements/conflict					
RO7. Is able to listen to others and be attentive					
RO8. Can cooperate and collaborate when working and playing in a group					

RELATIONSHIP WITH CURRICULUM (Predominantly Cognitive) *The dynamic interactions that make up the reciprocal activity between the learner and the curriculum. This involves being able and willing to access, process and respond to information available through the curriculum.*	Rarely	Sometimes	Fairly Often	Often	Always
Key Features	1	2	3	4	5
RC1. Is willing to engage with the curriculum; can remain focused/stay on task and avoid distractions					
RC2. Can take responsibility for own learning; can organise themselves and use equipment appropriately					
RC3. Is able to access the curriculum					
RC4. Is willing to try new things and 'take risks'					
RC5. Can make mistakes and 'move on'					
RC6. Is self-aware, knows how and when to get help					
RC7. Motivated to complete tasks					
RC8. Able to work unaided					
RC9. Follows classroom rules and routines					

This table can be used to collate information from the first three sections

List the pupil's strengths from the assessment		
Relationship with Self (RS)	**Relationship with Others (RO)**	**Relationship with Curriculum (RC)**

List areas of concerns from the assessment		
Relationship with Self (RS)	Relationship with Others (RO)	Relationship with Curriculum (RC)

Key focus areas identified based on assessment (RS, RO, RC)

Thank you

Appendix 2
Process for Primary Inclusion Development Service

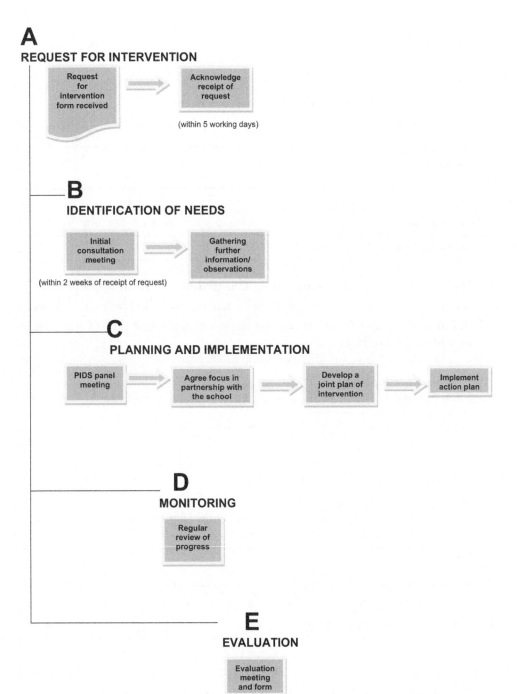

A

REQUEST FOR INTERVENTION

Request for intervention form received ⟹ Acknowledge receipt of request

(within 5 working days)

B

IDENTIFICATION OF NEEDS

Initial consultation meeting ⟹ Gathering further information/ observations

(within 2 weeks of receipt of request)

C

PLANNING AND IMPLEMENTATION

PIDS panel meeting ⟹ Agree focus in partnership with the school ⟹ Develop a joint plan of intervention ⟹ Implement action plan

D

MONITORING

Regular review of progress

E

EVALUATION

Evaluation meeting and form

Appendix 3
Joint Intervention Tool

Primary Inclusion Development Service

office use only	date received:	ref no.

Name of school:	**Date:**
Name & role of key school contact:	

1. **Is this request primarily concerning (Please indicate most appropriate)**

   ☐ whole school focus   ☐ targeted class/teacher focus   ☐ targeted group focus

   X individual pupil focus (If request is for an individual pupil focus please complete appendix 1)

   ---

2. **Reason/s for Request**
   Please give specific details of the main concerns related to the request, including year group and staffing.

   ---

3. **Strategies Already Implemented**
   Please provide brief details of any strategies already implemented and/or other services involved and the outcomes of this work.

   ---

4. **Staff views (as appropriate)**

   ---

5. **Anticipated outcomes; please relate to the individual/group/class/whole school needs** (What do you hope the outcomes of the support to be?)

Signature of Headteacher/Key school contact:

Signature of Parent/Carer (as appropriate):

Please return to: _____

Individual Pupil Information
Primary Inclusion Development Service

Name of School:
Form completed by: Date:

Pupil information

Name:					Gender:	
Date of Birth:		Year Group:		UPN:		
Attendance and Punctuality (Please attach print out)						
Current attendance?			Unauthorised Absence?			
Punctuality?						
EWAs Involvement?		No- school action only	Name:			
Ethnicity:		Language spoken at home:			EAL:	
Parent(s)/Carer(s): Current Address: Telephone:						
Siblings:						
Looked After Child?		Prioritised for EP involvement?		CP Child in need		
CAF completed? When? By whom?						
SEN level:		Medical needs:				

Child's strengths and interests:	
Parent/Carers work effectively with the school?	
Parent/Carers are actively involved?	
Parent/Carers work in partnership with the school to meet their child's learning and personal development needs?	
Parent/Carers support their child at home with their learning?	

Teacher's assessment of pupil's attainment (Please complete attainment data and targets up to current year)

Attainment Levels								
Subject	Yr1	Yr2	Yr2 Target	Yr3	Yr4	Yr5	Yr6	Yr6 Target
Reading								
Writing								
Speaking and Listening								
Maths								
Comments (Key learning issues)								

Exclusion history

Fixed term/ Permanent	Date	Duration	Reason

Other agencies involved

Please provide information on any involvement from external agencies that the child has had, is having or is planned for:

Agency:	Involvement	Contact Information
Social Services		
Educational Psychology		
Localities Team		
Speech and Language		
CAMHS		
Health		
Other		

Other relevant information

If the pupil has been offered a place in the PPRU, please complete the following section.

Do you require the PPRU to provide any of the following: –

Sex and Relationship Education   ☐
Drugs Education   ☐
Physical Education   ☐

Curriculum Coverage
Key points from discussion:

Primary Inclusion Development Service

Behaviour for Learning assessment

Date: _____   School: _____

Name of pupil: _____   D.O.B: _____

Completed by: _____   Relationship to Pupil: _____

RELATIONSHIP WITH SELF (Predominantly Emotional) *To want to, and be able to, include him/herself in the learning opportunities and relationships on offer in the classroom and school context. This includes how the learner feels about themselves, their self-esteem, self-efficacy and their perceptions of the relevance of school learning.*	Rarely	Sometimes	Fairly Often	Often	Always
Key Features	1	2	3	4	5
RS1. Is interested in learning					
RS2. Has a positive opinion of him/herself					
RS3. Can manage strong emotions such as anger and/or sadness					
RS4. Has a belief that he/she is capable of being successful					
RS5. Can independently make choices and try to solve problems					
RS6. Can accept responsibility for own behaviour					
RS7. Shows good self-control					

RELATIONSHIP WITH OTHERS (Predominantly Social) *Being able to take part in learning that involves others, and join in aspects of school life as a member of the school community. This involves being willing and able to interact socially and academically with others, including the teacher and other adults.*	Rarely	Sometimes	Fairly Often	Often	Always
Key Features	1	2	3	4	5
RO1. Is willing to work independently as appropriate					
RO2. Is socially aware of what is going on around him/her					
RO3. Is willing and able to empathise with others					
RO4. Is willing to ask for help					
RO5. Is willing to behave respectfully towards adults in school					
RO6. Is willing to behave respectfully towards peers					
RO7. Is able to listen to others and be attentive					
RO8. Can cooperate and collaborate when working and playing in a group					

RELATIONSHIP WITH CURRICULUM (Predominantly Cognitive) *The dynamic interactions that make up the reciprocal activity between the learner and the curriculum. This involves being able and willing to access, process and respond to information available through the curriculum.*	Rarely	Sometimes	Fairly Often	Often	Always
Key Features	1	2	3	4	5
RC1. Is willing to engage with the curriculum					
RC2. Can take responsibility for own learning					
RC3. Is able to access the curriculum					
RC4. Is willing to try new things and 'take risks'					
RC5. Can make mistakes and 'move on'					
RC6. Is self-aware, knows how and when to get help					
RC7. Motivated to complete tasks					
RC8. Able to work unaided					
RC9. Follows classroom rules and routines					

This table can be used to collate information from the first three sections

List the pupil's strengths from the assessment		
Relationship with Self (RS)	**Relationship with Others (RO)**	**Relationship with Curriculum (RC)**

List areas of concerns from the assessment		
Relationship with Self (RS)	**Relationship with Others (RO)**	**Relationship with Curriculum (RC)**

Key focus areas identified based on assessment (RS, RO, RC)

Thank you

Appendix 4
Joint Action Plan

Primary Inclusion Development Service
Name of School: Date:
Name of Pupil/Class/Project:
Contributors to Plan:

What are the anticipated outcomes of the intervention?

What changes will you be looking for? (for example, staff, parent/carer, pupils, environment)

What are your expectations of the Primary Inclusion Development Service input?

Specific Actions	Personnel	Timescale	Training & Development/Other Resources

How will you know that the actions are having an impact?

Appendix 5
Joint Evaluation of Intervention

Primary Inclusion Development Service

TO BE COMPLETED AT THE END OF THE INTERVENTION

What have been the outcomes of the intervention?

How has the input from the Primary Inclusion Development Service contributed to this?

Strategies/Systems/Actions that have made an impact

Sustainable Next Steps

Agreed Date of Follow Up Meeting

Appendix 6

Review, Evaluation, Next steps

Team/School/Individual/Focus area: **½ Term:**

PIDS Worker:

Work completed	Progress against outcomes
School/Service/Agency Hours Specify actions that have taken place – see action plan	Targets/Success criteria What progress has the pupil made following analysis of the BfL assessment by the school and school staff? What academic progress has the pupil made? Level of attainment Has attendance/punctuality improved? What is the pupil's view? What is the parent's view?
Barriers Is there anything getting in the way of action work identified on the action plan?	**Next Steps and timescales** Specific actions with times What is the focus going to be following the analysis of the assessment? Will it change or stay the same?

Appendix 7

Request for AP Academy Placement

CAPA ☐ BAPA ☐	Request for Primary AP Academy Placement

Office use only	Date received:	Date of first visit:	Ref no:

Name of learner: Date:	School:

Reasons for Referral – Nature of the social, emotional or behaviour concern (please be specific)

What interventions or strategies have been employed by the school to support the child? Please provide specific details.

What impact did the above interventions have on the learning, behaviour and attitude of the child?

What are the intended outcomes for this referral?

What are the child's views of the referral?

What are the parent(s) views of the referral?

Signature of Headteacher: **Date:**

Signature of Parent(s):   **Date:**

Learner Information:

Name:		Gender: M/F
Date of Birth:	Year Group:	UPN:

Parent/Carer Name:	2nd Parent/Carer Name:
Relationship:	Relationship:
Parent/Carer Address (if different):	Parent/Carer Address (if different):
Phone Number:	Phone Number:
Email:	Email:
Siblings:	
Who child lives with if different from above:	

Ethnicity:		Religion:	
Home Authority:	Language spoken at home:		EAL:
	Interpretation Needed? Yes/No		
Looked After Child? Yes/No	Prioritised for EP involvement? Yes/No		CP: Yes/No
CAF completed? Yes/No	When?		By whom?
SEN level:	Medical needs:		
Looked after by local authority? Yes/No	Subject to child protection plan: Yes/No	Child in Need: Yes/No	

Learner's strengths and interests:	
Parent/Carers work effectively with the school?	Fully/Partially/Not at All
Parent/Carers are actively involved?	Fully/Partially/Not at All
Parent/Carers work in partnership with the school to meet their child's learning and personal development needs?	Fully/Partially/Not at All
Parent/Carers support their child at home with their learning?	Fully/Partially/Not at All

Teacher's assessment of pupil's attainment: (Please complete attainment data and targets up to current year)

Attainment Levels								
Subject	Yr1	Yr2	Yr2 Target	Yr3	Yr4	Yr5	Yr6	Yr6 Target
Reading								
Writing								
Speaking and Listening								
Maths								
Comments (Key learning issues)								

Exclusion History

Fixed term/ Permanent	Date	Duration	Reason

Other agencies involved

Please provide information on any involvement from external agencies that the child has had, is having or is planned for:

Agency:	Involvement	Contact Information
Social Services	Yes/No	
Educational Psychology	Yes/No	
Localities Team	Yes/No	
Speech and Language	Yes/No	
CAMHS	Yes/No	
HEALTH	Yes/No	

Additional information

e.g., Child Protection Plan, Pastoral Support Plan, Safeguarding Issues

Behaviour for Learning assessment

Date: _____ School: _____

Name of pupil: _____ D.O.B: _____

Completed by: _____ Relationship to Pupil: _____

The numbers represent the percentage over time for each category	5	25	50	75	95
RELATIONSHIP WITH SELF (Predominantly Emotional) *To want to, and be able to, include him/herself in the learning opportunities and relationships on offer in the classroom and school context. This includes how the learner feels about themselves, their self-esteem, self-efficacy and their perceptions of the relevance of school learning.*	Rarely	Sometimes	Fairly Often	Often	Always
Key Features	1	2	3	4	5
RS1. Is interested in learning					
RS2. Has a positive opinion of him/herself					
RS3. Can manage strong emotions such as anger and/or sadness					
RS4. Has a belief that he/she is capable of being successful					
RS5. Can independently make choices and try to solve problems					
RS6. Can accept responsibility for own behaviour					
RS7. Shows good self-control					

RELATIONSHIP WITH OTHERS (Predominantly Social) *Being able to take part in learning that involves others, and join in aspects of school life as a member of the school community. This involves being willing and able to interact socially and academically with others, including the teacher and other adults.*	Rarely	Sometimes	Fairly Often	Often	Always
Key Features	1	2	3	4	5
RO1. Is willing to work independently as appropriate					
RO2. Is socially aware of what is going on around him/her					
RO3. Is willing and able to empathise with others					
RO4. Is willing to ask for help					
RO5. Is willing to behave respectfully towards adults in school					
RO6. Is willing to behave respectfully towards peers					
RO7. Is able to listen to others and be attentive					
RO8. Can cooperate and collaborate when working and playing in a group					

RELATIONSHIP WITH CURRICULUM (Predominantly Cognitive) *The dynamic interactions that make up the reciprocal activity between the learner and the curriculum. This involves being able and willing to access, process and respond to information available through the curriculum.*	Rarely	Sometimes	Fairly Often	Often	Always
Key Features	1	2	3	4	5
RC1. Is willing to engage with the curriculum					
RC2. Can take responsibility for own learning					
RC3. Is able to access the curriculum					
RC4. Is willing to try new things and 'take risks'					
RC5. Can make mistakes and 'move on'					
RC6. Is self-aware, knows how and when to get help					
RC7. Motivated to complete tasks					
RC8. Able to work unaided					
RC9. Follows classroom rules and routines					

List the learner's strengths from the assessment		
Relationship with Self (RS)	**Relationship with Others (RO)**	**Relationship with Curriculum (RC)**

This table can be used to collate information from the first three sections

List areas of concerns from the assessment		
Relationship with Self (RS)	Relationship with Others (RO)	Relationship with Curriculum (RC)

Key focus areas identified based on assessment (RS, RO, RC)

Thank you.

Appendix 8

Courtyard Partnership Agreement

School:		Year group:	
Learner:		Date of Entry:	

The Courtyard will:

- Provide skilled staff who can provide alternative short-term education provision.
- Promote a positive learning experience through a balanced and personalised curriculum and supportive and caring staff.
- Provide a safe learning environment where the learner can explore their difficulties and learn from experience.
- Work collaboratively with schools in developing their capacity to be the most effective they can be in responding to learners with SEMH difficulties.
- Communicate regularly with mainstream staff to review progress and the impact of the strategies implemented.
- To train mainstream staff to ensure a consistent approach if necessary.
- Lead a review of the learner's progress and readiness for reintegration following a 6- week placement.

The Mainstream School will:

- Complete the referral form and provide the CAPA with any relevant information, including the completion of a Behaviour for Learning questionnaire, SATS or teaching assessment results which may be useful to the CAPA staff.
- Provide CAPA with appropriate learning and curriculum information for the learner to maintain continuity in learning on a weekly basis.
- Provide opportunities for the class teacher and any other key adults to visit CAPA during the placement.
- Make any reasonable adjustments necessary, including those under the Disability Discrimination Act 2005, for the pupil to be able to succeed in the mainstream environment.
- Attend review meetings.
- Participate fully in the learner's reintegration to mainstream school.
- Work in partnership with the staff in the CAPA.

HOS Mainstream: _____   HOS CAPA: _____
Class Teacher: _____   Class Teacher: _____

Appendix 9

Mainstream Feedback

School:
Date:
Pupil/Class/Project:
School staff seen:

Relationship with self	Always	Often	Fairly Often	Sometimes	Rarely

Any comments:

Relationship with others	Always	Often	Fairly Often	Sometimes	Rarely

Any comments

Relationship with the curriculum	Always	Often	Fairly Often	Sometimes	Rarely

Any Comments:

Key Points

Signed:
Hours in school:

Appendix 10

Example of completed Mainstream Feedback

School: Courtyard AP Academy	
Date: 4.2.14	
Pupil/Class/Project: Karen	
School staff seen: Ms Jacobs	
Courtyard staff: Mr Long	

Engaged in learning	Always	Often	Fairly Often	Sometimes	Rarely
		x			

Any comments:

Karen demonstrated that for 75% of the day she was engaged with her learning. She was able to access her learning independently and started most tasks as soon as they were set. She remained on task for periods of up to 15 minutes at a time without any adult input. Occasionally, Karen asked for help and was able to seek this out appropriately within the classroom. Karen responded well to positive praise when she became disengaged and this helped her to continue with her learning. During numeracy, following the class teacher input, she returned to her table and put her head on the desk. She was asked if she was ready for learning and chose to take herself outside for a short period of time, after which she brought herself back to class to continue with her learning.

Positive Attitude to Learning	Always	Often	Fairly Often	Sometimes	Rarely
		x			

Any comments

For 75% of Karen's learning, she showed a positive attitude. She engaged quickly with the task and was keen and motivated to complete it and show the teacher. She was very proud of what she achieved. At the start of numeracy, she found it more difficult to engage but once she had come back to class, she was keen and willing to complete the work. During topic, Karen was able to contribute to class discussions and ask pertinent and topic related questions to find out more information.

(Continued)

Positive interactions with Adults and Peers	Always	Often	Fairly Often	Sometimes	Rarely
	X				

Any Comments:
Karen was polite and well mannered throughout the day. She was able to interact appropriately with all adults and children unsupported. She demonstrated that she was able to play and work in a small group and take different roles within the group. Karen was keen to work with her talk partner and was able to actively listen and be attentive.

Key points

- Use of positive praise has an impact on engagement.
- Routines in place help Karen to feel safe within the classroom.
- Calm environment enabled Karen to settle well into class.
- Ready for learning script is effective.

Signed: J Long
Hours in school: 6hrs

Appendix 11

Parent's/Carer's Questionnaire

The Courtyard AP Academy – Parent's and Carer's Questionnaire

We value your views and opinions about your child's experiences at the COURTYARD. We would be grateful if you could take the time to complete this short questionnaire.

No.	(Please circle)	Strongly Agree	Agree	Disagree	Strongly Disagree	Comment
1.	The Courtyard keeps my child safe.					
2.	The Courtyard encourages my child to have a healthy lifestyle.					
3.	The Courtyard staff keep me informed of my child's progress.					
4.	The Courtyard helps me to support my child's attitude to learning.					
5.	My child is encouraged to be independent in his/her learning.					
6.	The Courtyard makes sure my child is well prepared for the future (for example, returning back to mainstream, secondary transfer).					
7.	The Courtyard meets my child's particular needs.					
8.	The Courtyard deals effectively with unacceptable behaviour.					
9.	Overall the Courtyard promotes good behaviour.					
10.	My child's behaviour has improved since attending the Courtyard.					
11.	The Courtyard encourages my child to take responsibility for his/her actions.					
12.	The staff at the Courtyard take account of my suggestions and concerns.					
13.	The Courtyard is welcoming.					

No.	(Please circle)	Strongly Agree	Agree	Disagree	Strongly Disagree	Comment
14.	I feel comfortable approaching staff at the Courtyard with any questions, concerns or problems.					
15.	Overall, I am happy with my child's experience at the Courtyard.					

Completed By: .... **Pupil Name:** ....

Relationship to Pupil: ....

Date Completed: ....

Appendix 12
Pupil's Questionnaire

**LONDON BOROUGH OF HAMMERSMITH AND FULHAM –
PRIMARY INCLUSION DEVELOPMENT SERVICE**

The Courtyard AP Academy – Pupil Questionnaire

		Agree	Not Sure	Disagree
1	I understood why I started to learn at the Courtyard.			
2	I was made welcome when I started the Courtyard.			
3	I am making good progress with my learning at the Courtyard.			
4	My behaviour is getting better since I have been at the Courtyard.			
5	The Courtyard is helping my behaviour improve when I am at my school.			
6	The Courtyard is helping my learning improve when I am at my school.			
7	I feel safe when I am at the Courtyard.			
8	My learning at the Courtyard is interesting.			
9	The staff at the Courtyard are helping me to improve my behaviour.			
10	Behaviour is good at the Courtyard.			
11	The staff in the Courtyard treat all children fairly and with respect.			
12.	The Staff in the Courtyard care about me.			

13.	The staff in the Courtyard are interested in my views.			
14.	There is always a lot to do at playtime at the Courtyard.			
15.	School meals (breakfast and lunch) are good at the Courtyard.			
16.	I get on well with children from other backgrounds and cultures.			
17.	The Courtyard helps me to be healthy.			

Any other comments?

Name: **Year:**   **Date:**

Index

Note: Page numbers in *italics* indicate a figure and page numbers in **bold** indicate a table on the corresponding page.